Power Ball

Also by ROB NEYER

Rob Neyer's Big Book of Baseball Legends

Rob Neyer's Big Book of Baseball Blunders

The Neyer/James Guide to Pitchers (with Bill James)

Rob Neyer's Big Book of Baseball Lineups

Feeding the Green Monster

Baseball Dynasties (with Eddie Epstein)

Power Ball

Anatomy of a Modern Baseball Game

ROB NEYER

HARPER

An Imprint of HarperCollins*Publishers*

HarperCollins books may be purchased for educational, business, or sales promotional use. For information, please email the Special Markets Department at SPsales@harpercollins.com.

FIRST EDITION

Library of Congress Cataloging-in-Publication Data has been applied for.

ISBN 978-0-06-285361-5

18 19 20 21 22   LSC   10 9 8 7 6 5 4 3 2 1

This book is for A, and O.

Contents

Preface

The strongest thing baseball has going for it today is its yesterdays.

—LAWRENCE RITTER (1922–2004)

Ninety feet.

Sixty feet six inches.

Those numbers—the distance between the bases; the distance from the pitcher's rubber to the foot of home plate—have remained the same since 1893. You remember 1893, right? When a mustachioed fella named Grover was president?

No, you don't remember. The two dimensions that matter the most in baseball have been the same for way longer than you can remember. Or your grandparents can remember.

It's still ninety feet, and it's still sixty feet six inches, and you still gotta hit a round ball with a round bat and that's still really hard to do. Which is why we're able to compare Babe Ruth to Aaron Judge. Mickey Mantle to Mike Trout.

This is a wonderful gift for baseball fans. I just watched Game 7 of the 1960 World Series, and there was very little that didn't seem perfectly modern. Aside from a player they called the Little Round Man, anyway. When my wife's uncle Bruce tells me stories about seeing Jackie Robinson playing for the Dodgers in Brooklyn, it's not like trying to imagine Gettysburg or the Pony Express. I can *relate* to a baseball game sixty-some years ago at Ebbets Field. They've now been playing baseball at Fenway Park and Wrigley Field for more than a century, and a time-traveling baseball fan from 1917 would not need long at all to perfectly understand a game in 2017.

But even as the dimensions and the necessary skills and a few of the ballparks have remained largely the same for so many decades, virtually *everything else* is radically, dramatically, tremendously different than it was.

Most of the changes have been gradual, so we hardly noticed them as they were happening. But we're lucky enough to get the occasional literary snapshot.

Way back in the Dead Ball Era, more than a century ago, National League stars Johnny Evers and Christy Mathewson wrote—okay, had written for them—fairly sophisticated, revealing books about the game as it was then played in the major leagues. Alas, there really wasn't anything comparable published for some years. Not that there weren't any books published about the game on the field in those next few decades; it's just that none of them are today considered essential for one's understanding of the times.

For that sort of book, we must jump all the way to Game 1 of the 1954 World Series, when the wonderfully perceptive Arnold Hano sat in the center-field bleachers, just like any other fan, in Manhattan's Polo Grounds, and wrote an entire book about that single game. Hano's *A Day in the Bleachers* would be the first of a specific genre, and stands today as the single most vivid description of Willie Mays's nearly infinite talents.

In 1985, we were blessed with Dan Okrent's *Nine Innings*. Three years earlier, Okrent witnessed a Brewers-Orioles game in Milwaukee, and over the course of many months he reported the hell out of that single game. The book was worth the wait.

Five years later, George Will's megabestselling *Men at Work: The Craft of Baseball* came out. Will's book focused largely on Tony Gwynn (especially his hitting), Cal Ripken (fielding), Orel Hershiser (pitching) and Tony La Russa (managing). Will was *mostly* interested in how those supremely successful professionals went about their business. Their craft.

Thirteen years later, Michael Lewis's *Moneyball: The Art of Winning an Unfair Game* became a mega-megabestseller; to this day, you can hardly walk into an airport bookstore without tripping over a pile of *Moneyball* paperbacks.*

While Will focused on his four principals, and Lewis on Billy Beane and his Island of Misfit Toys, both books also serve as revealing windows into *what baseball then was like*. Will's primary interest was in how the *players* did their work, Lewis's on how *management* did their work, and Okrent seems to have been interested in everything. I'll cop to all of the above, while leaning toward management *and* taking a great deal of interest in those managing the managers: the people who run Major League Baseball, and the people who run the union.

Speaking of whom, you will see a form here you've maybe never seen before: not "baseball," which after all is just a game. Rather, *Baseball* with a big *B*.

Major League Baseball is a proxy for the teams and the league office, now headed by Commissioner Rob Manfred. But MLB's powers, while considerable, are hardly unilateral or unlimited. For roughly fifty years, the Major League Baseball Players Association—that is, the union—has been fighting like hell not just for larger salaries, but also for a wealth of other benefits and work rules, to the point where today *almost* everything is subject to negotiation.

Baseball (with the big *B*) is who determines and enforces (however loosely) the written *and* unwritten rules involving beanballs and machismo and bat flipping and all the other things that occasionally get the players so worked up. Baseball (with the big *B*) is who comes up with the new rules about rosters, and pushes the pitcher's complete game toward extinction, and ensures that every player has plenty of space on the airplane and a hotel suite all for himself during road trips.

This book is not about *baseball then*. It's about *baseball now*.

This book is full of the stuff you might have missed. It's full of

---

* *New! Improved! Now featuring Brad Pitt on the cover!*

the stuff that's changed since Arnold Hano and Dan Okrent and George Will and Michael Lewis wrote about the modern game—that is, wrote about *their* modern game. Which is to say, the game since free agency in the 1970s changed everything, and then again since the early '90s, when vast disparities in local television revenues changed everything again.

Inspired by Hano's *A Day in the Bleachers* and Okrent's *Nine Innings*, we're going to explore today's Baseball through the lens of a single game: Athletics vs. Astros in Oakland. September 8, 2017.

In many ways, this was a meaningless game. If you remember who won the World Series seven weeks later, you might think this was an important game on the way to that victory. It was not. The Astros would be in the playoffs and the A's would not. This game was not going to change that (although there was a *slight* chance that the results would affect the Astros' seeding in October, which can seem terribly important in the moment).

It does matter that these were two emblematic franchises: the A's of modern baseball, the Astros of (if you will) Postmodern Baseball. And it matters that much of the happenings in this particular game exemplify the sport as it was played, at the absolute highest level on the planet, in 2017.

It also mattered to the players on the field. Every game matters to the players, because most of them are intensely competitive and all of them are being evaluated by their employers, every inning of every game. And this game mattered to the fans who paid good money to see it. Even while knowing their team won't be playing in October, they still root like hell for that jolt of elation that comes with the last out of a victory.

For practically every person in the stadium that night, the game mattered.

I hope it matters for you too. Because just about anything could happen, even in just one game. Because Joaquín Andújar's single favorite word to describe baseball is nearly as true now as it was in 1985, when he said it: *youneverknow.*

Power Ball

Prologue

The art of hitting is the art of getting your pitch to hit.

—DR. BOBBY BROWN (B. 1924)

This baseball game seems just about over. The crowd in the stands has been sparse throughout this practically meaningless September contest; with the home team losing in the bottom of the ninth inning, there seems little reason to hang around.

See, the visitors are one of the best teams in Major League Baseball *and* they're bringing their lights-out, hundred-miles-an-hour closer into the game. His nickname is literally ONE HUNDRED MILES. Granted, not many people know this, among the few thousand fans still in the stands. Thirty or forty years ago, if you threw a hundred miles, you were a legend. You were on posters in kids' bedrooms. Today? Today you're just another guy who throws a hundred.

Oh, and the home team? They're one of the worst teams.

If you're losing, you lose games like this. Which any quick-thinking fan with a cell phone might actually quantify with just a few clicks. According to the FanGraphs website, the home team's chance of winning is just 1 in 5 . . . and that's assuming two evenly matched teams (these aren't) *and* ignoring what happens if the guy on the mound might be throwing aspirin pills, almost too fast to see (he does).

That guy on the mound, all six feet two and 200-some pounds

of him, throws his first pitch *almost* a hundred. The guy batting, a rookie at the very bottom of the lineup—you know, where they usually put the worst guy—takes the first pitch for a strike. He might have seen more than a blur (he might not have).

The next pitch is the same as the first. This time the rookie sees enough to get a splinter of wood on the moving target. Foul ball. Strike two.

The catcher and the pitcher now have a couple of options.

Another fastball close to a hundred? Because after all, the kid still hasn't proved he can hit something going a hundred. On the other hand, the kid *has* seen fastballs like this before. He just saw two of them, and he's seen them before. They grow pitchers big these days, and they throw real hard. They throw real hard in the majors, and in the minors, and in college too. And it's long been said that if your fastball is *straight*, it doesn't matter how hard you throw it; major leaguers, even kids like this rookie, will hit it. Kids *reach* the major leagues because they can hit fastballs. This kid, though, has been struggling against fastballs lately. And word gets around. Earlier in the game, the kid battled three different pitchers, and all three just kept cramming fastballs down his throat.

Still, maybe the slider instead? The traditional sequence is time tested: get ahead in the count with the fastball, finish him off with *spin*—a slider or curveball (most pitchers throw just one or the other). Behind in the count, the hitter must "protect the plate"— swing at anything that even resembles a strike, because he surely doesn't want to go down with (as they say) *the bat on his shoulder.* Unfortunately for our young fellow at the plate, a good slider looks like a strike upon leaving the pitcher's hand . . . only to veer sharply inside—that is, toward a left-handed hitter, like this hitter, when thrown by a right-handed pitcher, like this pitcher—often leaving the batter to flail at a foot of nothing. And Hundred Miles happens to throw not just a good slider, but one of the best sliders. In this pitcher's era, the smart set loves to talk about *tunneling*: distinct pitches that seem to travel the same path until it's too late for the hitter to react to any deviation in their flight. Hundred Miles's slider looks like his fastball, until it doesn't, by which point the hitter usually has little chance.

With an 0-and-2 count on the hitter, you're not supposed to throw *anything* hittable; there are old stories about managers who fined their pitchers every time they gave up a hit on 0 and 2. So if you throw the fastball here, you throw it too high to hit; if you throw the slider, you throw it too far inside to hit. Best case: strikeout. Worst case: it's a ball and you're still way ahead in the count. For a long time, the numbers have been quite clear on this one.

A few years ago, I sent away for a new book: *The Beauty of Short Hops: How Chance and Circumstance Confound the Moneyball Approach to Baseball.*

The coauthors, two brothers, grabbed me with the title. Because short hops *are* beautiful. Chance and circumstance *are* confounding (and also, in their way, beautiful). Sure, "Moneyball approach" sounds like an epithet (or a marketing tool). But if we don't keep an open, curious mind, what have we left?

Alas. Even before reaching chapter 1, I knew I would need more than my usual curiosity to enjoy *The Beauty of Short Hops*. I would need to switch off my mind. How else does one respond to this passage, from the preface?

> *It's bad enough that sabermetrics compromises a real appreciation of baseball, but making matters worse, it fails on its own terms. It cannot succeed in doing what its more ambitious adherents openly espouse: reducing baseball to a social science understandable wholly in terms of data. It often fails in the more limited effort to guide player selection and game decisions.*

I've met dozens of sabermetrics adherents. Hundreds, maybe. I have not met one who thinks the numbers might somehow explain everything. Even if they're around, they're not worth writing a book about; they're not actually working for baseball teams or even writing for one of the sabermetrically inclined websites. So just imagine: a whole book, lovingly written, edited, and designed, about straw men.

I did finish *The Beauty of Short Hops*. Quickly too. Underlining passages throughout.

There is a chapter toward the end, the book's longest chapter by far, that's essentially a list of wonderfully bizarre, utterly unpredictable things that happened during the 2009 baseball season. If you can enjoy all those (seemingly) random happenstances *and* admire the incredible efforts made by baseball people to *lower* the degree of unpredictability by just a smidgen here, a driblet there . . . well, then we've got something to talk about. Especially if you're willing to consider the possibility that sabermetrics—that is, the search for objective knowledge about baseball, in its infinite variety of forms—perhaps *has* cost us a smidgen of beauty, if only because it *has* brought about fewer short hops. Literally many fewer short hops.

With the count 0 and 2 on an anonymous rookie batting ninth, one of Baseball's top-rated relief pitchers threw a slider.

If you appreciate the beauty in a short hop, I suspect you'll love what happened next. . . .

Visitors First

This ain't a football game. We do this every day.

—EARL WEAVER (1930–2013)

It's a Friday in September, 2017. By 7:30 or 8 this morning, a complicated dance began when the head groundskeeper arrived at the Oakland-Alameda County Coliseum. A couple of hours later, the facility operations manager showed up for *his* long day at the office. The Coliseum is one of professional baseball's oldest stadiums, which doesn't make anyone's job easier. There are seats to wipe down, toilets to polish, concrete floors to mop, and a thousand other jobs to prepare the (relatively) ancient building for a few thousand paying customers tonight. And of course there's the actual baseball field, dirt and clay and some really expensive "natural" grass, which must be mowed and watered and pampered and then, at the last minute, watered once more.

All told, it took upwards of six hundred people working one long day to start this engine and keep it running. All in preparation for this moment: 7:07 Pacific Daylight Time in Oakland, California, when a young right-handed pitcher named Jharel Cotton fired a 93-mile-an-hour fastball to begin this Major League Baseball game on a typically cool East Bay autumn evening.

Cotton pitches for the last-place Oakland Athletics, whose opponents tonight are the first-place Houston Astros. Up in the broadcast booth, Astros radio analyst Steve Sparks offers a scouting report: "And from Cotton you'll get the fastball/slider/changeup combination. Fastball anywhere from ninety-two to nine-four, for the most part. The changeup is his best secondary offering."

Five months ago, after Cotton pitched quite effectively in an early-season start, Pedro Martinez tweeted, "Jharel Cotton reminds me a lot of myself. Nasty changeup, nice cutter, same arm angle and rotation, and same grip I used to have."

High praise from the Hall of Famer!

Since then, Cotton has not drawn many similar comparisons. In nineteen starts for the A's this season, he's won only seven games while losing ten, and posted a 5.53 ERA, largely because he's also given up twenty-four home runs in that stretch. This is 2017, and in 2017 home runs are flying over fences more than ever before. Still, twenty-four home runs in nineteen games is too many.

Before doing anything else, the Astros' first batter, center fielder George Springer—a joyful player who has described baseball as "the only place where being twenty-four and being a kid is allowed"— gives both the catcher and the umpires a little pat on the back, then turns and salutes the home team's dugout. It's not until he's completed this brotherly ritual that he sets himself in the batter's box and takes Cotton's first pitch for a strike. Springer does swing at Cotton's second pitch, a hard curveball, but fouls it off.

It's early in this game. It's early in this book. So with zero balls and two strikes on Springer, and before all the baseball onomatopoeia takes over—the *craaacks* and *bloooops* and *thwacks*—it's worth taking a moment for a quick primer on balls and strikes . . .

The strike zone, with nearly an iron grip, rules professional baseball. "The game," A's pitcher Bob Welch once said, "is the count." Similarly, Hall of Famer Greg Maddux observed, "The most important pitch in the count for me is one and one, because one and two and two and one are two different worlds." If you control the strike zone, you'll win. You'll win the at-bat, you'll win the inning, you'll win the game, you'll win the season. Not always. But close enough. The best pitchers control the strike zone. The best hitters control the strike zone. Always have. Always will.

This year in the American League—we have to make the distinction because American League games include designated hitters, National League games still include pitchers in the lineup, and tonight's game features two A.L. teams—the numbers are stark. As always.

After hitters fall behind in the count this season, zero balls and two strikes, they'll combine for a .166 batting average, .198 on-base percentage, and .262 slugging percentage.

Conversely, if hitters are *ahead* in the count, two balls and no strikes, they'll combine for a .284/.496/.499 batting line. How good is that? There aren't any real hitters with a line quite like that; that .496 on-base percentage is inflated because so many plate appearances that begin 2 and 0 finish with walks. Still, there are only three hitters in all the major leagues who have been roughly as productive over the last three seasons as our theoretical 2-and-0 hitter: Mike Trout, Joey Votto, and Bryce Harper.

Or to put it simply: When you're behind 0 and 2, you become one of the very worst hitters in the major leagues; and when you're ahead 2 and 0, you become one of the very best hitters.

This is *not* new. We've got data going back thirty seasons now—that is, pitch-by-pitch data that allows factual comparisons—and the story was essentially the same in 1988: .178/.208/.253 after 0 and 2, and .276/.502/.444 after 2 and 0. Before 1988? As Ted Williams said in 1951, "Make them pitch strikes. Make them get the ball over. Play the game that way and you'll be playing the percentage. The percentage will be with you. Take the base on balls."

George Springer's an excellent hitter, so you might guess he's an exception to the rule; that being down 0 and 2 doesn't matter so much to him.

Springer will finish this season with a career .173/.234/.296 line in plate appearances that began with two strikes. Yes, better than the average hitter in this spot. But terrible, still. Baseball is a zero-sum game. Pitchers are tremendously effective after getting ahead in the count, and Cotton's no exception. He'll finish this season having allowed just a .177 batting average after getting ahead 0 and 2.

Now Cotton doesn't have to worry about getting ahead in the count *or* walking the leadoff man, so he can throw just about anything he likes, which means Springer can't reasonably expect any particular pitch, except he can figure the pitch *probably* won't be anywhere near the middle of the strike zone. But that's not much. Cotton's been a borderline major leaguer this season and Springer's been one of the better hitters in the entire league. But at this moment, Jharel Cotton has George Springer *exactly* where he wants him.

And then he loses him. As pitchers will. Once every four or five times, the batter will wind up getting on base. Winning. Here, Springer takes a high fastball for ball one, an off-speed pitch in the dirt for ball two, and another high fastball for ball three. A year or two ago, Springer might already have struck out; neither fastball missed the strike zone by much. But like a bunch of his teammates, Springer is striking out less often this season, and now *he* has the edge in this battle.

Because Cotton certainly doesn't want to walk the game's first hitter. So he throws a fastball down the middle and Springer takes a big rip . . . foul ball, straight back. When I was a boy in the 1970s, listening to Royals games on the radio, the announcers often said that if you put that sort of swing on a fastball and fouled it straight back, that meant you had it timed. And maybe Springer did. But we won't find out, because Cotton's seventh pitch is yet another high fastball, this one even farther out of the zone than the others that missed. And so Springer trots down to first base with a free pass, having done what leadoff men were put on this earth to do: reach.

Next up: Astros second baseman Jose Altuve. All five feet six inches of him. On this Friday evening, with all thirty major-league teams in action and roughly three hundred players actually batting,

Altuve presents the smallest strike zone of them all. He might be the smallest player in all the major leagues, but he's definitely the smallest *great* player in the major leagues. Which makes him probably the most *interesting* player in the major leagues too.[*]

The history of short players in the major leagues is . . . well, the history is actually quite long, but the list is relatively short. In the 1970s, Royals shortstop Freddie Patek was listed at five feet four (or five feet five) and made a few All-Star teams. Toward the very end of his career in a game at Fenway Park, Patek hit three fly balls over the Green Monster, which almost certainly ranks as the unlikeliest three-homer game ever.[†]

From World War II through the 1980s, Patek was one of only two or three major leaguers who were somewhat famous *because* they were small. One of the others was Philadelphia Athletics pitcher Bobby Shantz, listed as five feet six, and the American League's Most Valuable Player in 1952. And the other was five-feet-seven second baseman Joe Morgan, who started his career with Houston in 1963 and later won consecutive MVP Awards with Cincinnati. Morgan's nickname was Little Joe, but what made him so impressive was not his height; there were plenty of shortstops and second basemen of similar stature. What made Morgan unique was his power, which was simply unknown in observers' living memories in a player his size.

Before Morgan, in fact, the list of "short" power hitters consisted of exactly one man: Lewis "Hack" Wilson, a fireplug-shaped outfielder who starred for the Giants, Cubs, and Dodgers in the late

---

[*] Altuve will lose this highly unofficial title in 2018, when Japanese star Shohei Ohtani joins the Angels of Anaheim and promptly (a) wins his first game as a starting pitcher, and (b) hits two home runs in his first three starts as the Angels' part-time designated hitter. Which probably makes Ohtani the most interesting player in the major leagues since Jackie Robinson or Babe Ruth.

[†] In his career, Patek averaged four home runs per 162 games.

1920s and early '30s. Listed at five feet six (and 190 pounds!), Wilson led the National League in home runs four times, and in 1930 he drove in 191 runs, which still stands as the all-time record for one season.

Morgan didn't have that sort of power. But during his five-year peak from 1973 through '77, he averaged twenty-three homers per season during an era when thirty got you on the leaderboard.

Oh, and here's something people forget. Or more likely, never knew: *Yogi Berra was short.* I don't mean toward the end of his life, when he resembled a wizened old gnome. In his prime, I mean, when he was perhaps the greatest catcher who ever lived (the competition usually comes down to Berra, Joe Morgan's Cincinnati teammate Johnny Bench, and black baseball's Josh Gibson).

Yogi stood only five feet seven, and he's one of only four twentieth-century players that height or shorter who hit more than one hundred career home runs in the majors. The list: Berra with 358, Morgan with 268, Wilson with 244, Jimmy Rollins with 231 . . . and then there's a weirdly massive gap before the fifth man on the list: 1930s infielder Tony Cuccinello with 94.

Which brings us to Altuve, an Astros second baseman (like Morgan) who's almost certainly shorter than every player on that list (and come to think of it, shorter than any other player in this entire book, unless we mention three-feet-seven Eddie Gaedel, because every baseball book should mention Eddie Gaedel at least once).

We can't say there's never been a player remotely like Jose Altuve before, because Altuve is remotely like Joe Morgan. Both are second basemen far smaller than most of their peers, who batted leadoff for a while and stole plenty of bases while also hitting for power you might not believe without seeing it.

In fact, for some years there were any number of otherwise observant baseball people who *did* see Altuve play, but essentially did not believe what they were seeing. Because they had never seen it before.

Altuve signed with the Astros in the spring of 2007 and batted

.343 with a hint of power and a bunch of walks in the Venezuelan Summer League. The next year, he came north and played for Greeneville in the Appalachian League, and more than held his own despite being among the circuit's younger players. The next spring, he returned to Greeneville and did even better in forty-five games, earning a promotion to the tougher New York-Penn League. He did struggle there, statistically speaking, but was nearly the youngest player on his team and played only twenty-one games.[*]

What did the world think of Jose Altuve at that point? *Baseball America* has been covering the minor leagues and generating prospect reports and rankings since 1981 and has been publishing an annual prospects book since 2001. Today there are voluminous reputable outfits publishing their own prospect lists—it's a growth industry, although I can't quite fathom why—but *Baseball America* remains the *most* reputable outfit, for many reasons.

After the 2009 season, *Baseball America* did not rank Jose Altuve among the Astros' ten best prospects. Or twenty best. Or thirty best. In the Astros section of that winter's *Prospect Handbook*, Altuve shows up just once, in the organizational depth chart—which excluded anyone with real major-league experience—at second base. Fourth on the depth chart. Behind three guys who *also* didn't rank among the organization's top thirty prospects. Which means *Baseball America* ranked Altuve, *at best*, as Houston's thirty-fourth-best prospect.

In reality, it's unlikely that he would have been considered among the top forty, and perhaps not the top fifty.

---

[*] Altuve's signing with the Astros has become legend. Among the elements: Altuve, then just five feet four, showed up for a tryout with the Astros. Al Pedrique, working as a special assistant for then GM Tim Purpura, told his boss Altuve "could be Freddie Patek with a little power." Pedrique was worried about getting approval from Purpura to spend even the fifteen thousand dollars it would take to sign Altuve. But Pedrique, Purpura says, "convinced me very easily. It was a low-risk investment and wound up being a pretty good signing for the money." (Purpura is a master of understatement, or perhaps modesty.)

That was before the 2010 season, when Altuve moved up a couple of levels on the minor-league ladder, and (again) acquitted himself well despite being (again) among the young players in his leagues. And hallelujah, this time he made *Baseball America's* list.

Twenty-eighth among thirty.

Ultimately, that list would include three outstanding major-league players: Altuve, twenty-eighth; Dallas Keuchel, twenty-third; and J. D. Martinez, sixth. The top five on the list: Jordan Lyles, Delino DeShields Jr., Jonathan Villar, Mike Foltynewicz, and Jiovanni Mier. (You might be excused, even if you're a passionate baseball fan, for not knowing what's lately become of any of those five.)

Mier makes for an interesting comparison with Altuve, as they were double-play partners for most of a minor-league season in 2010, and were born only a few months apart. Same team, same age, facing the same pitchers in the same ballparks. The results? Mier batted .235 with modest power and struck out 107 times in 131 games. Altuve batted .308 with real power and struck out 49 times in 94 games.

And coming off those performances, Mier was considered a potential Shortstop of the Future while Altuve was . . . well, basically an afterthought. Why? Non-professional, non-performance pedigree. Mier had been a first-round draft pick and signed with the Astros for nearly $1.4 million; Altuve had signed as a sixteen-year-old amateur for $15,000. Mier stood six feet two; Altuve was seven or eight inches shorter. As *Baseball America* wrote, "Altuve fits no standard profile. He doesn't lack tools, but he's difficult to compare to other players. . . . He may put up big numbers at Lancaster this season but will have to keep proving himself at higher levels to scouts who remain skeptical of a player with such a small body."*

The next season, Altuve batted .361 (with power, again) in the

---

* Over at the Baseball Prospectus website, Kevin Goldstein did quite a lot better, ranking Mier tenth—and Altuve eleventh. A year and a half later, Goldstein was

Double-A Texas League in thirty-five games—this was after he batted .408 in a couple of months of high Class A ball—at which point the Astros summoned him to the majors (bypassing Triple-A). Same season, Mier got hurt and didn't escape Class A. In the years since, Mier has split his time between Double-A and Triple-A, failing to hit at either level.

Meanwhile, had Altuve finally made believers out of *Baseball America*? Not really. In their 2012 *Prospect Handbook*, the editors offered a projected 2015 Astros lineup with . . . Delino DeShields Jr. at second base. And Jose Altuve? Nowhere to be found. At that point, DeShields had done very little in the minor leagues, but (wait for it) had been a first-round draft pick not long before. Pedigree over performance.

None of which is meant as a commentary on the good work done by *Baseball America*. Their m.o. has always included checking in with a bunch of scouts, and then synthesizing all those opinions into a consensus estimation of a player's likely future. Still, that's a pretty incredible series of inaccurate estimations! Here's the progression of *Baseball America*'s opinions through 2011; then, beginning in 2012, the facts on the ground:

2009	No prospect (Opinion)
2010	No prospect (O)
2011	Fringe Prospect (O)
2012	MLB All-Star (Fact)
2013	Solid MLB Regular (F)
2014	MLB All-Star (F)
2015	MLB All-Star (F)
2016	MLB All-Star (F)
2017	MLB All-Star (F)

---

hired to work in the scouting department of . . . the Houston Astros. Today he serves as the Astros' Director of Pro Scouting.

Remember the name Dallas Keuchel? In 2012, *Baseball America* ranked Dallas Keuchel as the number ten pitching prospect.

No, not the number ten pitching prospect in the minor leagues. The number ten pitching prospect in the Houston Astros organization. Three years later, Dallas Keuchel was named the American League's best pitcher. This year, he was an All-Star for the second time.

Young players are highly unpredictable. As we've seen. And pretending otherwise will lead to some serious misjudgments. As Sig Mejdal, an Astros executive who for some years was uniquely titled Director of Decision Sciences, says, "Sometimes it's just about reminding yourself that you're not so smart."*

Since World War II, Jose Altuve is the only five-feet-six major leaguer with more than *eight* home runs in one season. Which he's now done three times: fifteen in 2015, twenty-four last year, and twenty-one so far this year.

What's more, Altuve essentially willed himself to become a power hitter. Just as he'd willed himself to become a batting champion two years earlier. His first few seasons in the majors, Altuve was exactly what management might reasonably have hoped for: a nice little player (as the saying goes). But in the 2013–2014 off-season, he retooled his swing. He'd been tapping the front of his foot on the ground, as the pitch was being delivered. But on the advice of various coaches and teammates, he thought he should try a real leg kick. It's not something that comes overnight, though.

"It's a pretty interesting process," he tells me. "Because in batting practice and in the cage, you can try so many different things,

---

* For the last couple of years, Mejdal's title hasn't been nearly as poetic. Now he's Special Assistant to the General Manager, Process Improvement. Still unique. Also unique: Mejdal spent the last few months of this minor-league season *in uniform*, as "development coach" with the Tri-City ValleyCats.

and you are going to feel comfortable with ninety percent of those things, because the speed of the pitches is way lower; you hit off the tee, and the ball is just standing there. But then you get in the game and everything is fast and quick, and oh my God, the pitchers aren't the same, mechanics are different. That's when you really have to trust in what you are doing."

He used his new swing in spring training, "and it was good, good, good."

Then the real games started, "and it was like, oh my God. Those first twenty games weren't really good for me. But I trusted my coaches, trusted the people who really wanted to help me, and I trusted the process. 'Let's stay with it. Let's try it.' The next hundred and forty games were good. Then I stayed like that. If I would have quit my leg kick, different story. You know, you never know what will happen."

The next 140 games were better than good. Well, just being ridiculously precise about this, in Altuve's first twenty-two games in 2014, he batted .250 with little power at all. But the rest of the season? In 136 games, he batted .355 with 52 extra-base hits. Despite that slow start, he finished with a league-leading .341 batting average.

"Adjustments are part of baseball," he said. "The pitchers are going to adjust to you; you've gotta adjust back to them." But Altuve has done more than just adjust to survive, as so many players do. First he adjusted and became a batting titlist, then he adjusted again—swinging at fewer bad pitches, but more aggressively at good ones—and became a miniature power dynamo.

Obviously, nobody saw any of this coming. The scouts didn't, *Baseball America* didn't, the Astros' analytically minded front office didn't. How could you see a player like Altuve coming, when there's been only one player remotely like Altuve before, and some fifty years earlier? And *this* player's dramatic improvements came from within?

Before Altuve, the last little guy to make a big impression was probably David Eckstein. Growing up in Florida, Eckstein played a prominent role for a state championship team in high school. Nevertheless, he was just a walk-on at the University of Florida; he tried out for the baseball team, but the long-term goal was law school. Maybe because he was only five feet six. In 1996, having earned a scholarship, Eckstein was both a baseball All-American *and* an academic All-American. In 1997, Eckstein got drafted by the Red Sox. But not until the nineteenth round. Maybe because he was only five feet six (he was actually listed by the University of Florida as five feet nine, but the Red Sox probably knew better).

Eckstein thrived in his first three professional seasons, playing a solid second base and posting tremendous on-base percentages at each rung on the minor-league ladder. But in 2000, his fourth pro season, he was struggling with Boston's Triple-A farm club in August, and the Red Sox, needing to clear a spot on their forty-man roster, waived him. The Anaheim Angels were smart enough to pounce, and just two years later, with Eckstein now playing shortstop (!) every day, the Angels won the World Series for the first (and still only) time in their history. But after the 2004 season, instead of going through the arbitration process with Eckstein—which would have resulted in a goodly raise—the Angels "non-tendered" him; essentially, they released him rather than pay him around $2.5 million for another season. Instead, the Angels committed $32 million to free-agent shortstop Orlando Cabrera.

Granted, Eckstein was by then thirty years old. But so was Cabrera. By the Angels' lights, thirty-year-old Cabrera was worth $32 million, and thirty-year-old Eckstein was worth $0.0 million.

Because he was five feet six? Nah, probably not. Cabrera was the better player. But why not just get Eckstein signed for one year for a relatively paltry sum, and then trade him? Or use him as a utility infielder? It's a baseball mystery.

It was the St. Louis Cardinals' turn to pounce, signing Eckstein for three years and around $10 million. ESPN's Jayson Stark called it the off-season's *worst free-agent signing*.

It wasn't the worst. It wasn't close to the worst. Eckstein was an All-Star in 2005 and 2006, *and* earned Most Valuable Player laurels in the 2006 World Series, in which the Cardinals trounced the Tigers. Along the way, Eckstein became everybody's favorite poster boy for *grit*. For doing all the little things that *sabermetrics* just couldn't measure. A testament to the fallibility of the numbers.

Well, raw numbers are certainly fallible. Especially in the paws of amateurs. But the numbers always said that David Eckstein was a pretty damned good player who reached base reasonably often and somehow became a fine defensive shortstop.

And *Baseball America?* In their first-ever *Prospect Handbook*, they didn't rank Eckstein among the Angels' ten best prospects. Or twenty. Or thirty. In fact, they didn't mention Eckstein at all. Whether because he was five feet six or for some other reason, *Baseball America* and all their scout friends just *couldn't see David Eckstein*. They did rank a young shortstop named Brian Specht, who'd signed out of high school for six hundred thousand dollars, as the Angels' number three prospect.

Specht never escaped the minor leagues. And so it goes.

The Red Sox missed on Eckstein, and *Baseball America* missed on Eckstein, and it seems the Angels missed on him too. And they might not have, if only they'd believed in the numbers instead of Eckstein's Lilliputian dimensions.

Felipe Alou was a star outfielder in the 1960s, and much later would manage the Montreal Expos for ten seasons, then the San Francisco Giants for four. In Alou's 2018 memoir, he'll write, "I do fear that sabermetrics is encroaching too much into the game. . . . I especially think it can get ridiculous with Minor League players, where I believe data is accumulated and implemented too quickly. Players need time to develop, to learn the game, to adjust. A player at eighteen might be completely different than he is at twenty.

Young players should develop under a manager's care instead of by an edict from a spreadsheet. You should also give every Minor League player a fair opportunity to perform. Your prospects will get that opportunity. But the second-tier guy deserves that opportunity, too."

First, there are *hundreds* of "second-tier" guys in the minors every season. Many hundreds, probably. That's just a function of needing to fill the rosters of five or six farm teams per major-league franchise. And second, it's the *numbers* that actually help players who might not be considered real prospects otherwise. Today, Eckstein's numbers might get him on the prospect lists, or they might not. Either way, his numbers would get him the chance to play.

Which isn't to suggest that baseball people don't still look at the proverbial "tools." They do. They have to! When looking at young players in high school or in the Dominican Republic or Venezuela or any of the other baseball hotbeds, there essentially aren't any numbers worth looking at.

For a long time, though, scouts seemed to consider *size* as one of the tools, while *not* considering strike-zone judgment as a tool. Granted, it's difficult to evaluate the strike-zone judgment of a sixteen-year-old Dominican or an eighteen-year-old American high schooler, as the best teenagers are simply too talented to swing at terrible pitches *and* talented enough to hit pitches that aren't actually in the strike zone.

But while scouts might be impressed by a "little" player's fielding, they probably wouldn't trust his hitting. "They'll knock the bat out of his hands," the scouts might say.

Nobody's knocking the bat out of Jose Altuve's hands. Not anymore. And the Astros have a bench player, switch-hitting outfielder Tony Kemp, who's also listed at five feet six; both Altuve and Kemp are the products of an organization that places performance over the traditional scouting tools. And the Astros are hardly alone. In 2017, three of the first-place Boston Red Sox's best players— Mookie Betts, Dustin Pedroia, and Andrew Benintendi—are listed at five feet nine or five feet ten . . . and these listings are probably generous by an inch or so.*

Tonight Oakland's center fielder is a rookie named Herschel "Boog" Powell; at five feet ten and 185 pounds, Powell is the smallest player in the A's lineup (and half a foot shorter than his namesake, old-time slugger John "Boog" Powell). Five years ago, the A's chose Powell toward the end of the amateur draft. That late, a player usually can't be regarded as anything but a sort of prayer, as most of the best players are selected far earlier in the proceedings. But the A's saw something more than just Powell's relatively small stature.

Which is hardly surprising, considering the A's history. Fifteen years ago, in what would soon become immortalized as the "Moneyball draft," the A's owned eight of the first sixty-seven picks. With one of those picks, they drafted a five-feet-ten catcher listed at 226 pounds. Which was probably, uh, generous. With another, they drafted a five-feet-eight, 160-pound outfielder.

Of course, neither player fit anyone's preconceived notions about what a catcher or an outfielder should *look* like. But as A's general manager Billy Beane would tell Michael Lewis, "We're not selling jeans here."

That's probably the most famous line in Lewis's famous book . . . even though neither the 226-pound catcher nor the 160-pound outfielder really panned out. It's simply a useful shorthand for the idea that it doesn't much matter how you look, *if you can play.* And while there's a connection between the two—yes, most of the best players actually do look the part—it's not a perfect relationship, and you're foolish if you ignore performance just because . . . well, because a guy happens to fall well shy of six feet, or looks a little odd in baseball pants, or because you wouldn't look twice if you just saw him walking down the street.

---

* Next spring, a power-packed Braves rookie named Ozzie Albies will launch a batch of impressive home runs. Albies's listed height is five feet eight.

Jose Altuve enters this game with an MLB-leading .351 batting average, despite going 0 for 10 in his last three games. (He didn't play in the Astros' last game, two days ago; manager A. J. Hinch called it a "mental day off.")

With Springer taking his lead off first base, Cotton starts off Altuve with a fastball, for a called strike. Cotton's next pitch is a low-90s "cut fastball"—the pitch made famous by Yankees Hall of Famer Mariano Rivera—that rides in on Altuve, who chops a weak grounder to the third-base coach. Strike two.

So again, Cotton's got an Astro just where he wants him.

And again, he loses him. Loses him badly, with a fastball down the middle that Altuve drives well beyond the wall in straightaway left field. Two batters in, and as Altuve rounds third and touches home, the Astros are already up 2–0.

But wait. This is Major League Baseball, circa 2017. We can be a *lot* more specific about Altuve's two-run homer. Because it's 2017, we can report that Altuve's home run traveled 415 feet. Because it's 2017, we can report that the baseball left Altuve's bat with an *exit velocity* of 106 miles per hour—came in 93, left at 106—and spent 5.6 seconds in the air. And because it's 2017, we can report that the baseball left Altuve's bat with a *launch angle* of precisely 29 degrees.

We could report more, actually. Because it's 2017. But this is still just the top of the first inning, and we should save something for all the other innings.

Cotton does recover to strike out Astros shortstop Carlos Correa—who stands nearly a foot taller than Altuve, which simply must be the all-time differential record for a double-play tandem—but walks left fielder Josh Reddick after Reddick spoils a couple of full-count pitches by fouling them off.

Having now thrown twenty-three pitches and recorded just one out—when a pitcher gets to around thirty in one inning, warning klaxons start blaring in the dugout—Cotton has to work against first baseman Yuli Gurriel, a Cuban defector just finishing his first full season in the majors.

And once *more*, Cotton gets ahead with a couple of quick strikes. And once *more*, he can't finish the job.

Well, technically he does finish off Gurriel. In the box score, Gurriel hits into an inning-ending double play. Technically speaking. After a couple of foul balls, Cotton catches too much of the plate with a changeup, and Gurriel lines the baseball *right up the middle*. Cotton *just* has time to move his glove a smidgen, which is enough to slow the ball down and deflect it to second baseman Jed Lowrie, who underhands the ball to shortstop Marcus Semien, who's stepping on second base to force out Reddick before throwing on to first base to retire Gurriel and end the inning.

Before retreating to his dugout, Cotton bends down to reclaim his glove from the ground, fortunate that Gurriel hadn't instead knocked off a chunk of his ear.

Score: Astros 2, Athletics 0
Win Probability: Astros 65%

Home First

Data, data, data. I can't make bricks without clay.

—SIR ARTHUR CONAN DOYLE (1859–1930)

With shortstop Marcus Semien leading off for the A's, Houston's Collin McHugh takes the mound, already spotted a two-run lead. McHugh hasn't been particularly impressive this season, but prior to 2017 he was a providential find for the Astros: both quite good *and* practically free. Every baseball executive's dream.

With high-quality starting pitchers incredibly difficult to develop and incredibly expensive to acquire, the Astros simply plucked McHugh from the waiver wire after he'd been jettisoned by the perpetually pitching-starved Colorado Rockies. At the time, McHugh was twenty-six years old, and had gone 0-8 with an 8.94 ERA in his brief major-league career. In the rough-and-tumble, youth-obsessed world of professional baseball, if you're going to be great or even good, you're supposed to prove it before you turn twenty-seven.

So what did the Astros see in McHugh that the Mets and the Rockies apparently didn't?

Spin. They saw spin.

As A's television broadcaster (and ex-A's catcher) Ray Fosse now says, "It's all about the spin rate on the curveball. He's got a good one. Throws it a lot."

Which is true. From the 2015 through 2017 seasons, only eight major leaguers will throw at least three hundred innings *and* throw curveballs more than 25 percent of the time; McHugh's eighth on that list, just shy of 26 percent.*

"When we found McHugh, he was a sinker-slider guy," Astros pitching coach Brent Strom told me. "He got called up to replace Scott Feldman in the rotation, just for a couple of weeks. Warming up before the game, he's working horizontal in the strike zone. And I just said, 'With the backspin on your fastball and that curveball, why not work up and down instead?' He goes out there, gets twelve punch-outs in seven and two-thirds innings, and never saw the minor leagues again."

Sure, a dozen strikeouts aren't what they used to be. But a dozen's still plenty: in fact, the second most in franchise history for a pitcher making his Astros debut. But flashy beginnings were nothing new for McHugh. In his first major-league start, with the Mets back in August 2012, McHugh gave up only two hits in seven innings, striking out nine Rockies. This ranks as one of the two or three greatest debuts in Mets history. But then McHugh managed only fourteen innings and eight strikeouts the rest of the season. The next summer, the Mets traded him to the Rockies and he still struggled.

Struggled so badly that the Rockies waived him. But there was something about Collin McHugh that perhaps nobody else realized. Or if they realized the something, it wasn't something they found particularly interesting. McHugh's fastball sat right around 90 miles per hour; which (these days) is barely passable. Let alone interesting. But what *was* interesting? To the Astros, anyway?

What interested the Astros, more than anything else, was the spin rate on McHugh's curveball. A typical curveball *spins* at around

---

* When it comes to throwing curveballs, McHugh's teammate Lance McCullers, the Astros' second draft pick five years ago, finishes behind nobody. McCullers has thrown his curveball nearly *half* the time. McCullers is the champion curveballer of the last fifteen years, at least.

1,500 rotations per minute. But McHugh's clocked at roughly 2,000 RPM, among the highest rates in the game.*

But the Rockies had been more intrigued by McHugh's two-seam sinking fastball than his curveball, or his (high-spinning) four-seam fastball. They became considerably less intrigued when he posted a 9.95 ERA in four games.

If only they'd appreciated his curveball, right?

Ah, but the world is a complicated place. According to a metric published on the FanGraphs website, McHugh's curveball has *not* been a particularly good pitch for him. Generally speaking, his slider and (semirelated) cut fastball have worked better than his curveball, which has been particularly ineffective this season. Still, it's hard to argue against spin rate, which also comes into play not just with the curveball and slider, but also the high fastball Brent Strom prefers. If it's spinning more, it drops less . . . which allows a pitcher to fool batters *without* throwing more than around 90 miles an hour. As Strom told me, "Hitters don't hit the fucking radar gun. They hit what they see or can't see."†

But ten years ago, nobody knows any of this. Yes, scouts would talk about the spin on a pitcher's curveball. Yes, scouts would notice that a pitcher's fastball seemed to *rise*. Which is an optical illusion; it was really just dropping less than the brain expected. But optical illusion or not, the hitter can be fooled; there have always been a

---

* In 2014, McHugh's first season with the Astros, only four major leaguers threw at least one hundred curveballs and averaged a higher spin rate than McHugh's. One of them, Charlie Morton, would himself be acquired by the Astros after the 2016 season. And all Morton will do in 2017, at thirty-three, is set a career high with a team-best fourteen victories.

† Strom reached the major leagues as a pitcher with the New York Mets in 1972; the staff ace was of course Tom Seaver, who somewhat famously said, "The good rising fastball is the best pitch in baseball." Strom's never been a fan of the sinking fastball, which hasn't always gone over well with some sinker-centric coworkers.

few pitchers who didn't throw particularly hard but still managed to get plenty of swings and misses with their fastball.*

It's not until fairly recently, though, that anyone could *quantify* spin rate. And once you can quantify something, it becomes easier to evaluate players, who become more distinctive; decisions become more justifiable. As McHugh finishes his warm-up throws, we can look at him and be reminded, as we might be reminded so many more times through the course of every single professional baseball game, of the book that changed everything.

In 2003, W. W. Norton published Michael Lewis's *Moneyball*. You've probably read the book. Or seen the movie. Or quite likely, both.

Before *Moneyball*, for many decades the biggest drivers for hitters' salaries were home runs and RBIs. If you hit homers and drove in runs, they would call you a *run producer* and they would pay you plenty. There's an old quote, supposedly from perennial home-run champion Ralph Kiner: "Singles hitters drive Fords. Home-run hitters drive Cadillacs." Contrary to popular opinion, batting average was not valued so highly by the market. Most baseball executives did know an "empty" batting average when they saw one.

But in 2004 and 2005, in the immediate wake of *Moneyball*, on-base percentage became more valued, RBIs and home runs less valued, with the three essentially even in those years. OBP then leveled off, perhaps because once teams internalized that metric, they could move on to other, less obvious attributes. The A's, for example, made a brief (but notable) shift away from big, slow, OBP machines like Scott Hatteberg and Matt Stairs, to players with cryptically outstanding defensive talents.

In related news, *Moneyball* also propagated the notion that there's essentially *free talent* out there, just waiting for the canny

---

* Thirty years ago, New York Mets left-hander Sid Fernandez routinely posted superior strikeout rates despite a sub-90 fastball, which he threw most of the time. Nobody could quite figure out how he did it. Today it would be figured.

general manager to grab it. There are whole chapters in the book about Billy Beane's ability to see real value in Hatteberg and relief pitcher Chad Bradford—value that other, presumably more traditional baseball men simply failed to see.

But the A's weren't the only team that turned so-called Dumpster-diving into a sort of dark art.

Shortly after David Ortiz turned twenty-seven, the Minnesota Twins released him. *Released him.* So the Boston Red Sox took a flier. Someday David Ortiz will be in the Hall of Fame, purely because of all he accomplished after the Twins cut him loose.

Granted, Big Papi's an extreme case. Before he was released, Ortiz had posted a .500 slugging percentage in the 2002 season. What's surprising is not that the Twins had little use for Ortiz. What's surprising is that his value was so low that they weren't able to *trade* a future Hall of Famer for *anything*, and that nobody claimed him from the waiver wire before the Red Sox. In fact, Ortiz opened his first Red Sox season on the bench, below Kevin Millar and Jeremy Giambi on the depth chart. It wasn't until Giambi crapped out that Ortiz became an everyday player. And the rest, as they say, is history. Lots of World Series history.*

Does Dumpster-diving still work, all these years later? Can you still find those guys, essentially free? Well, Collin McHugh and stars J. D. Martinez and Justin Turner and Jake Arrieta and a few others we'll meet later are living proof that it doesn't just still work—it can still work spectacularly well. One of the *ideas* in *Moneyball*— and Michael Lewis will tell you that the book wasn't about the A's or Billy Beane or OBP, but rather it was about an *idea*—was that

---

* Speaking of history and Dumpster-diving, in the spring of 1986, a glowering right-handed pitcher named Dave Stewart signed with Oakland two weeks after drawing his summary release from the Philadelphia Phillies. He was twenty-nine, and eventually earned a spot in the A's rotation. From 1987 through 1990, Stewart averaged twenty-one victories per season, finishing second, third, or fourth in A.L. Cy Young balloting each year.

there are market inefficiencies out there, and there always will be, and the key to success is finding them. Yes, especially if you're on a tight budget. But it turns out that even the rich teams don't win without finding a few bargain surprises too. The Dodgers might be the best team in the National League this season, and two of their best hitters—Turner, and Chris Taylor—were both freely available; essentially any team with just a shred of interest could have acquired their services, quite cheaply, just before they broke out as hitting stars.

The key is knowing what to look for, and today you must look far beyond on-base percentage, since hitters' OBPs or pitchers' strikeouts per nine innings aren't any sort of secret these days. The Astros were intrigued by the spin rate on McHugh's curveball, and the Cubs were intrigued by Jake Arrieta's raw stuff (combined with their opinion that he'd been jerked around by too many different pitching coaches, and discouraged from throwing what looked like a pretty good cut fastball), and the Dodgers were intrigued by Turner's and Taylor's new swings.

There will forever be a search for new competitive edges, even as more and more teams are looking at essentially the same data. But there's looking, and there's *looking*. In 2014, there was a report that *some* major-league team had purchased a $500,000 Cray supercomputer. Speculation held that it was the Astros, but the next spring an official Cray blog said it wasn't the Astros, but another analytics-heavy team that won more games than the Astros.

Which left a lot of possibilities, since the Astros won only seventy games in 2014. Obvious candidates included the Dodgers, Red Sox, and Yankees; but if you throw in teams with usually limited budgets, the list triples in size. Anyway, it wouldn't be strange if other teams had supercomputers by now. For one obvious reason: Statcast.

Ah, glibness! If only the world were accurately described by glibness! (It's not.)

This era—beginning this year, or perhaps in 2015—will probably be remembered as *the Statcast Era*, for various and sundry reasons. But this story actually begins in 2008, when a system called PITCHf/x went online in twenty-eight of thirty MLB stadiums (the other two were added the next season). Using two highly specialized (and expensive) cameras, PITCHf/x measured just about everything about a pitch that could be measured: release point, speed, movement, spin, and location.

Prior to PITCHf/x, there were smatterings of such data available. Of course, radar guns had long been used to measure the speed of pitches, and various parties were manually charting where pitches ended up. But none of this data was particularly reliable, or organized in ways that were wildly useful for analysts.

PITCHf/x changed all that in a million ways. So we *could* call everything since 2008 the PITCHf/x Era. Except that PITCHf/x has disappeared from Major League Baseball. This season, a transition was completed from the technology powering PITCHf/x to the technology powering what Major League Baseball dubbed Statcast.

Statcast actually does far more than simply track pitches. Using both cameras and a sort of radar, if it's on the field and it moves, Statcast is watching. And recording. Yes, the baseball wherever it goes, but also every player and the hitter's bat.

So we're in the middle of the Statcast Era, instead of the PITCHf/x Era, largely because Statcast is a catchy name and the technology's fan-friendlier outputs are being promoted heavily by Major League Baseball Advanced Media, with its many internet and broadcast tentacles.

Oh, and about computing power? In a single game, Statcast generates several terabytes of data. Granted, according to a Deadspin story, "the final stored data is far more manageable, at 250 megabytes per game without video."

Still, you play 162 games in a season. So do the other twenty-nine teams. That's 2,430 games. They're generating data in minor-league games too. Now we're talking about some *real* information. If you're running a baseball team and you're smart, you want that information. You want all that information. And once you've got the information, you want to play around with it. You *need* to play around with it, if you're going to stay competitive in today's game.

Which is where a Cray supercomputer comes in. And $500,000 seems like a small price to pay, when you think about it. When you think about it, half a million bucks seems like a price that every franchise should happily pay with hardly a thought.

One thing about baseball franchises, though: even now, aside from paying the players, most of them are reluctant to spend more money than the barest minimum. So you can bet there aren't thirty supercomputers in the major leagues. Many clubs wind up scrimping on both computing power *and* the people who could use more computing power.

Back afield, McHugh toes the rubber and looks to catcher Brian McCann for the sign, his workday officially beginning. Which isn't to say he hasn't already been working. Just like Cotton, McHugh has studied video of tonight's enemy hitters twice in the last four days—half the lineup one day, then the other half—looking for tendencies and weaknesses: "Where they're going to do damage on fastballs," McHugh says, "where they're susceptible to fastballs, whether a curveball or slider is better, what's my bailout pitch, and can I throw my changeup.

"I go through all those guys," McHugh continues, "try and get a good visual picture of what they look like before I see them." Stats are available, but McHugh doesn't spend much time with them; one thing you hear from a lot of baseball players is the phrase "paralysis by analysis" (or its brother epithet, "information overload"). There *are* players out there who gobble up all the numbers, but most ballplayers (and regular people) have a limited capacity for reams of data. "Most of the time," New York Mets pitching coach Mickey Callaway will say next week, "it's pitch to your strengths.

We've kind of pulled back on some of the information and let them do their thing."*

This sort of game preparation occupies roughly an hour a day, so McHugh and Cotton spend most of their off days on physical preparation: trainer, masseuse, throwing, and (for at least a few pitchers around the league) a bit of yoga too. Oh, plus rest; Cotton describes the third day after his last start as *your day*: a bit of light throwing, but otherwise reserved for decompressing, just enjoying life outside baseball.

A couple of relatively minor injuries—which is to say, surgeons weren't involved—have limited McHugh to just eight starts all season, in which he's gone 2-2 with a 3.25 earned run average. It's striking that the Astros have been missing a key component of their pitching rotation for most of the season and yet here they are, fighting for the best record in the entire league.

After jumping ahead in the count against leadoff man Semien with a couple of well-placed pitches, McHugh unleashes his first slider. It's not supposed to catch the strike zone at all, but instead cuts through the heart of the zone. They'd call this a mistake if Semien *barreled* the pitch, but instead he swings just a bit low, lofting an easy fly ball to left fielder Josh Reddick.

That brings up lefty-hitting Matt Joyce, with one out. He rips McHugh's third offering, a cutter that also catches far too much of the strike zone, into the right-field corner for a double. There's no play at second base, as Joyce jogs to the bag, then bends down to remove a protective pad from his right shin. In the Astros' television booth, analyst Geoff Blum says, "In the past, if Collin McHugh

---

* Similarly, many catchers are reluctant to dive *too* deeply into the data. As brainy ex-catcher John Baker told me, "Catchers are generally the biggest skeptics of any information. We're more skeptical because our reputation, in the clubhouse and with our pitching staff, is on the line."

hasn't buried that pitch inside, it usually gets hit pretty hard." Once you start paying attention, you'll notice that even really good pitchers make mistakes in the strike zone; this was McHugh's second big miss in just two batters.

Next up: veteran infielder Jed Lowrie. At thirty-three, Lowrie's the oldest player in the A's lineup *and* is enjoying his best season, in part because he's been largely healthy for one of the few times in his career. It's a bit surprising that the rebuilding A's didn't trade him this summer for a prospect or two, especially considering Lowrie's team-friendly contract; he's earning just $6.5 million this season, and a bit less next season. Then again, there's that commonsensical belief that young teams need at least a dollop or two of veteran leadership, and $6 million might seem a small price to pay. Even for these habitually penurious Athletics.

McHugh feeds Lowrie three straight fastballs. The second of them (again!) catches too much of the plate, but Lowrie merely fouls the pitch into the stands. The third is up in the strike zone, just where Brent Strom likes them, and Lowrie lifts another easy fly to Reddick in left, with Joyce rooted at second base.

The A's cleanup hitter is Khris Davis, and for good reason: Davis hits home runs.

Khris Davis hits lots of home runs. Which hardly anyone seems to have noticed.

Ralph Kiner was the greatest power hitter of the immediate postwar era. Beginning in 1946, Kiner led the National League in home runs in seven straight seasons. Babe Ruth never (quite) put together a streak that long. Nor did Ted Williams or Mickey Mantle or Willie Mays or Hank Aaron or Barry Bonds or anyone else.

Yes, those were different times. In Kiner's era, power was rare. In those seven straight league-leading seasons, Kiner topped forty homers four times. Which was (and would be today) impressive. But Kiner was almost alone. In those seven years, only three other hitters hit more than forty home runs, and each of them did it just once.

By the close of this season, Major League Baseball will have seen *twenty* guys in the last seven years with more than forty homers in a season.

Aside from Kiner, the other three on that 1946–1952 list were Johnny Mize, Ted Williams, and Hank Greenberg. Hall of Famers, all of them. The 2011–2017 list of twenty includes Mark Trumbo, Adam Dunn, Chris Davis, Curtis Granderson, and various others who, while certainly fine players, aren't fine candidates for the Hall of Fame.

In Kiner's era, and for some decades after, if you hit thirty-odd homers with any frequency at all, you were a star. And you were driving whatever you liked.

In the 1970s and '80s, Dave Kingman was famous even though he was basically good for just one thing: power. He couldn't really run or play defense or draw walks. In Kingman's final season, he batted .210 . . . but also hit thirty-five home runs, and that was his final season not because of his batting average or his fielding, but because he was a pain in the ass. Thirty years later? Sure. Hit your thirty-five or forty home runs. We'll take them. But if you don't do something else at least decently, you're driving a Ford. Well, a metaphorical Ford.

In 2017, there's no greater example than Chris Carter.

Once an A's prospect, Carter never established himself with the big club despite numerous trials. Before the 2013 season, the A's traded him to the Astros for Jed Lowrie; mostly, the Astros wanted to shed Lowrie's contract and clear the way for Jose Altuve at second base.

With no real reason not to, the Astros installed Carter as an everyday player, and he led them that season with twenty-nine homers and eighty-two RBIs. He also struck out 212 times, then the third-highest figure in major-league history. Oh, and the Astros lost 111 games. In 2014, basically the same story, except the Astros lost only 92 games.

In 2015, Carter batted just .199 and didn't lead his team in anything except walks (and almost strikeouts). And so after the season, the Astros essentially released him, rather than go through the arbitration process and (win or lose!) give Carter a substantial raise over the $4.2 million he'd earned that season.

Carter signed a one-year contract with the Milwaukee Brewers. He took a huge pay cut, to $2.5 million (which, granted, even today will buy you plenty of Fords). And in 2016, all this ill-paid castoff did was win the Ralph Kiner Award, leading the National League with forty-one home runs.*

Jackpot for Chris Carter, right?

Nope. Like the Astros, the Brewers wanted no part of an arbitration process with Carter, and so they cut him loose too. He *did* get a raise this time, though, ultimately signing a one-year deal with the Yankees for $3.5 million in 2017.

In early July, having hit only eight home runs, Carter got cut loose once more. With half the teams in the majors still actively trying to get better and reach the postseason, Carter couldn't find another job. Ralph Kiner one year; the next, unemployed.

Obviously, Carter's an extreme example. Another extreme example? The Athletics' own Ryon Healy, who's DHing tonight and batting sixth. This season, starting nearly every game for the A's, Healy has hit twenty-three home runs, which is somewhat impressive. Less impressively, he's struck out 126 times while drawing only nineteen walks. That means he's good enough to play . . . but just barely. These days the strikeouts aren't really an issue—lots of guys strike out more—but without more home runs *or* more walks, a player like Healy's always going to be dispensable, and in danger of suffering Carter's fate once he's earning much more than the major-league minimum salary (this season, $535,000).

Another, less extreme example is Khris Davis, who went the op-

---

* That's the award they give you for leading the National League in home runs, which I just made up. You get a chrome Cadillac Escalade on a wooden platform that rotates and is powered by a tiny perpetual-motion machine.

posite direction of Carter: first Milwaukee, then Oakland. In 2015, Davis led the Brewers with twenty-seven home runs. And after the season, they traded him to the A's for a couple of middling (at best) prospects. In 2016, he hit forty-two home runs. Not enough to lead the American League, but one more than Carter hit in the other league. The A's did *not* cut Davis loose; instead they and he agreed on $5 million for this year; and he'll reward them with forty-three more homers this season. Over the two seasons, *nobody* in the A.L. will hit more home runs.

Leaving aside World War II, when nobody hit home runs because the baseball was dead and nearly all the stars were in the service, I'm willing to bet that essentially every player who's led his league in home runs over a two-year span was a star; that is, he was well known to most baseball fans, and often more famous than that.

Putting that another way, I'll bet Khris Davis is the most anonymous major leaguer in history with eighty-some home runs in two years.

Which might seem unfair.

It is not. In 2017, it's perfectly fair. Despite his imperfections, Khris Davis is a wonderfully talented athlete, and at this point in his career, a tremendous bargain for his employers.

What he's not is a tremendous *major-league baseball player.* Because, like Chris Carter, Davis doesn't really do much *except* hit home runs, at a particular moment when there are lots of players who also hit home runs.

Davis will finish this season with a .247 batting average. For the third straight season (which is crazy weird). He will also draw seventy-three walks this season, leading to a respectable .336 on-base percentage. He'll lead the A's in both runs scored and RBIs, and it's true that people *would* notice all this if the A's were playoff contenders.

But Davis is *not* a star and will probably never be *paid* like a star, for the simple reason that he doesn't win enough baseball games. He doesn't create a great number of runs because he doesn't control

the strike zone or run well, and he doesn't prevent many runs because he's a poor left fielder (more on this later). Over these two
seasons, Davis will rank number two in the major leagues in home
runs . . . and number ninety-three in wins above replacement (via
Baseball-Reference.com; WAR is relative to the contribution we
might expect from a good Triple-A player, or fill-in off the bench).
Not so long ago, if you hit forty-three homers and drove in 110 runs,
as Davis will this season, you were automatically an MVP candidate.

This year he'll finish tied for twenty-second in the balloting, appearing on just one voter's ballot, in the last slot.

Let's be clear! Being the ninety-third most valuable non-pitcher
in the major leagues is mighty impressive! Almost none of us will
ever be so good at anything in our lives! Let alone something as
quantifiable as "baseball player." In an open market operating with
perfect rationality, the sum of Davis's parts might be worth something like $25 million per season. On the presumption that on the
open market, a single win above replacement costs—or has cost, in
recent off-seasons—upwards of $8 million.

But *that* presumes that talent is distributed evenly; that a three-
win player like Khris Davis is just as rare a three-win player as, say,
Red Sox shortstop Xander Bogaerts or Astros super-utility player
Marwin Gonzalez. It also presumes that a single win above replacement is as valuable to a team like the A's as a team like the Astros.

It's not. The market doesn't operate with perfect rationality, and
wins are worth a lot more to some teams than others. And so it's
unlikely that Khris Davis will ever earn the sort of money his agent
has told him he'll earn. He's not Chris Carter. But he'll never be
Ralph Kiner either.

McHugh's not thinking about any of this while getting ahead
in the count, though he's surely thinking about Davis's ability to
tie up the game with a single swing. With Matt Joyce on, the A's
could mirror the Astros and be right back in the game. McHugh
can't tempt Davis with a couple of sliders well outside the zone, and

Davis ultimately draws a quiet walk. Uh-oh. Next: A's first baseman Matt Olson, who's been on quite a power surge lately. Since rejoining the lineup a month ago—after his *sixth* stint in the minors, just this season—Olson's hit eleven home runs in just twenty-five games. In any era, no matter how moribund the franchise, those numbers should inspire hope in even the bitterest of fans.*

Not this time, though. Olson gets a fastball on the edge of his happy zone—if you believe the "heat maps" that every pitcher and catcher look at now—but lifts yet another easy fly to left field, where Reddick ties an all-time record, held by many hundreds of other left fielders, by squeezing the third out.

Score: Astros 2, Athletics 0
Win Probability: Astros 70%

---

* Olson will finish this season with forty-seven home runs: twenty-four in the majors and twenty-three in the minors, his twenty-four with the A's coming in just 216 plate appearances. On the all-time list of players with at least two hundred plate appearances in a season, Olson's home-run percentage ranks fourth, behind one Barry Bonds season and a couple of Mark McGwire seasons.

Visitors Second

I have already written a treatise and it reads like this: Keep your eye clear and hit 'em where they ain't. That's all.

—HALL OF FAME OUTFIELDER WEE WILLIE KEELER (1872–1923)

With Cotton back on the mound, the Astros' first hitter is jack-of-most-trades Marwin Gonzalez, who doesn't have a regular position but does lead the Astros in runs batted in, plus the major leagues in killing time. Gonzalez is one of those players whose existence can, all by itself, explain a great deal of today's Baseball, and later we'll spend more time with him. He deserves it.

For now, Gonzalez takes a couple of high fastballs to get ahead in the count, then drives another heater, this one meant by Cotton to actually be hit—because almost anything's better than falling behind 3 and 0—to the wall in center field. There, Boog Powell takes a couple of stutter steps on the dirt warning track before leaping a couple of feet in the air to make the catch. Everything went according to everyone's plan: Cotton *didn't* fall behind 3 and 0, Gonzalez *didn't* miss an eminently hittable pitch, and Powell did what small, power-starved center fielders are supposed to do.

Next up: forty-year-old designated hitter Carlos Beltrán. While Gonzalez has far exceeded anyone's reasonable expectations this season, Beltrán's done the opposite. Signed for both his veteran leadership *and* his demonstrated run production, he's been the Astros' worst-hitting regular. Quite a disappointment considering Beltrán, earning $16 million, is the Astros' second-highest-paid player, just a tick behind catcher Brian McCann, who was acquired for essentially the same reasons: veteran leadership *and* run production.*

Beltrán doesn't exactly turn things around here. After fouling off a high fastball to reach a 2-and-2 count, he whiffs on a low changeup. And we're perhaps reminded that, hey guess what, now that players are getting tested for sports drugs, they're not aging quite as well as they were when, for a few years, you could take just about anything.

Which brings up the lefty-swinging McCann, and gets Oakland's inner defense moving around, in what's become for infielders (and fans) a familiar dance: first baseman Matt Olson and second baseman Jed Lowrie shift slightly closer to the first-base line than they would normally be, shortstop Marcus Semien swings all the way around to the *first-base side* of second base, and third baseman Matt Chapman sets up roughly where the shortstop usually would.

Statistically speaking, this is *not* a difficult call. According to Sports Info Solutions, *no* active player has faced more of these shifts than McCann; by the end of this season, he'll have faced 1,577 in his career—technically speaking, this counts only shifts on batted balls in play—and lost 136 hits in the process. He's also gained 77 hits because of the shift, but McCann's minus-59 net is also the largest loss over these eight seasons. If you're an extreme pull hitter (check) and extremely slow (ditto), there's just no reason *not* to shift against you, at least when the bases are empty.

So what does McCann do? Instead of hitting into the teeth of this lopsided defense, he slaps a high fastball into left field; even with the infield positioned normally, the ball probably would have

---

* In October, Beltrán will be consigned to part-time duties during the Astros' postseason run. Meanwhile, a good chunk of McCann's considerable salary is actually being paid by the Yankees, who were simply happy to trade McCann and relieve themselves of *most* of the $34 million they still owed him.

snuck between the shortstop and third baseman. But here, third baseman Matt Chapman has no chance, and McCann trots down to first base with one of the easier base hits of his life. Well, "easier" if we assume that he was trying to do that.

Which he probably wasn't, considering his history. Or his thoughts on the practical difficulty of hitting them where they ain't.

"I hear everybody talking about that all the time," he says, "and I laugh because, you know, the cutter changed the game. The cut fastball changed the game of baseball. When guys are throwing mid- to upper nineties with cut? Twenty years ago, even fifteen years ago when I first broke in, you maybe had four or five guys around the league throwing cutters. Maybe not even that. Now that's a very common pitch. When you can throw a cutter in on someone's hands, that's a pitch that you've gotta cover. And it's very hard to go the opposite way on that pitch."

Again, he's not the only one. McCann's merely an extreme example of a widespread phenomenon. In today's Baseball, strikeouts are up. But they've been going up for a long time. In today's Baseball, home runs are up. In fact, we'll see more home runs this season than we've ever seen before. But there have been home-run spikes before. Perhaps the most dramatic transformation in recent years has been the explosion in nontraditional defensive alignments, and particularly in the infield.

Just seven years ago, there were only 2,463 shifts on batted balls.

That's when Baseball Info Solutions—now Sports Info Solutions—began paying attention. BIS employed people to track a multitude of events for every batted ball, including: *was one of the infielders on the wrong side of second base?*

If so, BIS counted this as a "Williams Shift," for its most famous inspiration.*

---

* A few years ago, BIS dropped the term "Williams Shift," and now just calls them shifts.

It's important to reiterate here—important, for reasons we'll discover in a moment—that most of the data on shifts *still* covers just batted balls. (Commercially, that is. Every MLB team now has access to all positioning data for every pitch, since Statcast tracks the location of every player on the field at all times.)

Still, thanks to BIS we've now got systematic, publicly available shifting data for eight full seasons, including this one. In 2010, BIS recorded 2,463 shifts; in 2011, the figure actually fell off a little. But in 2012, radical infield shifting exploded and kept exploding for five seasons. Here are the season-to-season *percentage* increases, beginning in 2012: 95, 50, 93, 34, 57.

The raw numbers? There were 2,350 shifts in 2011 . . . and *28,130* in 2016. Which, if my math's correct, is roughly a 1,197-percent increase in shifts on batted balls. Which, assuming my math is correct, is approximately three additional (metric) shit-tons of Williams shifts.

You're forgiven for suspecting that radical infield shifting is a modern invention.

In Tom Verducci's book about the 2016 Cubs—which, just being honest here, plays out as a sort of group hagiography—he traced today's shifting to a game in 1998, when then Angels coach Joe Maddon, who kept hitting spray charts for every opposing hitter, told manager Terry Collins that Ken Griffey Jr. "almost never hits a ground ball to the left side of the infield. What do you think if we shift the shortstop over and play three infielders on the right side?"

"Let's do it," Collins (reportedly) said.

So according to Verducci, "The modern shift was born on September 20, 1998."

Which is true! At least if you've got a terribly loose definition of "modern." In fact, there must be millions of fans who witnessed such "modern" shifting in the 1970s and '80s without really noticing.

Without the man-hours and the hypersoftware, it just wasn't practical for anyone to closely track shifting and its efficacy. I watched a lot of baseball games in those years, and I just *barely* remember some occasional shifting. I would *almost* swear that teams used to shift against Royals first baseman John Mayberry . . . or was it Royals first baseman Willie Mays Aikens? Both were big, slow power hitters looking to drive every pitch into the right-field stands. And I wouldn't be surprised if both faced shifts. Occasionally. But it's impossible for us to ever know how often; it's one of the few interesting things about baseball we will never, ever know. When we're talking about the historical trend toward shifting, we're at a huge disadvantage, for the simple reason that—and I believe this is literally true—we've got absolutely no data before 2010.

No reliable data, anyway. We do have a few numbers from the late 1940s, though accompanied by a giant asterisk.

In 1946, Lou Boudreau, the Cleveland Indians' young shortstop *and* manager, came up with a novel tactic against Ted Williams, then the greatest hitter on the planet by quite a lot. In the second game of a July 14 doubleheader—in which Williams had already racked up eight RBIs—Boudreau deployed the so-called Williams shift for the first time: first baseman deeper than normal, and near the foul line; second baseman in short right field, not far from the foul line; shortstop roughly where the second baseman would usually play; third baseman at the edge of the outfield grass, just to the first-base side of second base; right fielder deep and swung around toward the foul line; and center fielder swung around to medium-depth right center.[*]

Oh, and the left fielder? He alone was left to guard the entire left side of the field, essentially playing an exceptionally deep shortstop.

But it wasn't only Boudreau's teams that were shifting. Not at all. In the process of working on his book *Facing Ted Williams*, journalist Dave Heller spoke to 236 former major leaguers who faced

---

[*] It was often called the Boudreau shift for some decades, but that eventually faded as Williams's legend grew and Boudreau's shrank.

Williams during his playing career; 84 of them are actually in Heller's book. Of those, 20 were infielders. As it happens, Heller seems to have asked *everyone* about the shift—infielders, outfielders, and pitchers alike—and it seems that nearly *everyone* shifted against Williams, at least occasionally. Just among the infielders, six of the seven non-Williams (that is, not the Red Sox) American League teams are represented, and players from all six talk about shifting . . . oh, and the seventh? The seventh is the Kansas City A's, managed for most of two seasons by Boudreau. A's pitcher Ned Garver says they shifted too.

As I said, it's impossible to know for sure, but we might reasonably guess that from 1946 through the end of his career in 1960, Williams somewhat routinely faced shifts that would look highly familiar to us sixty-odd years later.

Did it work?

From 1947 through 1960, Williams batted .340/.480/.627 overall, with Mickey Mantle the only American League hitter *remotely* in Williams's class.

How did Williams fare with the bases empty, when there was no obvious reason *not* to shift on him? With the bases empty in those years, he batted .332/.452/.611, which suggests the shifts worked *some*. Maybe just a little. Except pitchers have a small natural advantage with the bases empty, because the fielders don't have to worry about baserunners. Considering the small differences between the percentages, I think it's safe to say that Williams lost little, if anything, to the shifts he did face. Granting, again, that we can't know how often he actually faced them.

It's quite possible that the original Boudreau/Williams shift was unique in its radicalness. But Boudreau has long been popularly credited with being the first manager to shift his shortstop—in his case, himself—to the other side of second base, and that's just flat-out wrong. I mean, way, way, nineteenth-century wrong.

In 1877, just the second season of the National League, Brooklyn

Hartfords player-manager Bob "Death to Flying Things" Ferguson reportedly positioned his second baseman on the third-base side of second base for *righty* pull hitters. Two years later, Ferguson—by then captaining the N.L.'s Troy Trojans—shifted his infield against lefty hitters in *exactly* the same way it's done in 2017.*

We've got nothing like a comprehensive history of shifts since good ol' Bob Ferguson. But according to researcher David Nemec, lefty power hitters Ken Williams and Cy Williams both faced shifts in 1922. Probably Babe Ruth too.

In fact, 1946 wasn't even the first time Ted Williams faced a shift. In September 1941, with Williams on his way to a .406 batting average, Boudreau's Indians—at twenty-four, he wouldn't be named player-manager until after the season—shifted against Williams under the direction of skipper Roger Peckinpaugh, who probably got the idea from White Sox manager Jimmy Dykes, who had shifted against Williams earlier that season.

By now you might be wondering why shifting, so popular from 1946 through 1960 against Teddy Ballgame, didn't catch on with other pull hitters.

But it did catch on! And people just don't remember or talk about it! Maybe because it didn't seem so notable at the time, or maybe because, in those days before instant replay and microanalysis and nearly every game on television, most people just didn't even notice. Or they noticed, but only for a moment. In 1978, the Royals used four outfielders against Red Sox slugger Jim Rice. But it wasn't particularly extraordinary. As Orioles pitcher coach Ray Miller observed, "The Rice Shift is an eye-catching version of what many teams are doing. We chart what every pitch is, where it is, and where it is hit."

---

* When you do a bit of historical research, you quickly realize that there's very little in baseball that's new, except for the electronics.

The only reason so many of the players mentioned shifting in *Facing Ted Williams* was that the author directly asked them about it; shifting against Williams was just something you did.

What's so wonderful about all the data today is that even though everyone's got essentially the same numbers, they're coming up with remarkably different questions and answers. This season the Cubs will shift for only 526 batted balls and post the second-best defensive efficiency rating in the National League; that is, they'll rank second in the percentage of batted balls that get turned into outs by the defense. The Reds will shift for 1,235 batted balls and post the fourth-best rating in the league.

But while teams have all sorts of approaches, the sluggers keep doing the same thing: slugging. Almost always, just slugging.

Should they bunt more often? Make the defense pay, with easy base hits dropped into that massive area of unprotected grass? Probably! When you look at Dodger slugger Cody Bellinger's batting average on bunts, you say of *course* they should bunt more. But there are two downsides to bunting. The obvious one is that it's tremendously difficult to hit a home run when bunting. The less obvious one is that bunting is not actually so easy. Especially against guys who throw as hard as guys throw today. If you miss the bunt or foul it off, now you're probably behind in the count.

Of course, there are also the two upsides: the high batting average when getting the bunt down, and the long-term likelihood that if you bunt with some frequency, you'll see shifts less frequently.

But if you're going to bunt for a hit just once every month or so, there's practically no deterrent effect at all. So now it's just for the batting average. Which is fine. If they're just giving you first base, why not take it once in a while?

The other suggestion is to simply hit the ball "the other way." Do what Brian McCann just did, and keep doing it until the other manager gives up. With just one player guarding that entire half of the infield, why not? That's what Ty Cobb told Ted Williams to do. But Williams just couldn't do it. "I'm not going to tamper with my style just to hit a few extra singles to left," he said. "I've spent too many years learning how to pull the ball to right to take chances. If I change my style now, I might lose my power to right. I'll keep swinging away even if they put the catcher out in right field. If I smack the ball over the fence they'll have a hard time fielding it."

Stubborn? Okay. Maybe. But are we sure Williams was wrong? He used essentially the same argument when writers said he should expand his strike zone with runners on base. Sure, he'd walk a bit less and strike out a bit more. But the extra RBIs (they said) would be worth it. Williams told the writers to pound sand. That would be a great way to develop bad habits, he figured.

And it's awfully hard to argue with the results. Could Williams have changed his approach and done *better*? Would Einstein have been a better physicist, if only he'd gotten more sleep? While Williams peaked, as most hitters do, in his middle to late twenties, he remained one of the game's most devastating hitters until the day he retired. At forty-two.

Plus, it should be said that Williams *did* try to beat the shift by going the other way. Back then, they said he wasn't. "The hell I wasn't," Williams would later say. "I was just having a hard time hitting to left field. Every spring after [1946] I'd experiment, shifting my feet, trying to drop balls into left field, blunking them into short center"—*blunking them*—"seeing what could be done. But I was having a hard time. Ty Cobb, who used to give me a blast every now and then for not swinging at close pitches, wrote me a 2-page letter outlining how *he* would beat the shift."

But Ted Williams wasn't Ty Cobb. Cody Bellinger isn't either.

Essentially, we're talking about something that's probably real but can be found only when measured closely, and that's while ignoring the psychological and physiological ramifications. In fact, Boudreau himself wrote, "As for myself, I have always regarded the Boudreau Shift as a psychological, rather than a tactical, victory. At any rate, it was a lot of fun while it lasted."

So can you blame a big strong fella for not wanting to change his game, when the upside might be an extra dinky single every few weeks?

When a lefty pull-hitter like the Cubs' Anthony Rizzo first bunted for a hit, he became an instant Twitter hero.

In these last four seasons, Rizzo has bunted for a hit seven times. He's tried fourteen times. For those of you scoring at home, that's a .500 batting average. Granted, his slugging percentage in those fourteen at-bats is also .500. But so's his on-base percentage! Granted, we're not considering the times he missed the bunt attempt, or fouled it off, thus (usually) falling behind in the count. But, you know . . . fourteen times in four years? Roughly one bunt every two months? And he's one of the hitters who's *tried* to adjust? How stubborn are these guys, really?

Bottom line, today it's almost certainly easier for the manager to place his fielders where the batter hits the ball, than for the batter to *change* where he hits the ball. Which is symptomatic of basically everything that's happening in baseball. *Almost everything* that's changing is changing in favor of the pitchers and the fielders. The pitchers are throwing harder and better than ever. The umpires are getting better, which generally favors the pitchers because now they're (correctly) calling more strikes, especially low in the zone. And of course the fielders have more going for them than ever, with all that information about batted balls.*

In 2014, scoring around the majors was down significantly: 20 percent lower than its recent peak in 2000. Which has led some to call for a dramatic measure: outlawing the Williams shift. Now, I've little tolerance for the use of *some* to start an argument; *some* might be a couple of random egg boys on Twitter. But you

---

* It also helps, at least a little, that runners are no longer permitted to throw body blocks at middle infielders unfortunate enough to be doing their jobs. But more about Chase Utley later.

have to take the prospect at least semiseriously if the *Commissioner of Baseball* seems to. As Commissioner Rob Manfred has, more than once. Just last March, he told Rich Eisen, "This is something we are having conversations about, and it's one of those changes in the game, the number of shifts, I think went from three thousand two years ago, to ten thousand. Just crazy numbers, yes. It does affect particular kinds of players. It also exacerbates what I was saying about home runs and strikeouts, right? You get a left-handed pull hitter, you shift on him, he's much more likely to *not* be able to put the ball in play. That's just the reality. So we are looking at it."

That's just the reality.

Is it, though? Really?

No, not really. Yes, they're losing some hits. But most of them aren't losing *that* many hits—in fact, the *league* batting average on balls in play (BABiP) seems to have changed barely a tick as shifting has exploded—and of course they might lose fewer hits if they'd just learn to bunt, or take Wee Willie Keeler's advice. Just a little of it. Yes, there are some reasons to believe shifting ultimately isn't good for the game. But it's not why scoring was down in 2014, and it's certainly not why strikeouts are taking over the sport. And in fact, if shifting ever does lead to significantly more bunting, it'll be *good* for the sport, because baseball will be more aesthetically pleasing; more interesting, more exciting.

With McCann aboard, there are two outs, and a guy on first who isn't going to score unless the ball gets to the wall (or over it). Cotton's got a good chance to escape the inning if he can take down Cameron Maybin, the nine hitter. Maybin sets up, wearing white shoes, uniform pants cuffed just below his knees, and bright orange batting gloves. This is Maybin's seventh game with the Astros, who snatched him from the waiver wire just before the September 1 deadline, which means he'll be eligible for postseason play. He was added simply to provide outfield depth (which will prove quite

fortuitous just a few days from now, when outfielder Jake Marisnick suffers a season-ending thumb injury).

Maybin chops Cotton's first pitch to shortstop, and so the inning
ends with a fielder's choice, 6 to 4, McCann forced out at second
base.

Score: Astros 2, Athletics 0
Win Probability: Astros 66%

Home Second

Don't tell me about the pain. Show me the baby.

—BILL PARCELLS (B. 1941)

A's designated hitter Ryon Healy leads off the second with a short-hop liner that third baseman Marwin Gonzalez can't initially corral; Healy's awarded a base hit when Gonzalez's hurried throw pulls Gurriel off first base.

Lefty-hitting catcher Bruce Maxwell's next up, and he takes one of McHugh's modest heaters just inside the outside edge of the zone for strike one. McHugh follows up with almost the same pitch, but this time *on* the edge of the zone: strike two. And after fouling off an inside curve, Maxwell whiffs on yet another McHugh fastball "on the black"; that is, the outer inch or so of the strike zone, named for the stripe of black rubber that outlines home plate, and is practically invisible to anyone except the three men within a few feet of the thing.

Matt Chapman, the A's first draft pick in 2014 and the twenty-fifth overall, is McHugh's next foe, with Healy still on first base. Chapman's a perfect example of just how hard baseball really is, at this highest level. He was a first-round pick, he did *well* in the minor leagues, and yet didn't debut in the majors until this June, a couple of months after turning twenty-four. And to this point he's actually been the most successful major leaguer among all the players drafted after the fourteenth pick that June.[*]

Which is why the amateur baseball draft cannot be a big event, the way the NFL and NBA drafts are big events. The lag time is simply far too long for nearly every player drafted. It's now more than three years later, and Chapman's one of just five or six hitters even playing regularly. Let alone starring. In the NFL and the NBA, players can, and every year do, jump straight from the draft to stardom. In Baseball, that literally never happens; occasionally, with the rare outlier like Ken Griffey Jr. or Bryce Harper or Kris Bryant, it could happen if the executives weren't quite so cautious. But no, even those guys probably weren't quite ready to become *stars* the day after the draft. Even they probably needed a few weeks or months of seasoning. Which they got.

It's been awhile since anyone's gone straight from college (let alone high school) to the major leagues. In 1989, there was the Amazing Jim Abbott, who didn't seem to need seasoning *or* a right hand. (Just being honest, though? Abbott didn't really pitch *well* until his third season in the majors.) And a few years before him, there was Pete Incaviglia. A devastating, record-breaking slugger in college, "Inky" was drafted by the Montreal Expos and simply refused to play in the minor leagues. When he finally signed, five months after the draft, it was only because the Expos agreed to immediately trade him to the Texas Rangers, who acceded to Incaviglia's plan. Which didn't really work out. As a rookie in 1986, he set an American League record with 185 strike-

---

[*] Six players drafted between one and fourteen have already become fine major leaguers: pitcher Carlos Rodón, then-catcher (but future DH) Kyle Schwarber, pitcher Aaron Nola, pitcher Kyle Freeland, outfielder Michael Conforto, and shortstop Trea Turner.

outs, and while Incaviglia wound up playing in the majors until he was thirty-four, he never hit more than thirty homers, never drove in a hundred runs in a season, never played in an All-Star Game.*

So even though Chapman's twenty-four, as a college guy drafted with the twenty-fifth pick, he's right on schedule.

McHugh's first pitch misses low, but his second is a four-seam fastball up in the zone—some people call this pitch a "Brent Strom fastball," although Strom scoffs—that Chapman foul tips into Brian McCann's mitt for strike one. After Chapman fouls off a low cutter, Astros radio play-by-play man Michael Coffin describes the A's as "a very young ball club," which isn't precisely true. They're young, yes. Especially since trading a few veteran players earlier this summer. But *very* young? No. Not with Jed Lowrie (33), Matt Joyce (32) and Khris Davis (29) in the lineup.

Continuing the discussion, Steve Sparks quotes A's manager Bob Melvin: "When the A's were at Minute Maid Park the last time, he was saying that he felt, and a lot of teams are probably going with the Astros' template on how to rebuild. Of course, that was to go young, and it's important to have veterans like Lowrie, to help these young players along."

Fair enough. Still, one might reasonably wonder if they need Lowrie *and* Joyce *and* Davis, all of whom have played well enough this season to elicit interest from teams *not* in the middle of a rebuilding process.

What the A's do need are players like Chapman, Matt Olson (23), Ryon Healy (25), and Marcus Semien (26) to become good or great

---

* In the middle of his pro career, Incaviglia did spend a season in Japan, where he played so poorly that he was fortunate, the next year, to be invited to spring training with the Phillies. Oh, and he actually spent most of his last five professional seasons in the minor leagues. *La vengeance des Expos!*

players for whole seasons. Which, at least to this point, none of them has quite done.[*]

Olson looks like the best hitter among the younger players, but Chapman might be the best *player* among the younger guys, because his fielding at third base is among the finest in the major leagues. Both visually/subjectively and statistically/objectively.

McHugh misses outside with a fastball, then makes a mistake with a slider in the strike zone. In center field, Cameron Maybin gives up at the warning track, as the baseball flies over the fence and lands 410 feet away from the plate. McHugh didn't even look. He just took a few steps toward his catcher and waited for a new baseball. It's Chapman's eleventh home run, all of them coming since the All-Star break in July, and ties the game. Not bad for a number eight hitter.

"Well," Sparks says, "the A's have at least one homer in each of their last nine games now, here at the Oakland Coliseum. And that's kinda their game, the long ball."

More than kinda. Some years ago, then–Baseball Prospectus writer Joe Sheehan came up with a junk stat called the Guillen Number, in honor of the all-or-nothing White Sox teams led by manager Ozzie, that simply tracks the percentage of team runs scored as a result of home runs. And the A's will finish this season with the second-highest Guillen Number in the league, just a touch behind the Blue Jays. Nearly 49 percent of the A's scoring comes on home runs. Meanwhile, the more balanced Astros will actually finish the season with a few more homers than the A's, but just sixteenth in the majors in Guillen Number, around 42 percent.

The A's ninth hitter is young Boog Powell, who arrived via a midseason trade with the Mariners. Just as he did against the lefty-

---

[*] They also need a similar number of young starting pitchers to break through, but it seems unlikely that Moneyball-era stars Barry Zito, Mark Mulder, and Tim Hudson are walking through the clubhouse door anytime soon.

hitting Maxwell, McHugh attacks away against the lefty-hitting Powell, one of the few major leaguers you'll see who chokes up on the bat (if just an inch or so). Powell fouls off a couple of McHugh's fastballs, but finally lifts an easy fly to Reddick in left field. The same Reddick who last winter signed with the Astros for four years and $52 million, and is putting together the finest season of his career.

With the lineup turned over and number one hitter Semien up again, it's amazingly hard to remember the Astros of just four or five years ago, when spending that sort of money on any player, let alone a middling free agent like Reddick, wasn't even a remote possibility. Perhaps that's one of the game's charms—that the seasons overlap in our memories, overwriting themselves so neatly—but we're barely removed from an era when Houston baseball appeared bleaker than bleak, with 0.1 local cable ratings and sub-$20-million payrolls. Four years later, only five members of the 2013 roster are still around to recall their own sad labors: Altuve, Gonzalez, Keuchel, pitcher Brad Peacock, and occasional catcher Max Stassi.

And yet the rebuild worked precisely for the same reason that made it so easy to mock at the time. The template for how to build a franchise, while never guaranteed (see: Pirates, Pittsburgh), is more likely to bear fruit by following this simple advice:

If you can't win ninety games, you should lose ninety.

Billy Beane, or maybe it was some other smart fella, told me that, or something very much like that, a long time ago. Oddly enough, Billy Beane's A's have not followed the advice particularly well. Or maybe it's just that the advice didn't go far enough. It's certainly an elegant-enough equation, but does it prove out? Because if you believe the recent history, the advice actually should have been this:

If you can't win ninety games, you should lose a hundred.

Or maybe the first number is eighty. Or was. Back in 2006, Nate Silver—now famous for parsing electoral polls, but then writing for Baseball Prospectus—concluded that a team's ninetieth win was worth six times more than its seventy-eighth . . . and until reaching eighty or so, there's practically *zero value in winning additional games at all.*

Before exploring the practical ramifications of this "strategy" any further, it's necessary to consider a popular sports epithet: *tanking.* This will require, I'm afraid, a brief detour among other, lesser sports.

Tanking—for the uninitiated—historically has been largely about *losing games on purpose,* usually with the aim of improving one's position in the next amateur draft.

Beginning in 1966, the two National Basketball Association teams with the worst records in their division—now there are conferences, with divisions; but back then, with only ten teams in the whole league, there were just the two divisions—were eligible for the first pick in the college draft; the number one pick went to the winner of a coin flip.

Nobody seemed to pay this much mind.

Until 1983.

In 1982, the Houston Rockets made the playoffs with a 46-36 record. One year later they cratered to 14-68, easily the league's worst record. In the other conference—by then there were conferences—the 20-62 Indiana Pacers finished last. The Pacers lost the coin toss. With the second pick, they drafted Missouri center Steve Stipanovich, an outstanding prospect. But Stipanovich was merely a consolation prize. With the first pick, the Rockets drafted seven-four center Ralph Sampson, who had already been on the cover of *Sports Illustrated* five times.

There had been *whispers* about the Rockets losing on purpose, to get themselves that fifty-fifty shot at Sampson. If so, it seems to have started early; they lost seventeen of their first twenty games, thirty-four of their first forty, forty-nine of their first sixty, and finally sixty-eight of their eighty-two games. There was no pattern, except losing, all season long. Which isn't to say management might not have tried a *bit* less to win, once it became obvious that the conference's worst record was well within reach.

Sampson delivered as a rookie, averaging twenty-one points and eleven rebounds per game. Yet somehow the Rockets managed to *again* finish with the conference's worst record. Somehow, by just a nose, they did. And *again* they won the coin flip, this time beating out the Portland Trail Blazers for the first pick. With the second pick, the Blazers (infamously, in Portland) drafted Sam Bowie. Which left Michael Jordan to the Bulls with the third pick. And the Rockets? They missed on Jordan, but hit big anyway with Hakeem Olajuwon.

In Bill Simmons's opus, *The Book of Basketball*, he calls this the birth of tanking:

> *With Hakeem and Jordan looming as draft prizes, both the Rockets (blew 14 of their last 17, including 9 of their last 10) and Bulls (lost 19 of their last 23, including 14 of their last 15) said, "Screw it, we'll bastardize the sport," and pulled some fishy crap: resting key guys, giving lousy guys big minutes and everything else. Things peaked in Game 81 when a washed-up Elvin Hayes played every minute of Houston's overtime loss to the Spurs. Since none of the other crappy teams owned their picks, only Chicago and Houston controlled their destinies (hence the tanking). . . . The unseemly saga spurred the creation of a draft lottery the following season. And even that didn't solve the tanking problem; Team Stern has changed the lottery system five times in twenty-five years, and we're probably headed for a sixth soon.*

All these years later, tanking remains an issue in the NBA; in addition to draft consideration, now teams will occasionally rest their star players, particularly in road games during a particularly tiresome stretch. The thinking—informed of course by analytics—is that whatever hit you take in your chances of winning that game, you make up for down the road, with your stars better rested for both regular-season and (especially) playoff games. In the 2016–2017 season, for example, Lebron James skipped eight games. Back in 2012, Spurs coach Gregg Popovich was fined $250,000 for flying four of his best players home *before* the last game of a long road trip.

That's tanking, of a sort. Just not the sort we care much about (unless we happen to have paid good money to see LeBron play in our fair city). It's one thing to lose a game here and there—and actually trying to win those games, despite personnel limitations—in pursuit of a championship *this year* . . . and quite another to actively try to lose, in pursuit of a championship *in some later year.*

All that must be said, before saying this: *Baseball teams do not tank.*

Not like that, anyway. They don't lose games on purpose. They just don't.

For one thing, *it's really hard to lose a baseball game on purpose.* It's just a different sort of game, with different sorts of rosters. Until September, when the rosters are expanded, you basically have to play most of your best players every game. What's more, thanks to the all-knowing nature of baseball statistics, players are actually penalized statistically for bad games, unlike in basketball (or football), where you can take plays off without anyone (except your coaches) really noticing.

For another, getting a slightly higher draft pick just isn't a great advantage.

With one important exception. There is a real difference, historically, between the first pick and the second. And theoretically a team could maneuver its way into that first pick. But it wouldn't really be a season-long strategy, as there's simply too much pressure to . . . well, to play your best players.

In 2006, the Royals entered the season's last weekend with an MLB-worst 59-100 record. Their last series: three games in Detroit against the first-place Tigers. Kansas City's record was two games worse than the next-worst Tampa Bay Devil Rays.

The Royals' bizarro magic number was one: if they lost just once *or* the Rays won once, the Royals would own the first pick in next June's amateur draft.

You might imagine what happened. Because it's baseball. You-neverknow. Friday the Royals won, 9–7 in eleven innings. Saturday the Royals won, 9–6. Sunday the Royals won, 10–8 in twelve innings.

Meanwhile, not far away in Cleveland, the Rays were getting swept by the Indians.

Bizarro bingo. In the span of fewer than forty-eight hours, the Royals went from almost surely owning the first pick in the draft to owning the second. Which, again, has been a big deal. Historically.

With the first pick, the Rays drafted David Price, who had been the consensus choice for best amateur player available.

With the second pick, the Royals drafted a high school shortstop named Mike Moustakas.

You might argue that the draft actually worked out for the Royals. After all, in 2014 they reached the postseason for the first time since 1985, and in 2015 they won the World Series. Both years, Moustakas was their everyday third baseman.

On the other hand, in the first *decade* after the draft, Moustakas earned eleven wins above replacement. And Price? Thirty-four. On the other other hand, all those WAR for Moustakas did come with the Royals, while the Rays, with Price's free agency looming, traded him to Detroit in 2014. Which made sense at the time; alas, none of the three young players the Rays got in that deal really did much for them. Still, Price earned four All-Star nods as a Ray, played a key role on three postseason teams, and won a Cy Young Award in 2012. Leaving aside the Royals' two World Series (1-1) and the Rays' one (0-1), any moderately sentient baseball man, given a chance to redraft in 2007, would still choose Price over Moose.

The difference between number one and number two is large enough that one can see the incentive for tanking a game at the end of a season, maybe even a whole series. In some other dimension, someone whispered all this in Royals manager Buddy Bell's ear back in the fall of 2006, and so the Royals wound up drafting

David Price and today everything is different. Well, some things are different.

But this is how tanking works in *our* dimension, in the NFL and in the NBA, where a single player—a quarterback in the NFL, a superstar in the NBA—can almost singlehandedly turn a losing team into a winning team *immediately*. In Major League Baseball, you could do it. But it's harder to lose on purpose, there's usually not a great deal of competition for the worst record . . . and even if you *do* get your man in the draft, he probably won't help you win much for two or three years. *At best.* And no matter how good he is, he'll need a lot of help. Just ask Mike Trout (who was, by the way, drafted with *the twenty-fifth pick* a few years ago).

But when people talk about baseball tanking—and here's looking at you, Joe Sheehan, pal o' mine—they're not talking about giving less than 100 percent toward the end of the season (let alone earlier). What they're talking about isn't deliberately losing a few games; they're talking about deliberately not *really* trying to win *all of the time.* They're talking about entering a season with no intention of winning more than sixty or sixty-five games. If you wind up winning seventy or seventy-five, that's okay; it just isn't what the roster was built to do. But it's important to remember that all the players still have every reason to do their best; what's more, there are enough instances of underdogs actually winning that players can easily find historical reasons for optimism. Regardless of the preseason projections. Just look at the Rockies, the Diamond-backs, the Brewers, and the Twins this season; all four teams were practically written off last winter, and all four are currently fighting spirited battles for postseason berths.

Is that tanking? It's not tanking as we first came to understand the term a few decades ago. And the word carries with it a scurrilous accusation that *in the game I'm watching right now*, one of the teams is not doing its best to win. Which of course runs counter to the very idea of sports, and especially professional sports, where "professional" literally means the athletes are being paid to win.

This has always been the covenant in pro sports, for at least the last century or so: We pay to watch, and you try to win.

The difference, perhaps, between the Washington Nationals' template and the Astros' template is intent. The Nationals' general manager probably never went to ownership and said, "Hey, we're going to lose a ton of games these next couple of years. But it's okay! Because then we'll get to draft Stephen Strasburg and Bryce Harper, and both will make us better almost immediately! Cool, right?"

The Nationals were, by the way, *exceptionally* lucky four times: when Stephen Strasburg was available, when Bryce Harper was available, when Stephen Strasburg quickly became great, and when Bryce Harper quickly became great.

Wait. Make that five times. Because in 2008, when the Nats lost 103 games and earned the chance to draft Strasburg the next summer, the Mariners lost 102 games. Obviously, it could *easily* have gone the other way.*

But if the Nationals weren't tanking, not really in any sense of the term, what about the Astros? Well, sure. But they weren't the only ones. We might just as accurately describe "the Astros' template" as "the Cubs' template" or "the Epstein Gambit" or something.†

You might not think of the Cubs and Astros as similar franchises, and the differences are obvious. But here's one key fact: Chicago is the third most populous metropolitan area in these United States, and Houston ranks fifth. Objectively speaking, neither franchise

---

* With the second pick in the draft, the M's selected Dustin Ackley, a highly regarded college hitter. Ackley reached the majors less than two years later and looked great as a rookie for three months. Since then, he's been a below-average hitter in the majors and has spent all of 2017 back in the minors.

† Joe Sheehan would probably prefer that the word "racket" or "scheme" be in there somewhere. But Joe and I come at this particular thing, unlike most other things, from different angles. When I think about modern team building, Joe's counterarguments are always in the back of my mind.

would seem to have any natural right to cry poor. And that's without even considering that both franchises are (of course) owned by billionaires who purchased their teams largely as playthings for themselves and their families (with perhaps a dollop of civic pride mixed in there too).

In 2010, the Cubs finished 75-87. Not good, but respectable. This was new owner Tom Ricketts's first year. The Cubs were no better in 2011, and Ricketts fired general manager Jim Hendry that August. Shortly after the season ended, Ricketts hired Theo Epstein away from the Red Sox. But Epstein didn't promise to make the Cubs contenders in a year. Or two. Or three.

Still, Epstein figured he and his management team didn't have forever. He didn't have the eight years it took the Royals to go from worst to first. "We had five-year contracts," Epstein told Tom Verducci, "and that seemed like an awfully long time in a big market."

In Epstein's first three seasons, the Cubs lost 101 games, 96 games, and 89 games. Progress, but hardly the sort of progress that stirred the hearts of men, women, or school-age children.

But all the while, the Cubs were drafting well—well, drafting Kris Bryant, anyway, with the number two pick in 2013—and building their talent base with a number of advantageous trades, and when the time seemed right, targeted free-agent signings.

Funny thing about progress: it usually doesn't progress exactly how you think. Following the progression of Cubs' wins during Epstein's first three seasons—sixty-one, sixty-six, seventy-three— what would you expect next? Eighty-two, maybe? Finally a winning season after five straight losers?

Ninety-seven.

Oddly enough, in 2015 those ninety-seven wins were good enough for just third place in the Cubs' division, as the Pirates won ninety-eight, the Cardinals one hundred. But those ninety-seven wins *were* also good enough for a postseason berth, a year or two ahead of schedule. Just like the Astros.

Epstein was hired on October 12, 2011. Eight weeks later, Jeff

Luhnow was hired away from the St. Louis Cardinals, where he had originally been hired because owner Bill DeWitt Jr., who'd grown up in a baseball family and become "obsessed with statistics," concluded that the Cardinals weren't taking advantage of the new information that was available in the early 2000s. DeWitt's son-in-law had worked with Luhnow at the consultants McKimsey & Co., and told DeWitt, "I've got the greatest guy; why don't you interview him?" Luhnow got hired, despite having exactly zero experience inside baseball, and during his years running the Cardinals' amateur drafts, no organization produced more major-league players than St. Louis did.*

In 2012, their first seasons at the helm, both Epstein and Luhnow watched their new teams lose more than one hundred games, including once while playing in the same division. The Astros didn't finish last, but only because they were in the Cubs' division.†

Both teams finished last in 2013 and 2014. And in '15, both teams skyrocketed to the postseason. Yes, the Cubs did win ninety-seven games compared to the Astros' mere eighty-six . . . but those figures are misleading, in terms of their *progress*. Because believe it or not, the Astros actually finished with a significantly better run differential than the Cubs. The Cubs, considering their run

---

* *Moneyball* wouldn't have happened without Billy Beane, who wouldn't have happened without Sandy Alderson, who encouraged Beane's transition from playing to working in the front office. "The reason *Moneyball* became so important," Alderson told Howard Bryant, "was because so many of the owners read it. For years, the baseball people would tell the owners, 'Leave the baseball to us. You wouldn't understand.' They kept saying they were different. Then the owners realized the dynamics of baseball—of assessing risk—were the same as the ones they faced in their outside businesses."

† The next season, the Astros moved from the National League Central to the American League West, a condition placed on Astros owner Jim Crane upon his purchase of the franchise. From 2011 through 2013, Houston put together the worst three-year stretch, purely in terms of wins and losses, since the legendarily hapless early '60s New York Mets.

differential, were fortunate to win ninety-seven games; the Astros, considering their wins and losses, were fortunate to qualify for the postseason. In October, the Astros won three postseason games; the Cubs won four.

Essentially, the two franchises were on *exactly* the same trajectory.

Until 2016. The Astros took a small step backward, and the Cubs won the World Series for the first time since 1908.

In 2017? The Astros are well on their way to first place, and the Cubs are well on their way to a third straight trip to the playoffs. So was all of this tanking? In the historical sense, it was not. But for those first three seasons, both the Astros and Cubs were not making any real effort to win more than sixty-five or seventy games. So what should we call that? (Assuming that we can't simply call it "rebuilding," which used to be a generally accepted term for stockpiling young players with theoretically bright futures. There's also "full rebuild," which just means you're fully committed to rebuilding.)

Oddly, people are likely to take the wrong message away from the Cubs and Astros and their high draft picks. Kris Bryant is the *only* player drafted by Theo Epstein who's made a real dent in the standings. I mean a real, wouldn't-have-made-the-playoffs-without-this-guy dent.[*]

When the Astros reached the playoffs in 2015, it wouldn't have happened without Rookie of the Year Carlos Correa. Back in 2012, Luhnow & Co. used their first-ever draft pick, the overall number one, on Correa. Which was at least mildly criticized by various draft experts, because it was widely believed that Correa wasn't actually the top talent in the draft. But that allowed the Astros to spend a

---

[*] Yes, slugger Kyle Schwarber was instrumental in the Cubs beating the Pirates in the 2015 Wild Card Game, and this year Ian Happ has been superb in the super-utility role. But while both Schwarber and Happ have been better than people expected, or at least jumped into the fray sooner, neither's made a real dent in the standings yet.

bit less to sign Correa, and save enough of their league-mandated budget to also draft and sign Lance McCullers Jr. with the forty-first overall pick.

And while it's tempting to suggest that the Astros owned the number one pick in 2012 because, the summer before, then general manager Ed Wade convinced Jim Crane to give up on 2011, the Astros probably would have finished with MLB's worst record even if they had *not* traded two of their better players—outfielders Michael Bourn and Hunter Pence—in July. In fact, the Astros kept *all* their good (or decent) pitchers, including (and perhaps unaccountably) veteran starters Brett Myers and Wandy Rodriguez, and closer Mark Melancon. The Astros lost 106 games in 2011. That was seven more than any other team, yes. But they probably should have traded those pitchers for prospects, and lost even more.[*]

But not because of draft position. Because if you're going to tank or whatever you want to call the full rebuild, you might as well *commit to that* and get the hell started. Which is what happened the moment Luhnow took over. And Epstein too.

Again, the fundamental question: Draft position?

Here are the Astros' picks in the amateur draft's top fifty since Luhnow & Co. took over:

2012   Carlos Correa (1), Lance McCullers Jr. (41)
2013   Mark Appel (1), Andrew Thurman (40)
2014   Brady Aiken (1), Derek Fisher (37), A. J. Reed (42)
2015   Alex Bregman (2), Kyle Tucker (5), Daz Cameron (37), Tom Eshelman (46)
2016   Forrest Whitley (17)
2017   J. B. Bukauskas (15)

---

[*] Shortly after taking over in December, Luhnow traded Melancon, and the next July he traded Myers and Rodriguez for prospects. None of whom panned out.

The Astros drafted number one overall three times, and the only one of those three picks who panned out is the one experts said they shouldn't have made (Correa). Appel was a supposedly can't-miss pitcher from Stanford who did miss, big. After drafting Aiken, the Astros spotted something in his medical reports they didn't like, and significantly lowered their offer. He didn't sign, and Astros management got ripped in some quarters for their supposedly ill-treatment of Aiken. Which mostly went away when he was diagnosed with a serious elbow injury in 2015, shortly after Cleveland used *their* first-round pick to draft him.*

Actually, the Aiken pick did work out nicely for the Astros; as compensation for not signing him, they received the number two pick in 2015. And Alex Bregman, who's getting tonight off—it's his turn for a mental break—has been terrific as their regular third baseman this season.†

So, Correa: sure. Bregman, somewhat indirectly: you bet. But the Astros aren't good because of high draft picks. They're good for a few dozen reasons, just one of which is getting to draft early. You can call what they've done the Astros' template or the Cubs' template or anyone else's template. Just don't call it tanking, because that does nearly everyone involved a disservice, if not an injustice.

Yes, you *could* argue that the owners—men like Tom Ricketts and Jim Crane, to name just two of many—are so wealthy, and MLB's coffers generally so full, that there's simply no excuse for not spending ever-more piles of money. The Cubs weren't going to win ninety games in 2012, Epstein's first season, no matter what they

---

* He's since returned to the mound, showing some promise in 2016 but struggling terribly with the strike zone this year.

† Oh, and shortstop too. Correa, who would otherwise have been an MVP candidate this season, missed seven weeks this summer with a thumb injury. In his absence, Bregman enhanced his already considerable value by sliding over to start nearly two dozen games at shortstop.

spent. But if Ricketts had been willing to throw money at three or four big-time free agents, they might have won seventy-five, and spared their fans a fair amount of heartache. Especially if they'd been willing to trade a few minor leaguers for guys who could help win *now*. Sure, they still would have missed the playoffs. But their fans would have enjoyed those "extra" fifteen or twenty wins, and isn't it just *unseemly* for a billionaire to cry poor, even as he's (a) probably making money, thanks to various revenue streams, and (b) fully confident that the value of his franchise—and this is demonstrably true of *all* franchises, thanks to the large number of billionaires always casting about for new toys—will just keep going up and up and up?

The previous paragraph was brought to you by the letter *A*, the number 100, and my friend Joe Sheehan's spirited opinions. If I'm not doing justice to the latter, my apologies to the former. (Joe, I mean. The letter *A* and the number 100 don't give a damn.)

While Joe's critique might resonate loudly if you're a fan of one of the teams that's not trying to win *now*—and there were plenty of Cubs fans who weren't enthused about the Cubs' template—let's play out this scenario . . .

What if every billionaire owner spent whatever it took to win ninety games every season?

Oh. Wait. That would mean 2,700 wins every season. Which is a problem, mathematically speaking, since there are only 2,430 wins to go around. Here's another problem: there are only so many free agents to go around. Most are overpriced, in the long run especially, and few are good enough to actually move the W-L needle much.

Just last winter, for example, the top three free-agent hitters were all in their early (or middle) thirties; as it happened, two of the three re-upped with their current employers. Next on the list: closers Kenley Jansen and Aroldis Chapman, both of whom signed new five-year deals for roughly $16 million per season. Not coincidentally, both also signed with teams—the Dodgers and

Yankees—that have more money than they can possibly spend, and it's unlikely that both will remain top-flight for all five years. Among the best bargains last winter was actually Josh Reddick, who signed with the Astros for four years and $52 million. But even Reddick, now thirty, figures to be battling for an everyday job by the time his deal's expiring in 2020.

Which highlights, by the way, an oft-ignored risk of signing high-quality, needle-moving free agents. Most of them won't sign for fewer than three or four years, and (of course) large piles of dough. So let's say you do sign him; what happens when, two years later, you've got a young, cheap prospect who's ready to grab that position? Now you've got some hard decisions to make. As someone once observed, "The right plane can't land if the wrong plane is blocking the runway."

So, yes. If I'm a Royals fan, I might reasonably wonder why owner David Glass doesn't invest more of *his own money* in putting a better team on the field. In 2017, *Forbes* reported that the Royals suffered an operating loss of $900,000 during the previous year. But these days $900,000 is essentially a rounding error. Or, more likely, an accounting trick. And that's without even knowing how much money Glass might have paid himself, not to mention his kids, who serve on the Royals' board of directors. Especially when one considers that *Forbes* estimates the value of the franchise as $950 million—seventeen years after Glass purchased the Royals for just $96 million. Baseball has been very, very, very, good to David Glass and his heirs. Even if Glass chucked, say, $20 million of his personal savings into the kitty every year, wouldn't he still make out handsomely someday if he sold the Royals?

Yes. He would.

But, again: We can say much the same about almost every team. Glass could personally afford to spend more, and so could Jim Crane and A's owner John Fisher and the two brothers who run the New York Yankees. And, again: To what end? Ultimately, the only (predictable) effects would be (a) more money flowing from billionaire owners to millionaire players, and (b) little real change in the standings, since (1) the Yankees and Dodgers would probably still insist on outspending everybody else, and (2) there just isn't enough talent on the open market for more than a few teams to measurably improve by signing free agents in the off-season.

For these reasons and probably a few others, there seems to be a sort of gentlemen's agreement among the owners: We won't dip into our personal wealth. Not often, anyway, and not much of it. Which is why team payrolls so closely echo market size and revenues, and hardly at all the owners' non-baseball wealth.

And however much the fans want to rail about *their* skinflint owner and his willingness to watch his team lose a hundred games—on a humongous plasma screen on his yacht, no less—if just a few owners spend "whatever it takes to win"—as the ancient Tigers owner Mike Ilitch did, a few years ago—before long "whatever it takes to win" wouldn't actually be enough to win. Plenty of money sloshing around, but not enough free agents out there. Not enough wins.

Finally, it should be said that *if* owners of noncontending teams were to systematically spend more money, there would be two, and perhaps only two, practical results: free-agent players, the great majority of them past their natural prime, would get more money; second, there would be somewhat less playing time for truly young (and relatively cheap) players, with so many veterans locked into lucrative contracts.

Essentially, if you're arguing for owners to spend many millions more dollars on old players, you're also arguing for a less elegant, less efficient, less fair enterprise.

Thanks, but no thanks. What you should be arguing for is a system that winds up with less money in the pockets of veterans, and more in those of younger players who actually deserve to play.

Back to the game, which has just gotten exciting, with the score now 2–2, two outs. With the lineup turned over, leadoff man Marcus Semien falls behind 0 and 2. McHugh misses way outside with his next two offerings, but the 2-2 pitch, a low fastball, is grounded to shortstop Correa, who throws out Semien by a step. That looked like a really close, exciting play if you haven't seen much baseball, but it was close only because Correa knew exactly how much time he had, and used most of it. These guys are just so damn terrific at their jobs.

Score: Astros 2, Athletics 2
Win Probability: Even!

Visitors Third

Everyone has a plan until they get punched in the face.

—MIKE TYSON (B. 1966)

After two innings the Astros' lineup has turned over, too, so Astros leadoff man George Springer gets to actually lead off again. And just like in the first, Cotton gets ahead in the count, this time 1 and 2. But Springer grounds a mid-90s fastball toward left field; shortstop Semien is able to corral the baseball but doesn't bother throwing it: infield single.

Jose Altuve takes Cotton's first pitch for a ball, then "grounds out."

Officially speaking, that is. Officially, Altuve pulls a grounder toward third base, where Chapman fields the ball and throws to second, forcing Springer out; Chapman was playing fairly shallow, because in addition to the power that Altuve's already demonstrated in this game, he's also perfectly capable of laying down a good bunt. Officially it's a fielder's choice, 5 to 4.

But this play's hardly routine. Altuve *scalds* the baseball, which is what you're supposed to with a "middle-in" fastball; the exit velocity of the batted ball is 102.5 miles per hour, and in the next half inning we'll see a HOME RUN with almost exactly the same EV.[*]

---

[*] In fact, later in the game we'll see three home runs with significantly lower exit velocities than Altuve's grounder.

And even aside from the exit velocity, this is a "grounder" only in the most technical sense; in the realest sense, the most visceral sense, this is a line drive that just happens to hit the dirt just before getting snared in Chapman's glove. So this might look routine in the official account, perhaps even from the upper deck. But if you're close, you can't help realizing just how gifted major-league infielders must be, even granting that Chapman is among the *most* talented third basemen in the sport.

But yes, Springer's retired and Altuve's on first base. Which brings up Correa, since it just never gets easy with this lineup. After throwing Correa a low-90s fastball that just misses low, Cotton comes back with almost the same pitch, but a bit higher. Correa takes a rip and drives a liner up the middle. This will actually be *the hardest-hit baseball of the entire game:* 109.7 miles an hour off Correa's bat.

Back in the first inning, Cotton had been fortunate to escape with a double play instead of a brain injury. This time the baseball strikes the mound dirt first, then caroms off the back of his right thigh toward Chapman, who gathers the ball and fires to first base in time to get Correa, with Altuve safe on second. So that's now two shots off Cotton's body, and three outs. Just like you game-plan.

He's also lucky to still be pitching after two close calls. Squired to the mound by plate umpire Sam Holbrook, manager Bob Melvin and trainer Nick Paparesta both check in with Cotton, but he's cleared to continue after a few practice throws.

Almost exactly five years ago—September 5, 2012—then-A's pitcher Brandon McCarthy was pitching from exactly the same hillock as Cotton. In the top of the fourth inning, McCarthy threw a low-90s sinker to Anaheim's Erick Aybar, who ripped a line drive that struck McCarthy on the right side of his head, next to his ear.

McCarthy sank to the ground but never lost consciousness; after a few minutes, he stood up and walked off the field. What nobody could know was that McCarthy had actually suffered serious trauma: skull fracture, brain contusion, *and* life-threatening epidural hemorrhage. Quickly evaluated and diagnosed, McCarthy shortly underwent a two-hour surgery to relieve the pressure on his brain.

I was at Fenway Park in September 2000—exactly seventeen years ago tonight, actually—when Red Sox pitcher Bryce Florie took a line drive flush to his face, suffering three different fractures around his right eye socket, plus damage to his retina. There was a great deal of blood. As I wrote at the time, "Florie will live, but nobody's willing to guess whether or not he'll pitch again."*

McCarthy returned to the mound in the spring of 2013, seemingly none the worse for wear (it does take a special sort of bravery to face down the world's greatest hitters from just sixty feet away, even if you've never been skulled by a screaming line drive). But that season, Tampa Bay's Alex Cobb and Toronto's J. A. Happ both were struck in the head by line drives; Cobb missed two months, Happ three.

Those two incidents, following so closely upon McCarthy's scare, did seem to create a real sense of urgency to somehow protect the pitchers from all those missiles rocketing toward them.

When Herb Score nearly lost an eye to Gil McDougald's line drive back in 1957, it was simply assumed that nothing could be done. Same in 1993 when Willie Blair suffered a broken jaw, and in 1998 when Billy Wagner suffered a concussion, and in 2000 when Florie left so much blood in Fenway Park.

But today we've got better technology, and we're somewhat less willing to accept (supposedly) inherent dangers. Also, there's clearly a commercial opportunity here. So now there are plenty of smart people working on it. Just imagine how much money could be made

---

* Bryce Florie did pitch again, returning to the Fenway mound roughly ten months later. But after seven relief appearances and an 11.42 ERA, he drew his release from the Red Sox. Florie would later sign contracts with the Tigers, the A's, and the Marlins, but never made it back to the majors.

if every baseball pitcher in America, from ages six to sixty-eight, were compelled to wear some sort of protective headgear. We're talking about millions of dollars every year. Many millions.

Well, that's not the situation on the ground, yet. But it's hardly for a lack of options.

In the wake of McCarthy's near-death experience, there were serious efforts by various companies to create something major leaguers would actually, you know, wear. And before the 2014 season, MLB approved a product from isoBLOX that essentially was a cap with plastic and foam inserts. Aside from looking odd—which matters quite a lot to most of the pitchers—there were other issues, particularly the weight; the isoBLOX caps weighed roughly three times as much as the standard caps. Granted, we're only talking about ten or eleven ounces. But that's actually a lot of ounces when it's on your head. There was also a breathability issue. McCarthy tested one, but found the headgear both "too big" and "too hot."

That June, though, San Diego Padres relief pitcher Alex Torres donned the isoBLOX cap and wore it the rest of the season.

He was the only one.

In 2015, Torres switched to a different isoBLOX product, this one a sort of padded ring that wrapped around a standard cap.

He was the only one.

Another "prospect" arrived before the 2016 season. In spring training, twenty pitchers were slated to receive a visor/helmet hybrid from a manufacturer called Boombang; to avoid the dreaded visor *look*, the helmets were designed to be worn over a skullcap, so from a distance the whole contraption would resemble a slimmed-down batting helmet.

Alex Cobb told ESPN, "If I put it on and it's close to wearing a baseball hat and I've got nothing to complain about, I think I'd be open to it."

Alas, what Boombang called the Half Cap reportedly weighed ten to twelve ounces, and it still didn't look the way major leaguers want to look. And with Alex Torres getting released near the end of spring training, not a single pitcher used anything so obvious during that season. Or in this one either.*

In the summer of 2007, a minor-league coach named Mike Coolbaugh was struck in the neck by a line drive while coaching first base. A helmet would have done absolutely nothing for Coolbaugh, who died almost instantly. But less than four months later, Major League Baseball decreed that all base coaches in the minor *and* major leagues would henceforth wear helmets. One coach—longtime MLB shortstop and manager Larry Bowa—complained, even said he simply would refuse to do it. But he capitulated before the next season; it was that or lose his job, as coaches and managers have little control over work rules.

That's what baseball players call eyewash; MLB couldn't have reasonably thought the move would make much difference, but death has a way of eliciting dramatic responses, however unlikely to prevent a future catastrophe.

You can *almost* bet that if a professional pitcher were killed in the line of duty, MLB would push hard for something, eyewash or not, and the union would be ill-equipped to resist. That said, MLB *could* mandate, right now, protective headgear for pitchers in the minor leagues, and has not. At the very least, Baseball could push harder for more major-league pitchers and perhaps *all* minor leaguers to experiment with the products out there now.

When Brandon McCarthy was struck, then A's reliever Sean Doolittle was in the clubhouse, he told me, "because the night before I'd taken a liner off my shin. I knew that could have been me, and it made me realize how vulnerable we are."

So does Doolittle wear anything now? Nope. "I think I'm where

---

* Nearly two years later, Boombang's website will continue trumpeting the February 2016 press coverage, but with no follow-ups at all. And in 2018's spring training, there won't be a single story about any new headgear with a real shot at adoption by major leaguers.

a lot of guys are," he says. "You try something and say, 'I wanna wear something, but this isn't it.' The tech has to be there, lighter weight."

What makes this inaction all the stranger? There actually is a piece of equipment that's both light and reasonably protective, and Collin McHugh's wearing it tonight.

Not that you'd ever know. McHugh's SST Pro X Performance Head Guard, a thin pad constructed of carbon fiber, weighs just 1.7 ounces and slips easily between the body of McHugh's cap and the interior headband. McHugh's been using the SST since 2014, when the product's inventor—not coincidentally, a high school friend of McHugh's—introduced it to him.

"I was skeptical," McHugh says, "because I had seen the other things they'd done, the isoBLOX. But I said sure, I'll try it out. I looked at it, gave it a couple of runs in bullpens, and it just made too much sense. It was like, if I can wear this without feeling uncomfortable, and it gives me an extra layer of protection, why not? So I'll probably never throw another pitch without it."

That was two years ago. So is McHugh surprised that he's still one of just a dozen or so pitchers who use the SST? "Extremely surprised," he says. "They've come up with the other products, but guys aren't going to wear them; they're too blocky, they're big, they're uncomfortable, they're gimmicky. Baseball players, and pitchers in particular, are pretty obsessive about their comfort level, about the way they *feel* on the mound. But for me, this is comfortable. Maybe a sleeve would help, since some guys maybe don't want to worry about something sliding around every time they take off their hat. I don't see it as a big impediment. But a lot of guys do."

You talk to McHugh, and you just can't help wondering why they're not *all* using what he's using. But there's an awareness issue too. When I asked Jharel Cotton about adding protection, he seemed sincere about his worries. "I would wear something if they make it comfortable," Cotton said. "It's like wearing a cup. I do wear a cup; some pitchers don't, but it's comfortable so I wear one.

I like my life, and would do anything to protect that." He also said he's never even seen an SST Head Guard.

Granted, none of the headgear actually being used, or considered for use, in professional baseball would necessarily have done anything for the likes of McCarthy, Cobb, or Happ, for the simple reason that most of them were, like Coolbaugh, struck *below* the areas that would be protected. It's probably true that *most* of the worst injuries would be prevented only by a technologically superior device that incorporates a face mask, the sort of thing women's softball players have been wearing for a few years (and not just the pitchers; infielders wear them too). So, technically speaking, there's little preventing major-league pitchers from wearing something that would *significantly* cut their risk of suffering a serious injury.

And yet . . .

Today, almost exactly five years after Brandon McCarthy might have suffered a fatal injury on this very spot, Jharel Cotton remains entirely unprotected, just as hundreds of other pitchers in all the other stadiums—or thousands, if you want to include the minor leagues—remain unprotected. There's nobody to *blame* for this, really; the pitchers don't want an additional hindrance, no matter how minor, and they also don't want to look different, or scared. And you know, they're young; young men with tremendous physical talents tend to think they'll live forever.

But as the pitchers keep growing and throwing harder, and the hitters keep growing and swinging harder, there will be more concussions and fractured skulls and shattered jaws and dental disasters and ruined careers. Unless something is done. And I suppose if we do insist on blaming someone, we should blame the MLB Players Association for not doing more to create awareness; at the very least, why not send a dozen SST Head Guards to every major-league clubhouse, and see what happens?

Meanwhile, Cotton seems unfazed by this second close call; with Altuve on second base, he quickly jumps ahead of the next hitter, Josh Reddick. But just as he did twice in the first inning and once in the second, Cotton fails to take advantage, hanging a 1-and-2 curveball that Reddick lines down the left-field line for a double, pushing Altuve across the plate with the go-ahead run.

Worse: Cotton follows up *that* poorly aimed curve with another, which Yuli Gurriel deposits far beyond the left-field wall for a two-run homer and a 5–2 Astros lead. A's pitching coach Scott Emerson trots to the mound to check on Cotton but doesn't stay long, and Cotton remains in the game. Gurriel's blast is the twenty-sixth home run that Cotton's given up in 117 innings. Even in this era, that's a phenomenal figure.*

Cotton's career got off to such a promising start too. Roughly thirteen months ago, he was one of three prospects the A's received in a trade that sent starting pitcher Rich Hill and Josh Reddick— who's in the Astros' lineup tonight, of course—to the Dodgers during their pennant push.

Upon joining the A's organization, Cotton pitched even better for their Triple-A farm club than he'd pitched for the Dodgers' team in the same league. Last September, Cotton made his major-league debut with a start against the Angels, pitching into the seventh inning and giving up just one run. He ultimately made five starts and posted a sterling 2.15 ERA; most impressively, he struck out twenty-three hitters and walked only *four* in twenty-nine innings. Cotton did give up four home runs in those five starts. But when you strike out six times more hitters than you walk (with a 2.15 ERA) it's easy to forget the homers.

This season, Cotton's strikeout rate has held steady, at a respect-

---

* Cotton will finish the season having given up twenty-eight homers in 129 innings, tying him for ninth on the all-time list among pitchers with a similar workload (120–140 innings). The eight pitchers ahead of Cotton on the list—two others also this season, by the way—combined for a 40-94 record, with an execrable ERA. Even today, it's nearly impossible to give up that many home runs and still pitch reasonably well; in fact, since they started climate-controlling the baseballs in dry, mile-high Denver, it might *be* impossible.

able seven per nine innings. But his walk rate has roughly tripled, so he's striking out just twice as many batters as he's walking. A few decades ago, this ratio would have been quite good; but with today's elevated strikeout rates, Cotton's strikeout-to-walk ratio this season will rank just fiftieth among the fifty-seven American League pitchers with at least 120 innings. Toss in the home runs, now with a lot more baserunners ahead of them, and . . . well, Cotton's 5.58 ERA for the season will wind up fifty-first among those fifty-seven pitchers.

Meanwhile, as Cotton's early promise last season has turned into something else this season, Gurriel's early struggles last season have also turned into something else.

Back in 2006, Gurriel was regarded as the best baseball player in Cuba. But that's where he stayed for the first thirteen seasons of his career, with the Sancti Spiritus club. In 2014, Gurriel was permitted by his government to play a season in Japan; then it was back to Cuba for two more seasons. But in February 2016, Gurriel and his younger brother, while in the Dominican Republic with Cuba's national team, defected. As so many Cuban stars had before him. And the following July, Gurriel signed a five-year, $47.5 million contract with the Astros.*

Gurriel was thirty-two at the time, so there was obviously some real risk for the Astros. After just fifteen games in the minors, Gurriel was summoned to the majors in late August and played nearly every game the rest of the season. The results weren't terrible, but age and adjustments and rust gave fans plenty of red flags to choose from, as Gurriel didn't hit much in his thirty-six games

---

* Gurriel's father, Lourdes, was a tremendous player in Cuba, and batted .400 for his country's Gold Medal–winning team in the 1992 Summer Olympics. Gurriel's brother, Lourdes Jr., is nine years younger and signed with the Blue Jays last winter for seven years and $22 million. Like Yuli, Lourdes Jr. will struggle in his first pro season, but break through in his second, debuting in the majors next April.

with the big club. At that point, it seemed that maybe committing $48 million to a thirty-two-year-old Cuban with essentially zero professional experience might not have been the wisest decision ever.

As this season opened, it was hardly clear that Gurriel would play well enough to hold down an everyday job. Nevertheless, he was the Astros' Opening Day first baseman. And his performance this season is a real tribute to the Astros' patience. He went just 1 for 15 in his first four games; in the last of those, a close one, he was replaced in the seventh inning by a pinch-hitter. After six games he was just 2 for 21 and both hits were singles.

A. J. Hinch just kept writing Gurriel's name on the lineup card, though. And it's a funny thing about April batting statistics: You can turn things around in a hurry. After going 0 for 3 on the ninth, Gurriel's average was .095 . . . and by the end of the month, thanks to a bushel of multihit games, he was batting .329.

With one walk.

One walk in a month is fairly stunning.

Not quite as stunning: also in April, Gurriel struck out only eleven times. Which these days is an absurdly low number for a hitter with some power.

Entering tonight's game, Gurriel had struck out only fifty-two times . . . and drawn only eighteen walks. By season's end, among the 145 major leaguers with at least five hundred plate appearances, Gurriel will boast the seventh-lowest walk percentage *and* the fifth-lowest strikeout percentage. Meanwhile, he has been among the league's more productive first basemen while placing among the league leaders in hard-hit balls.*

While you might understand why pitchers wouldn't want to add much protection—*It's heavy and it's bulky and it's damn funny-*

---

* As measured by Statcast, Gurriel will finish the season tenth in the majors with 203 batted balls with exit velocities of 95 miles an hour or more.

looking, and hell, maybe I'll just work very carefully to Mike Trout and J. D. Martinez and all the rest of these beasts—it's even harder to understand why hitters wouldn't.

But most haven't. Marwin Gonzalez, now batting with the bases empty, is one of the current exceptions. His batting helmet includes a bolted-on extension called the C-Flap, which protects the left side of his jaw.

The *idea* for such a thing goes back to the 1970s at least, when various players used similar jerry-rigged devices for short stretches. The actual C-Flap was patented in 1987, and in 1988 A's catcher Terry Steinbach was probably the first to use one in the majors. The world first noticed the C-Flap that summer, when Steinbach homered off Dwight Gooden in the All-Star Game.

But Steinbach, like those before him and nearly all of those after him, wore the accessory in the wake of an injury, and eventually gave it up when the risk of recurrence seemed low enough. But a sea change might have come a year ago in June, when Cardinals beat reporter Derrick Goold dropped this item toward the end of a story:

> Cardinals catcher Yadier Molina sported a faceguard on his batting helmet during all of his at-bats Saturday, saying that he had the protective addition affixed as "a precaution." Molina ordered the piece awhile back and added that there wasn't an incident that prompted his use of the addition, which comes down from the ear flap and covers his left cheek and jawline. He said he didn't have any discomfort with it and intends to continue using it.

Molina might be the first major leaguer to adopt the C-Flap not *reactively*, but proactively. He's now hardly alone, though. Four months ago, Arizona Diamondbacks catcher Chris Iannetta was struck in the jaw by a fastball and suffered a couple of broken teeth and a busted nose. After seeing the video, Carlos Correa and

Marwin Gonzalez both ordered C-Flaps and began wearing them in late May.

They're still wearing them. And really, it seems just a matter of time until they're standard gear for just about everyone.*

In the first three innings, almost nothing's been easy for Jharel Cotton. But with a full count, Gonzalez lifts an easy fly ball to Khris Davis in left field. In a season hallmarked by poor luck, Cotton's actually lucky to be where he is right now: walking off the field under his own power, his team still in the game.

Score: Astros 5, Athletics 2
Win Probability: Astros 77%

---

* In 2018, the Milwaukee Brewers will purchase five hundred C-Flaps, making their use mandatory for all their players below the Class AA level, while strongly encouraging them for Double- and Triple-A players. Also in 2018, young superstars Mike Trout and Bryce Harper will open the season using C-Flaps, completely proactively. It's simply becoming the fashion.

Home Third

The future is already here—it's just not evenly distributed.

—WILLIAM GIBSON (B. 1948)

A s the Astros television broadcast returns from commercial, with
Collin McHugh finishing his eight warmup throws and leadoff
man Matt Joyce thinking about high fastballs and low sliders, Todd
Kalas says, "Sixteen in a row for the Cleveland Indians, the most
since these A's won twenty in a row, about fifteen years ago." In
fact, it was almost *exactly* fifteen years ago: fifteen years and four
days ago, the A's set the all-time American League record with their
twentieth straight victory, capped by Scott Hatteberg/Chris Pratt's
Hollywood-friendly home run. So this seems like a good time to
wonder: Has the Moneyball team been out-Moneyballed by (among
other teams) the Indians, and the Astros?

Essentially the A's—or if you prefer, Michael Lewis and his run-
away bestseller—touched off an arms race in which they seem to
have fallen well behind much of their competition. Actually, this
might have been true even before *Moneyball* (the book) came out
in 2003. Already the Red Sox, at the direction of new owner John
Henry, were engaged in the formation of a "baseball think tank."
Shortly after the 2002 season, in which the Red Sox won ninety-
three games but didn't make the playoffs, Henry fired placeholder
general manager Mike Port and hired wunderkind Theo Epstein,

then all of twenty-eight years old. Of course, this was after Billy Beane accepted, then turned down the job (a tale artfully embellished in *Moneyball* the movie). And not long after hiring Epstein, Henry hired sabermetrics pioneer Bill James.*

And while Bill was the highest-profile hiring for the think tank, he was hardly the only one. Early in that process, I asked Beane what he thought about the Red Sox's efforts to pile up talent not just on the field, but also in the front office. His response, as I recall these many years later, was essentially, "All those guys are great, but I wonder if you can have too many cooks stirring the pot."

Well, all those cooks a-stirring hardly seem to have hurt the Red Sox. Or in recent years, the Cubs or the Dodgers; both clubs have particularly expansive analytics departments. Now, the A's "shop" was never just Billy Beane and Paul DePodesta, despite what the movie might suggest. But the difference between the 2017 A's and the 2017 Astros is striking. Once you get past the usual assistant general managers and the like, the A's have literally three employees on the masthead whose jobs sound at least vaguely Moneyball-ish: Director, Baseball Systems; Research Scientist; and Baseball Operations Analyst. Three.

And the Astros? Man, the Astros.

Their list: Assistant General Manager, Player Acquisitions; Special Assistant to the GM, Process Improvement; Senior Director, Baseball Operations, Research and Innovation; Director, Research and Development; Manager of Amateur Scouting Analysis; Manager of Pro Scouting Analysis; Senior Technical Architect; and Sport Science Analyst.

(Process Improvement! Research and Innovation!)

---

* I played a tiny role in this transaction. John Henry, familiar with my book about spending a season at Fenway Park, contacted me to ask for Bill's email address. Bill is . . . well, I was never sure how accessible Bill wanted to be. So I asked him first. His response: "Any time a billionaire wants my email address, give it to him." Today Bill's got three World Series rings stashed away somewhere.

Oh, wait. One more: Analyst, Research and Development.

Oh, wait again. Five more. The Astros have five Analysts, Research and Development.

Among teams with an avowed, established interest in modern analysis, the Astros are *not* outliers. The Cubs, Dodgers, and Rays all boast large contingents of (for lack of a better term) objective analysts. And aside from Beane's personal preference, there is hardly a good explanation for Oakland's relative paucity. Yes, the A's annually spend less money than just about every other franchise, on just about everything. But the same might almost be said of the Rays. Analysts are cheap, man. Really, really cheap. C-h-e-a-p cheap. Turns out, there are so many bright young people wanting to work in baseball, you just don't have to pay them much.*

On the open market for major-league players, one win above replacement—again, replacement level essentially describes a player who might be easily and cheaply found in the minor leagues, or on the waiver wire, or at the end of the bench—is valued at roughly $8 million. On average.

In the real world, the number varies wildly. This season, Alex Gordon is earning $16 million in the second year of a four-year contract, while giving his team (the Royals) essentially zero wins (again, relative to replacement level). Meanwhile, last winter Matt Joyce signed with the A's for two years and $11 million . . . and is on track to give the A's nearly $20 million in "value" this year alone.

But that's the standard shorthand: an extra win will cost you between eight and ten million bucks on the open market.

And if you believe that math, doesn't it then become obvious that a good analyst, at perhaps 0.5 percent the cost, is literally worth his or her weight in gold? With so much potential marginal value—

---

* Come to think of it, the same is true of talented young people who want to *play* baseball. But more about that later.

that is, value beyond cost—why *not* hire a bunch of people to run the numbers?*

It wasn't recently, but I have heard one good, or at least good-*sounding* argument against more data, more analysis, more everything: *everything* can be overwhelming. Sounds reasonable enough. On the other side of the argument: the Astros, the Red Sox, the Dodgers, and the Rays (but not the Indians, who have been saber-metrically inclined for many years, but like the A's, continue to maintain a small shop). To make *everything* work, it seems you need two key ingredients: a top decision maker who's comfortable with lots of things going on, some of which he is but dimly aware; and a software suite that can both handle *and* elegantly present the fruits of all this labor and thought and raw data.

Not really so long ago, even when teams did have computers, there wasn't a single repository for all the information. All the organizational scouting reports, for example, were probably rotting away in file cabinets. Today, though, practically every team has an in-house data management system. So if you punch in a player's name, you can immediately see all the data and scouting reports and transactions and medical reports and videos and psychological evaluations that you've bothered collecting. All of them, at once (and if you're not collecting all of them, you're doing it wrong).

When Jeff Luhnow arrived in Houston in 2011, the Astros did not have a system like that. So now the Astros have their Ground Control—"the repository of all our baseball knowledge," Luhnow described it, three years ago—just as the Cubs have their "Ivy" and the Red Sox have their "Carmine" and other clubs have their own. Not all, though, and some are just now ramping up. In Detroit,

---

* A few years ago Lewis Pollis, a bright young fellow then at Brown University, made a compelling argument in his senior thesis that "in the current league market, an extra dollar put towards acquiring front office talent will go further than an extra dollar spent on players."

for example, the Tigers' "Caesar" won't turn a year old until this winter.*

So the Astros have a lot of people working the problems, and the A's don't. Relatively speaking. Does all this really explain anything?

Since Luhnow took over, the Astros have won 46 percent of their games, and the A's almost exactly 50 percent. But of course the Houston franchise, organizationally speaking, was making very little effort toward *winning* during Luhnow's first few years, when they averaged 103 *losses* per season. If we're measuring success, do we start with 2015, when the Astros began spending real money and fighting for competitive respectability? Sure. We can do that.

Except then we lose the A's three straight postseason appearances (2012–2014), following a five-year drought. Which obviously isn't fair to them.†

Except. Except it's probably more important now than ever, probably far more important, for a front office to have plenty of bodies to throw into the fray, for one simple, highly complex reason: Statcast.

Today, there's more information than there's ever been, and there is always, *always*, more that could be done with it.

One thing that's already done? Fairly precise measures of fielders' two most important attributes: their quickness in getting started—

---

* Ground Control became infamous in 2015, when news broke that the St. Louis Cardinals had hacked into the database, probably via Sig Mejdal's account. In 2016, ex-Cardinals executive Chris Correa was sentenced to forty-six months in federal prison, and a few months later the Commissioner's Office levied a penalty against Correa's former employer: $2 million, plus the Cardinals' two highest picks in the 2017 amateur draft, which were the fifty-sixth and seventy-fifth overall. St. Louis wouldn't pick until the ninety-fourth spot, with the Astros having made five picks already.

† In all three of those postseason appearances, the A's lost a winner-take-all elimination game, continuing a pattern from four straight Octobers during the "Moneyball era," starting in 2000. Back then, Billy Beane famously said "My shit doesn't work in the playoffs." But he could hardly have imagined it would keep not working for another decade. At least.

their *jumps*—and their acceleration and speed once they're moving. Prior to Statcast, I've been told by front-office executives, publicly available metrics like defensive runs saved and ultimate zone rating were roughly as good as anything the more astute teams were generating internally. Probably not *as* good, because teams could throw more money and bodies at the problems, which were many. But close.*

It's still fairly close, but with the money and bodies *plus* the Statcast data, which tracks every moving object on the field, there's now very little guesswork involved. Postmodern front offices don't need scouts, or ultimate zone rating, to inform their evaluations of a fielder's skills; Statcast tells them almost everything they would want to know. As ex-MLB center fielder Doug Glanville says, with perhaps a hint of envy, "A player like Kevin Kiermaier"—Tampa Bay's tremendous center fielder—"will never be undervalued or underestimated again."

Another thing that's already done? Measuring spin rate, of course. Collin McHugh doesn't throw particularly hard, but lately we've been taught that if your spin rate's high enough, you can still get away with such fastballs up in the zone.

Except somebody forgot to tell Matt Joyce. He's the first hitter up in the inning, and McHugh's fourth pitch is one of those high fastballs.

Which Joyce drives over the center-field fence for a home run. On TV, Geoff Blum says, "You don't see that happen too often with Collin McHugh. He's not afraid to pitch up in that zone."

---

* One unfortunate consequence of all this new data: Because much of it's not public, most of the best analytical work being done these days is probably *not* being done publicly, which means "amateur" sabermetricians aren't doing as much top-flight work as they were a few years ago. Relatively speaking. So as Baseball-Reference.com's Sean Forman observes, "The privacy of Statcast data leads to inefficient hiring. 'We can't see the best work anymore, so we'll just hire more Ivy League guys.'"

For many years, and especially against power hitters, the mantra was down, down, down. Especially in high-power eras. The idea being that low pitches are harder to drive a long distance. But in recent years, and in part because of Astros pitching coach Brent Strom, that's been (literally) turned upside down, with many pitchers working higher in the zone: vertically, instead of horizontally (as Strom would put it). And there's plenty of statistical evidence that it works (granted, in this game a few quite-high fastballs are driven quite far). After all, it's not so much about how hard you throw, as how hard you *seem* to throw, from the hitter's perspective. "Deception is everything," Strom says. "Is the fastball ninety-eight to the hitter's eyes?" There's even a relatively young term for this concept: effective velocity (which we might abbreviate as EV, except exit velocity for batted balls now has a headlock on that one).

But if high fastballs are effective, one might reasonably wonder what Baseball would look like today with *low* fastballs. If low fastballs were in vogue once again, whether by hook or by crook, would the game look more like it once did, not actually so long ago?

It's often said that baseball is *cyclical*, and to some degree this is true. It's both naturally cyclical *and* artificially cyclical. When there's a dearth of outstanding young catchers in the major leagues, or shortstops or whatever, writers will scurry about looking for explanations, while generally ignoring the best, most likely reason: "major-league catchers" is an inherently small sample size, so basic probability tells us that sometimes there will be fewer great catchers than usual, and sometimes more. That's perfectly natural.

When the game begins to seem particularly even dramatically unbalanced, the officials will step in and attempt to restore equipoise. Of course it never works perfectly, because the officials' tools are too blunt, their interests too compromised, their intellects too rigid to seriously weigh the potential for unintended consequences. But they do try, historically anyway, and so those trend lines rise and fall, fall and rise. Artificially.

Not that *everything* is cyclical. At least three things have generally trended upward since about as far into the past as you'll care to check: strikeouts, use of relief pitchers, and (of course) money in all its lovely manifestations.

Usually, though? Toss out a *cyclical* or a *random variation* and you won't be far wrong. Knowing this, that's always my first instinct.

It was my first instinct in the closing stages of the 2015 season, when home runs had made a *dramatic* uptick after the All-Star Game. We were looking at just two months of data, so *cyclical* and *random variation* seemed like perfectly appropriate reactions. Just guessing, one might have thought about lucky hitters, unlucky pitchers, or unseasonably warm weather (the warmer it gets, the easier the hitting).

Wait. Just wait, and the power will fall off. Because nothing *structural* in baseball has changed, right? Or rather, nothing structural changed overnight, at the All-Star break in the middle of the season, that would lead to elevated home-run rates. Right? Because what could change overnight?

In the months and (now) years that followed, there would be a great deal of loose talk—some of it from the Commissioner Himself—about launch angles and maple bats and probably a few other *external* factors contributing to the tremendous power surge since the middle of 2015.[*]

Well, let's talk about launch angles. Because launch angle has become a real story this season. When you make a list of experienced hitters who have, in the last few years, become outstanding hitters practically overnight, in nearly every case their transformations have been attributed to radically revamping their swings, usu-

---

[*] Maple bats? Sixty-two years ago in the *Sporting News*, columnist Oscar Ruhl asked Cardinals manager Harry "the Hat" Walker about *the modern epidemic* of home-run hitting. Walker's response: "We've got fellows up there now swinging 30-ounce sticks, with pencil-like handles and all the wood bunched in the fat end. The hitters just swish those things around like batons and pop! You're liable to be licked any old time." So, yeah: there's not a lot new out there.

ally in the off-season under the tutelage of *personal* hitting coaches (this, by the way, in an era when most MLB coaching staffs include not one but two hitting instructors; there would probably be more, but there's only so much room in the dugouts).

Two of the Dodgers' best hitters, third baseman Justin Turner and super-utilityman Chris Taylor, were slap-hitting backups until they developed new swings, and today they're both brilliant. Before the A's traded him a few weeks ago, first baseman Yonder Alonso was enjoying his finest season by far, thanks largely to nearly *doubling* his average launch angle on batted balls: 10.3 degrees last season, 19.4 degrees this season.

At least the A's got something for Alonso: Boog Powell, who's patrolling center field tonight. The Astros didn't get anything at all for J. D. Martinez, save for some measure of everlasting regret.

Toward the end of spring training in 2014, the Astros released Martinez, then twenty-six years old. Flat-out released him.

Looking just at the statistical record at that moment, this was a perfectly defensible move. If a hitter's going to be a good, reasonably useful major leaguer, typically he'll show some real signs by the time he's twenty-six. To that point, Martinez had nearly a thousand big-league plate appearances under his belt, and he'd been significantly *below* league average . . . while playing a position (left field) where you really shouldn't be playing unless you're hitting significantly *better* than average. And by the way, not playing the position all so well.

But the Astros' front office knew more than just the numbers. They knew, for example, that Martinez had, over the off-season, completely retooled his swing. They knew he'd batted .312 with big-time power in Venezuelan winter ball. And yes, they must have known other things that the rest of us don't.

In spring training, Martinez was given hardly a chance. On the twenty-second of March, having batted only twenty times all spring, Martinez got released. In part because—at least if you believe the public reports—management had more faith in a young outfielder named L. J. Hoes. And it probably didn't help that then-manager Bo Porter wasn't wild about Martinez's future.

When the Astros traded for Hoes the previous summer, Luhnow told MLB.com, "The thing we like about him the most is that he hits and knows what pitches to go after, with a high batting average and on-base percentage—both things that we value and look for. He'll be able to help our club a lot offensively at this level, immediately."

Immediately, Hoes joined the Astros and hit decently the rest of that season, with respectable batting and on-base averages. Since then, though? Hoes has played in just sixty-three major-league games, batting .182 with three home runs. In 2017, he played for the Southern Maryland Blue Crabs in the Atlantic League, an independent organization peopled largely by players who have essentially aged out of the MLB-affiliated minor leagues. Hey, who knows. Maybe Hoes will stage a huge comeback. Probably not with the Astros, though.

J. D. Martinez, on the other hand.

After getting dumped by the Astros, Martinez signed with the Detroit Tigers. Who shipped him to the minor leagues. Where he *destroyed* pitchers for a couple of weeks before the Tigers summoned him back to the majors.

In his first fourteen games with the big club, Martinez failed to hit even one home run.

Then he started hitting home runs, and essentially has not stopped. He hit twenty-three home runs that season, thirty-eight more in 2015, and would have been just as productive in '16 if not for six weeks on the disabled list.

Early on, there were skeptics. I was one of them. Figured Martinez was probably just a decent player on a nice little hot streak. If he was really that good, the Astros wouldn't have released him, right? Because *the Astros know what they are doing.*

The Astros do know what they are doing. Also, Martinez really was that good. In 2017, still with the Tigers, Martinez sported a .305/.388/.630 batting line in mid-July when Detroit traded him to the contending Diamondbacks. In his very first game with his new club, Martinez got hit on the hand by a pitch in the fourth inning and had to leave. Four days later he returned to the lineup, and from that point was one of the greatest hitters in the league.

Martinez will finish this season with a .690 slugging percentage, the highest in the majors. By a lot. Higher than Giancarlo Stanton and Aaron Judge and Mike Trout and everyone else. By a lot.[*]

Who cares about J. D. Martinez? I'll bet Jeff Luhnow cares, at least a little. Although the Astros' outfield this season has been plenty good enough, Martinez would make a tremendous designated hitter . . . while instead, the Astros' designated hitter in this game (and most games) is Carlos Beltrán, who's literally been the Astros' worst hitter this season, at least among those with more than a smattering of action. As good as they've been this season— and Houston will ultimately lead the majors in scoring, with one of the most potent attacks in quite a number of years—they presumably would be even better with Martinez. Roughly speaking, replacing Beltrán with Martinez—assuming of course that Martinez wouldn't have been adversely affected by his (hypothetical) teammates and coaches in Houston—would result in the Astros scoring around fifty more runs than they figure to eventually score. And perhaps winning 106 games rather than the 100 or so they figure to wind up winning.

Not that the Astros need to win 106 games; 100 will be plenty

---

[*] Technically speaking, Martinez's slugging percentage will count as only .670 when figuring league leaders. Largely because of an injury that cost him the first six weeks of the season, Martinez finished with only 489 plate appearances. You need at least 502 to qualify for ownership of a "percentage" title . . . except if by adding enough "empty" plate appearances your percentage would *still* lead the league, you qualify.

enough (although Martinez's bat in October would look pretty good).*

And finally, even closer to home: Jake Marisnick, who's sitting on the Astros' bench at the moment, but in part-time play this season has finally established himself, at twenty-six, as a legitimate major-league hitter after four seasons of futility. Is it coincidental that Marisnick retooled his swing last winter, and gone from an average launch angle of roughly 10 degrees to nearly 16 degrees? Probably not.

So yes, launch angle is real, for some players it's been fantastic, and the launch-angle revolution started even before Statcast gave everyone precise readings on their swing paths. And yes, perhaps the bats today are better than ever; certainly, a number of players swear by their maple bats, first popularized by Barry Bonds.

The problem for the commissioner is that none of these external factors, or even all of them *together*, could possibly account for the observed phenomena in 2015 and since, for the simple reason that none of those factors, let alone all of them, changed overnight.

Which essentially leaves us with two explanations: the mother of all random variations, continuing now for almost two and a half seasons . . . or the baseballs.

So now we're just left to guess? No. We're not. Even though much or most of the best data is now closely held by Major League Baseball, there are ways of answering this fundamental question: If the

---

* Meanwhile, the Diamondbacks won't really need Martinez either. By the end of the season, they'll sit atop the wild-card standings . . . with the next-place (and still qualifying) Rockies six games behind. They won't need him to beat the Rockies in the Wild Card playoff, and they won't need him to get swept three straight in their Division Series against the Dodgers. Martinez is eligible for free agency after the season, ultimately signing with the Red Sox. And due to a new rule designed to keep winning teams from stockpiling draft picks, the D-backs will receive zero compensation. This was a pure "rent-a-player" situation, and it's hard to argue that it actually worked so well in the end.

baseballs became livelier overnight—after the 2015 All-Star break, that is—what would we expect to see? Aside from more home runs, that is.

Well, we would definitely expect to see bouncier baseballs! Baseball tests their baseballs, but they don't let the public see detailed results. Not usually, anyway. At this year's All-Star break, Commissioner Manfred would say only two substantive things on the matter.

I do know with absolute certainty that the baseball falls within the specifications that have existed for many years. Absolutely certain about that.

And

We've kind of taken it for granted that the bats aren't different.

Again, though! The bats didn't change overnight! Nor did launch angles or (among other Manfred-floated theories) general managers' opinions about power hitters or pitchers' ability to throw hard or hitters' comfortableness with trading strikeouts for power. These all *sound* reasonable. Except they simply cannot explain, alone or in concert, the dramatic turn in the numbers two years ago.

Manfred's not stupid, and he's got squads of non-stupid people working for him. His lines about everything except the baseball itself are throwaways, perhaps purposely couched as half-assed theories with no supporting data, when there is literally nobody on the planet with more access to the data than the commissioner. Either he knows the data, or his non-stupid people have told him it's largely irrelevant. Which it probably is.

Manfred's not stupid, and so he probably would not out-and-out lie about the baseballs. But when he says the balls "fall within the specifications that have existed for many years" . . . well, he might not be lying, but he might also not be saying quite what people think he's saying.

People think he's saying the baseballs have not changed. He did not say that. He said the specifications have not changed, and the baseballs continue to fall within those specifications. Which are two utterly different things.

Some years ago, I became friendly with a couple of fellows who had built what was then probably the most sophisticated pitching machine in the world. Hell, might still be. It was designed to duplicate essentially *any* pitch thrown by a real pitcher, from Tim Wakefield's baffling knuckleball to Randy Johnson's nuclear slider. In fact, I once "batted" against Johnson's slider, which would have been terrifying except it all happened too fast to be scared.

My friends ran into a problem, though. Their machine couldn't be tested, or calibrated—which is to say, it couldn't be safely operated—without essentially identical baseballs. Which they wound up having specially manufactured. Because falling "within the specifications" set by MLB for *their* baseballs wasn't nearly good enough.

Which is to say, *It's the specs, stupid.*

Nobody's been on this case with more care than Ben Lindbergh, who used to write for the Baseball Prospectus and Grantland websites, and now toils for The Ringer. After repeated requests from Lindbergh, this spring MLB finally shared a detailed, 11-page study cited by Manfred last year. Lindbergh wasn't permitted to publish all the underlying data from the study, but was permitted to "relay its content and conclusion, which back up the commissioner's comments and indicate that the baseball hasn't been altered in any way that would explain the dramatic dinger surge."

The actual conclusion from the actual report: "There is no evidence from the results of this study that the performance of the 2016 regular-season baseballs used by these five clubs would have resulted in any difference in on-field performance from those used during recent seasons."

Alan Nathan, a professor emeritus of physics at the University of Illinois and the acknowledged authority on baseball physics, backed up the report, telling Lindbergh, "I saw nothing in the data that was presented that suggests that the ball has been altered at all."

Again, all this was in May of this year. And seemed to leave us exactly where we started, a couple of years ago: wondering how in hell all these baseballs started flying over the fences, all of a sudden. Ben's story was a real back-to-the-ol'-drawing-board moment.

And then a month later, Ben was back with contradictory evidence. Mitchel Lichtman, a professional gambler, longtime sabermetrician, and sometime consultant with major-league teams, gave Ben the results of his *own* study.

Yes, his own study. Lichtman had gone on eBay and purchased a few dozen game-used, MLB-authenticated baseballs.

That was actually the easy part. Frankly, it speaks quite poorly of our sports media that nobody—not ESPN or *Sports Illustrated* or the *New York Times* or anyone else with money to burn, plus an avowed hunger for the truth—had not already studied a few dozen baseballs. Or a few hundred.

Of course, you need more than just the baseballs. You have to do something with them. Lichtman spent around twelve hundred dollars on eBay for the balls, and another couple of grand to have them tested at Washington State University's Sports Science Lab. And the results? Compared to seventeen baseballs used in 2014 and early '15, the ten baseballs from 2016 had *higher* coefficients of restitution—that is, they were bouncier—along with *smaller* circumferences and *lower* seam heights.

There is more.

Among the many terabytes of data now available, in great detail, is the exact speed of a pitched baseball just after leaving the pitcher's hand and then again as it's crossing the plate. Of course, the speed drops on its way to the plate, at a constant rate . . . but that rate depends on *the air resistance of the baseball*. The lower the resistance, the lower the amount of velocity loss on the way to the plate . . . and the farther the ball, if struck, will travel.

Put another, perhaps more relevant way: If baseballs are traveling farther because of lower air resistance, we would also expect to observe lower drops in velocity as the pitch travels from pitcher to batter.

This summer, FiveThirtyEight's Rob Arthur checked, and found that *this is exactly what the data show.*

"In total," Arthur wrote, "the changes in ball drag explain about 25 percent of the variation in the ratio of home runs to fly balls over the last four years." Further, Arthur "also found a significant decrease in the drag on the ball in general over the past four seasons, with the MLB-wide average drag coefficient dropping by about 0.01 from 2015 to 2017. That might not sound like much, but . . . even a change that small can add up to five feet of distance on a well-hit fly ball, which in turn would be enough to make 10 to 15 percent more balls leave the yard in a given season."

Well. Five feet. That's a lot of feet. Ten to 15 percent. That's a lot of percent.

Essentially, everyone who claims to study the baseballs with any seriousness *except Major League Baseball* concludes the same thing: the baseballs are significantly, measurably different from just a few years ago, which accounts for the great majority of the massive increase in home runs since 2014.[*]

Yes, MLB presumably has the best data. MLB also has an incentive to . . . well, let's just say MLB has good reasons to obfuscate what might seem a pretty clear situation. Because if the balls *are* livelier and MLB acknowledged this, they would open themselves to criticism from the media and from the Players Association. Or at least the half that's pitchers. But it's more than just the criticism. If MLB were to acknowledge that the balls are livelier—even while remaining technically within the specified ranges—there would almost certainly be a call to tighten the specifications, which would almost certainly mean refining the manufacturing process, at some great expense.

---

[*] This season's new MLB record for home runs—6,105 across the majors—represents an utterly stunning 46 percent increase since 2014, when only 4,186 homers were totaled.

Or, putting it simply: more expensive baseballs.

Now, you might be thinking, hey, what's a few cents per baseball? Well, it would probably be more than a few cents.

In the old days, they might get through a whole game without using more than two or three baseballs. You know, a hundred years ago nobody hit home runs, and foul balls hit into the stands were usually sent back to the field and returned to the small stock of game balls.

Today? Depending on the weather and everything else, a single game will see somewhere between twelve and eighteen *dozen* baseballs. Which adds up to roughly three hundred thousand baseballs per season . . . with another six hundred thousand that don't actually get used in the games. So yes, we're talking about nearly a million baseballs in just one season. Tack on two or three dollars per baseball—just a wild guess at what it might cost to make all the baseballs the same, and *well* within the specs—and we're talking about some real money. Well, at least to a business that still can't seem to find enough real money to support youth baseball in a meaningful way.

Major League Baseball would like to be treated—in some ways, is treated—as a sort of public trust, given innumerable tax breaks and other public subsidies, and not subject to normal antitrust laws. But of course MLB also wants to—and does—generate enormous revenues, along with less enormous profits, while keeping a good deal of information deep inside a locked vault. Metaphorically speaking.

While we've been unlocking the mysteries of Postmodern power hitting, Jed Lowrie was digging into the batter's box to face McHugh, with nobody on and nobody out, his team now trailing by just a couple of runs. Lowrie gets ahead in the count, two balls and no strikes, then—hallelujah!—bunts against the shift. Leans right into it!

Alas, the ball rolls foul by a few feet; it *might* have been his second bunt single of the whole season. Alas, Lowrie gives up on leaning, and lifts the next pitch into short right field, where Altuve makes the grab after a long run, Springer peeling off at the last instant. Khris Davis follows with a solid drive to center field, easily snagged by Maybin.

Then Olson steps in, and he *too* bunts.

Later I'll ask Olson about bunting to beat the shift. "Down the road," he says, "if teams continue to do it, I think it's something I'd wanna work in a lot, because, (a) it's baserunners, and (b) just to have them respect it could open up other holes." But he also says it's difficult to justify the bunt when you're "swinging the bat well"—as he's been doing, actually a lot more than well, for the last couple of months—and giving up any chance for an extra-base hit. Which is a pretty good argument!

So here's a wild bit of advice for Olson, though. . . . How's about bunting more often against lefty pitchers, against whom you're not nearly as likely to homer? When we look at the cost-benefit analysis of bunting, we tend to look at overall numbers. But Olson, for all his demonstrated talents—and he's demonstrated a great deal of talent over the last month or so, perhaps because of a completely revamped batting stance—is *not* a great hitter against lefty pitchers. Probably never will be. So if you're ever going to bunt, that's the time.

Collin McHugh is a righty. Unlike Lowrie, Olson gets his down fair, but it's too close to the mound, and McHugh throws him out by five or six steps. Olson will finish this season with three bunts; all three times, he's out at first base. Before bunting more often, perhaps just a bit more practice . . .

Score: Astros 5, Athletics 3
Win Probability: Astros 73%

Visitors Fourth

The choice we face isn't between digital and analog. That simplistic duality is actually the language that digital has conditioned us to: a false binary choice between 1 and 0, black and white, Samsung and Apple. The real world isn't black or white. It is not even gray.

—DAVID SAX, *THE REVENGE OF ANALOG:*
REAL THINGS AND WHY THEY MATTER (2016)

Carlos Beltrán leads off the fourth against Cotton, who's already surrendered five runs and more than five laser blasts, and once again we're reminded that the Astros are paying Beltrán $16 million this season to serve as approximately the worst hitter in their lineup.

Of course the Astros didn't plan it this way. They always said they would spend money when the time seemed right, and last winter it seemed right, especially with a medium-sized hole in their designated hitter slot, and Beltrán willing to sign for just one season. Yes, $16 million might seem like a great deal of money. But in 2017, it doesn't constitute a particularly large commitment, especially considering Beltrán's solid 2015 and '16 seasons, with the Yankees and (briefly) the Rangers.

Fifty years ago in baseball, the decision-making process might have been 90 percent gut feeling and subjective experience, plus 10 percent objective information: batting average, home runs, earned run average, maybe a few others. Ninety/ten, maybe 80/20, but somewhere in that range. To be sure, baseball men loved statistics. But they rarely considered the context. If a pitcher won eighteen games in a season, it was because he was the sort of pitcher who won eighteen games; not because his teammates scored a lot of runs when he was pitching. If a pitcher posted a low earned run average, it was because he was the sort of pitcher who did that; not because he pitched his home games in a pitcher-friendly ballpark and was blessed with fast outfielders.

Today, that ratio has essentially flipped, at least among the more . . . uh, progressive clubs. As Billy Beane says, "In God we trust; all others must bring data."

The *data* suggested that Beltrán, even at forty, could still hit (even if aging patterns in recent years have returned to their normal, pre-Steroids Era cruelty). But beyond the data, there remains a lingering belief in probably every executive suite that yes, *chemistry* really does matter, and absent at least a sprinkling of veteran leadership, your chemistry might well go awry. The 2014 Giants won the World Series with thirty-nine-year-old Tim Hudson, the 2014 Royals *reached* the World Series—after so, so many years wandering in the desert—with forty-two-year-old Raúl Ibañez, the 2016 Cubs won the World Series with thirty-nine-year-old David Ross, and the 2017 Astros have Carlos Beltrán. If you win, it worked.[*]

Here, Beltrán falls behind in the count against Cotton, then grounds out to shortstop. But management still won't begrudge him that $16 million one bit. Especially if October goes well.

Since we mentioned Billy Beane, we might also mention that (a) we'll probably never quite flip that historical ratio to 90/10 or even

---

[*] Beltrán's reputation is so sterling that after officially retiring this winter, he'll be interviewed for the job as New York Yankees manager, despite his complete absence of managing, coaching, or front-office experience. However, the job will wind up going to Aaron Boone. Another ex-Yankee with zero experience.

80/20 objectivity/subjectivity, because (b) these are still human beings making decisions about other human beings, so the potential for emotions and cognitive biases mucking up all the fancy
equations is always high. Or at least higher than everyone involved
might prefer. Not to mention the fact that *chemistry* remains highly
amorphous; as historian Jill Lepore has observed, not everything
can be lashed to a ruler.

Before the 2015 season, Billy Beane's team signed ex-Royals
slugger Billy "Country Breakfast" Butler for three years and $30 mil-
lion. By the time the A's released Butler, five months into his second season—this was shortly after he'd been on the disabled list
with a concussion, suffered while brawling with a teammate—he
had accounted for approximately zero wins above replacement.
Which meant the A's would have done just as well spending that
$30 million on literally anything else, and just handed Butler's
759 at-bats to some fresh kid from the minor leagues.

Or the A's could have husbanded that $30 million and used it to
pay Josh Donaldson.

Donaldson ranks as one of the all-time great surprises, on the
same sort of list with J. D. Martinez. At twenty-five, Donaldson
was still down in Triple-A for the whole summer, hoping to reach
the majors as a backup catcher or maybe a third baseman of sorts;
at that point, it was far from clear *where* Donaldson's future lay. At
twenty-six, he was the A's Opening Day third baseman . . . only
to get demoted within a few weeks, then promoted, then demoted
again in June with a .153 batting average in nearly a hundred at-bats.

But Donaldson was *raking* in Triple-A (thanks to a J. D. Martinez–
style, reinvented power swing). So two months after that second
demotion, he was back in the majors—this was in the middle of
August 2012—and this time he hit. In 2013, by then twenty-seven,
Donaldson ranked among the best players in the major leagues. No
one-year wonder, he was nearly as good in 2014.

And then, just before Donaldson's twenty-ninth birthday, Billy
Beane traded him to the Blue Jays for a quartet of lesser players. At

the time, I half-heartedly defended the move, largely because one of those lesser players was Brett Lawrie, who had shown flashes of top-shelf talent when not convalescing on the disabled list.

In his first season with the Blue Jays, Donaldson was named the American League's Most Valuable Player. Brett Lawrie was not. In the three seasons since the trade, Donaldson has been good for roughly twenty wins above replacement. Lawrie plus the other three guys have not been good for twenty wins (the actual figure, give or take, is about ten; granted, one of those players, Franklin Barreto, is still quite young and might yet make Beane look like a genius).

If the A's had simply kept Donaldson, they would today be measurably better (although it's not clear where he'd play, as the A's now feature a fine young third baseman in Matt Chapman). If they had kept Donaldson for just one more season, or half season, before trading him, they would likely be measurably better today. Because they would have made a different, probably better trade.

Not to pile on Billy Beane. As we've already seen, everybody makes mistakes, or at least makes decisions that later look like mistakes, especially if we're not privileged enough to see the reasoning behind the decisions. Even the Astros. My point is that these "mistakes" are the products of human thought, regardless of the *process* supposedly employed with such great care. One group of smart people determined that J. D. Martinez wasn't worth a spot on the forty-man roster, and a different group of smart people determined that he was.

Actually, my real point is that as long as human beings are making decisions about other human beings, *of course* it's impossible to remove the *analog*—the human element—from the equation.

And yet still there are people who habitually bemoan the impending demise of *the human element* in baseball.

The decline of *the human element* in the evaluation of players is often bemoaned; the impending death of the scouting profession is lamented. Which would be worthy of the most spirited lamentations. Except there are more scouts now than there were twenty years ago, for the simple reasons that (a) Baseball people are casting wider nets than ever before, all around the globe, and (b) Postmodern Baseball people just *crave* information, and hiring scouts is a fairly cheap way of collecting information.

The demise of *the human element* in umpiring seems terrifying too. Specifically, the prospect of "robot umpires"—which is a stupid term, but what are you gonna do?—who will call the balls and strikes. To an outside observer, it might seem odd: the idea that we actually *want* our game officials to make the wrong call roughly 10 percent of the time, as even the best human umpires do, when calling balls and strikes.

Oh, and by the way? It's not their fault! With perhaps a few exceptions, mostly the older umpires who can't be fired and are either (relatively) incompetent or just don't give a damn, today's umpires are probably the best in the world, and the best there's ever been. But they can't get much better. They might not even be able to keep up. Pitchers are throwing harder all the time, their curveballs and sliders and cutters and changeups all the more devilish. Wouldn't it follow that those pitches are also harder to call?

So in the absence of an automated strike zone—my preferred terminology—we're going to keep seeing that 10-percent failure rate. At least.

Yes. How very human. But the game was not designed, any more than any other game is designed, for the human element to include errors by the officials. If the men who invented baseball could have eliminated umpires from their new sport, they would have. If they could have eliminated umpires' *errors* from their sport, they would have.

Today the people who run Baseball *can* eliminate those errors. Or at least a huge percentage of them. If the technology isn't ready yet, it could be soon.

When the human element can be removed, it *will* be removed, just as sure as the streets will soon be patrolled by driverless cars and our carpets will be kept spotless by robot—er, automated vacuum cleaners.

Oh. Right. Already happening. Well, more Roombas are coming. More driverless cars. More everything else, too. Robot umpires are coming, friends. Just as sure as tomorrow's sun. For the simple reason that today's technology, available to anyone with a cell phone or wi-fi, often makes it obvious when the umpire misses one, and nobody pays good money to see umpires be wrong. And there would still *be* a home-plate umpire doing various things, so anyone actually watching the game would hardly notice a difference at all.

Once that *particular* human element is gone, though, we'll still be blessed with the human element of players' training habits; the human element of pitch selection; the human element of guessing pitches; the human element of managers' cognitive biases; the human element of executives' and owners' emotions; and, oh, a few million other human elements that won't just disappear because a bunch of smart kids are writing code. Promise.

On TV, now they're talking about Brian McCann's beard, while he (and it) draws a one-out walk against Cotton. But on the Astros, McCann's whiskers take a backseat to those of ace starting pitcher Dallas Keuchel, whose beard has been described by *Sports Illustrated* as "the most lush" in the majors.

On the radio, with McCann sticking close to first base, now they're talking about Houston outfielder Cameron Maybin's high socks, which stand out because in the twenty-first century, most players don't show any socks at all, preferring the cuffs of their pants all the way down to the tops of their shoes (if not lower). Maybin's style looks best when traveling at high speed, but he just returns coolly to the dugout after swinging at a low changeup for strike three.

It's too late in the season to make a real dent in Cotton's statistics, but it's that changeup, a pitch that behaves for him very much like the old-school screwball, that got him to the major leagues. It's that changeup that Pedro Martinez raved about back in April. "Yes,

I saw that," Cotton says. "I watched it on TV a bunch of times after the game."

So why has Cotton thrown fewer changeups this season, and especially since early in the spring? "I was scared to throw it," he'll say next spring. "I thought it was going to be out of the strike zone every time. So I would throw my fourth-best pitch instead."

Tonight, Cotton will actually throw his highest percentage of changeups all season. It's not working, but at least he's committed to his strength (and will continue to lean on his changeup in his two remaining starts before season's end).

With McCann still on first base, a two-run lead and two outs, George Springer bounds to the batter's box. He's having a good night, having already walked and singled. Watch Springer enough, and you can't help remembering something Hall of Fame catcher Roy Campanella once said: "You gotta be a man to play baseball for a living, but you gotta have a lot of little boy in you, too."

With his tremendous talent and infectious enthusiasm, Springer's one of those players, and there are plenty of them, who might well be household names if, you know, baseball players were still household names. He's young and handsome and has a splendid personality and oh, he's also a tremendously talented athlete. But they're not household names. Which doesn't stop people from complaining that Baseball doesn't do enough to *market* its stars.

Baseball does try. It's probably never going to work. But Baseball tries. For example, today's players are generally encouraged (or at least permitted) to be themselves, at least within certain fairly prescribed boundaries. You wanna shave your head? Shave your head. You wanna grow out your hair? Grow out your hair; the Mets' Noah Syndergaard earned the nickname Thor with blond hair that flows below his shoulders, and now half the teams in the majors seem to have at least one pitcher with long locks. Meanwhile, Maybin doesn't just have the high socks; he's also wearing white shoes (which probably violate MLB's rules about uniform footwear) and a long, spectacularly orange sweatband over his left wrist and forearm.

Stylewise, players will do whatever they can get away with; now more than ever they can get away with a lot, as long as their choices don't interfere with official MLB uniform licensees.

Yes, a sign in every clubhouse says a player's pants "cannot extend over the tip of heel of the shoe, cannot have shoes laced through them and cannot have straps attached to the bottom of the pants. Pants cannot be worn so excessively baggy that it provides a competitive advantage." Further, "All footwear must be of a standard club color as determined by club management."

Which apparently leaves a great deal of leeway. Most players wear their pants so low that you can't see any socks at all, while a few players have their cuffs nearly knee high. And if they *do* show their socks, you might see just about anything. Especially now that Major League Baseball's got big *sock deals*. Jharel Cotton looks particularly stylish tonight, with his pant cuffs pulled high, showing green socks with yellow stripes and the A's logo in white. There's not a better-looking player on the field tonight.

In his book about establishing himself as a young player in the 1970s, now Mets broadcaster Keith Hernandez writes, "Everything from how we played to how we looked—socks lined up, shirt tucked in with letters showing—was important . . . It fostered pride and dedication to ourselves and to the organization." And in the minor leagues, it's still largely expected that each player will wear his uniform . . . well, *uniformly*. But all that goes completely out the window in the major leagues. All nine players on the field will wear the same cap and the same jersey and the same pants, but otherwise you might not find a single pair of players with the same pants length, socks, and shoe color.

This trend might have peaked (or cratered, depending on your perspective) a few weeks ago, when the inaugural Players Weekend included every team wearing garish jerseys, most of them with players' nicknames on the back—but not all! Jed Lowrie went with "Jed," while Boog Powell and a few notable Astros stuck with their last names—and all manner of other nontraditional, nonstandard accoutrements.*

So today's players are permitted, and sometimes even encouraged, to express their own tastes, sartorially and otherwise. Hell, we haven't even mentioned walk-up music, or closer entrance songs.

On the other hand, there are still a few *qualities* that remain largely taboo.

For one thing, you're still not supposed to show a great deal of emotion on the field. At least when it comes to "bat flipping" upon hitting a home run. Four years ago when Brian McCann was still catching for the Atlanta Braves, he took such great offense with Carlos Gomez's flip that when Gomez (almost) finished circling the bases, McCann simply stood in front of the plate and refused to let Gomez touch the plate.

Which wasn't the first time for McCann, and that's how he briefly became somewhat infamous on the internet as "Brian McCann: Fun Cop." There haven't been any incidents with McCann recently, but it's not clear whether that's because McCann's mellowed, or he and a few other (mostly U.S.-born white) veterans have beat all the enthusiasm out of younger (mostly Latino) players. But every year, Bryce Harper wins the "most hated" category in the *Sports Illustrated* poll, and it's largely because he really seems to enjoy playing baseball.

For another thing, it's 2017 and somehow there's *still* never been a gay major leaguer. Not who was out.

To be fair, there's also never been a publicly gay NFL player or

---

* A sampling of nicknames: "Squeaky" (Jharel Cotton), "Baby Prince" (Bruce Maxwell), Snap Dragon 2 (Collin McHugh), "Red Dawg" (Josh Reddick). In MLB's press release for Players Weekend, Tampa Bay third baseman Evan "Longo" Longoria was quoted: "It's America's Pastime, and it's steeped in a lot of history. I think a lot of the gear and the dress code was founded around that belief, and we were really behind [the weekend] in terms of guys expressing themselves on the field with what they wear." If you can figure out what that's supposed to mean, please write in care of my publisher.

a publicly gay NHL player, and there's been just one publicly gay NBA player: Jason Collins, who came out in 2013, toward the end of his career. Afterward, he signed with the Brooklyn Nets, playing just a bit in what would be his final season.

To be accurate, of course there have been *lots* of gay players in all the big leagues. Or so we might assume. Even without the data. While seven NFL players have come out after their playing careers ended, only two MLBers have: Glenn Burke, who played for the Dodgers and the A's in the late 1970s; and Billy Bean, who earned trials with three different teams from 1987 through 1995.*

Aside from Collins, just one NBA player has come out: Englishman John Amaechi, when his autobiography was published in 2007, four years after he'd left the NBA. And somehow, at least if I'm consulting my sources correctly, the number of closeted NHL players who later uncloseted themselves stands, in this Year of Our Lord 2017, at exactly zero.

Of course, there was a time when being publicly gay would have gotten you blackballed. Probably. If (say) Pete Rose had come out in 1973, would the Reds have released him? Would his teammates have refused to take the field with him? It's impossible to say, as we simply have no historical precedent, even all these years later. But while it's routinely said that gay players remain closeted because of their teammates, it's also true that in the late '70s, some of Glenn Burke's Dodger teammates knew he was gay, and yet he remained on fine terms with practically everyone in the clubhouse.†

---

* Here's your Most Important Footnote: This is *not* the Billy Beane of Moneyball fame. And if you think you've got problems keeping them straight, just think how Pat Corrales must have felt. In 1988, Corrales managed the minor-league Toledo Mud Hens, and for much of the season both Billy Bean and Billy Beane were in the lineup together. They called the six-feet-four Beane "Big" and the six-foot Bean "Little."

† On the other hand, his manager wasn't so thrilled when Burke spent a fair amount of time with his manager's gay son. And according to Burke, the front office offered him a bonus if he'd just get married (to a woman).

That was forty years ago.

Yet since then, Billy Bean remains the only major leaguer to come out *after* his career. His memoir, *Going the Other Way*, was published in 2003. Which now seems like a long time ago. Two years ago, the U.S. Supreme Court ruled, in a 5–4 decision, that all states must grant marriage licenses for same-sex marriages, and recognize same-sex marriages from other states. Today it's simply the law of the land, and so far the Republic has not fallen.

In 2017, you can say a lot of things you wouldn't say, not so long ago. You can say you've suffered from depression (as Cleveland pitcher Trevor Bauer has). You can say you were sexually abused as a youngster (as then-Mets knuckleballer R. A. Dickey did, in his 2012 memoir). You can say almost anything. But you can't say you smoke marijuana, even though it's now legal (to varying degrees) in a number of U.S. states. It seems you still can't say you're gay. You also can't say much that's obviously insensitive to our modern sensibilities. One year ago, a third-string catcher on the disabled list fired off a few anti–Black Lives Matter, racially insensitive Facebook posts—on a private account, no less—and was erased from the roster in less than twenty-four hours.

There seems little doubt about this, though: most fans, most front-office personnel, and *most* players would have few real problems with a gay player (or players!) on the roster. But in the cauldron of the six-month season, there would undoubtedly be a few players who would not handle it well, who would not want to answer the early questions about it, who would not want to share a clubhouse or shower room with a gay teammate. And perhaps it's because of those few that not a single gay player has yet come out in the majors. Even though in 2015, two active minor-league players *did* come out: Sean Conroy, a pitcher with the independent league Sonoma Stompers; and David Denson, a first baseman on a lower rung of the Milwaukee Brewers' farm system.

But Conroy never got out of indy ball, Denson never advanced beyond Class A, and neither played at all in 2017, which means this year is yet another year without a single publicly gay player in the entirety of professional baseball. Which, despite all the supportive words from the Commissioner's Office and the continuing presence of Billy Bean—since July 2014, Bean's held a high-profile role within Major League Baseball—and the occasional Pride Days in major-league stadiums, seems a sort of step backward, however blameless.

The bottom line on Denson and Conroy? Both simply were not talented enough to reach the major leagues. Most minor leaguers are not. The first publicly gay major leaguer might come out in high school or college or in the minors, and simply work his way up the ladder. Or he might be an established major leaguer. Different people have different theories on which of these avenues would be "easier." Some even think it should be a big star. Because what are you gonna do? Tell the guy making $20 million he can't play anymore? Because he prefers dudes?

We do have a fine recent example of an exceptionally smooth transition from in to out, on the field. Three years ago, veteran MLB umpire Dale Scott came out. Scott's employers and his colleagues had known for a few years that he was gay, with a long-term partner, and had offered nothing but their full support. But this didn't become public until December 2014 (through a somewhat convoluted series of events that aren't worth enumerating here). In Scott's first spring-training game the next February, he was stationed at third base during the middle innings when Reds outfielder Marlon Byrd came bounding up and said, "Buddy, I'm so proud of you. You're free. You're free." The same day, superstar first baseman (and data-friendly hitting guru) Joey Votto said much the same. As Scott told me, "For the most part it was business as usual. I never heard anything from the stands. Not once." Hell, even the retired Curt Schilling, a knuckleheaded Neanderthal in so many ways, tweeted, "Dale Scott might be one of the nicest guys I've ever met, and was a HELL of an umpire."

So the players seem to have been okay with a publicly gay umpire, and it seems likely they'd be fine with distaff umpires as well. This season, there are two women umpiring games in the low minor leagues, and by all accounts the response from players and managers has been almost uniformly positive, often downright supportive. Some of the ancient barriers *are* breaking down.

And yet, no player's come out in the majors. So there are limits, then, in 2017. It seems you're supposed to stay in the closet, if you're gay. And you're not supposed to express your affection for cannabis, even if you spend half your season in Denver or Seattle (where pot isn't merely legal, but celebrated as just another local avocation, like hiking or craft beer).*

George Springer's batting, with McCann still on first base. Just as he did in the first inning, Springer falls behind in the count against Cotton. But again he fights back, this time shooting a liner toward right field. Jed Lowrie's in the way, though, and makes the routine grab to finish off the Astros in the fourth.

Score: Astros 5, Athletics 3
Win Probability: Astros 69%

---

* Major-league players are *not* tested for pot. But minor leaguers are, and more than a few have been suspended in recent years for fifty games at a time. Or more. Jon Singleton, once among the Astros' top prospects, was suspended for fifty games early in 2013. The next year, Singleton signed a five-year, $10 million contract with the Astros, and spent most of '14 in the majors. But he has floundered since then, and this winter he'll fail a third drug test, resulting in a hundred-game suspension.

Home Fourth

You've got to be lucky, but if you have good stuff, it's easier to be lucky.

—SANDY KOUFAX (B. 1935)

Collin McHugh's out of the game, after just three innings. While waiting for official word from below, upstairs it's generally theorized that McHugh's been knocked out by a blister.

Could be lots worse. McHugh opened the season on the disabled list, with tendinitis in his throwing shoulder. On his way back, he stopped off in the minors for a rehab start . . . and was removed after just one inning because of "discomfort in his throwing elbow," which was later diagnosed as "posterior impingement."

That was in early April, and McHugh was supposedly going to miss just six weeks or so. In the event, though, he didn't pitch again in the majors until late July, so this is just his ninth start for the Astros all season. The good news? Before tonight he'd pitched well, with a 3.25 ERA and fine peripheral statistics, right in line with his fine career numbers.

Later in the game, the broadcasters will report that McHugh actually left the game because of a "right middle fingernail avulsion," which they find amusing because "fingernail avulsion" is just a fancy way of saying his fingernail started to come off.

This isn't the first time for McHugh. Back in the summer of 2014, his first season with the Astros, McHugh missed three weeks with the same injury (they called it an avulsion then too).

What's different is that McHugh's yet another data point for what's been described as an epidemic.

Among McHugh's colleagues, there have been all kinds of complaints this season about the baseballs. Not so much about how lively they've been, perhaps because pitchers don't want to sound like they're making excuses for giving up so many home runs. Or maybe because they recognize, all things considered, that they've got things pretty good. You know, with all the strikeouts. What they're complaining about is all the damned blisters. Because when you've got a blister you can't pitch. And if you're a pitcher, there's little worse than not pitching.

In June, Boston's David Price told *USA Today*, "Never have I ever gotten a blister on my ring finger. I had a huge one. And now that's gone, I have a cracked nail on my middle finger."

Also in June, then-Tiger Justin Verlander told the *Detroit Free Press*: "There's not much of a seam on the ball anymore. That was always the case. When you got up to the big leagues, if you picked up a minor league ball to a big league ball, the seams were always wound tighter, just a little smaller. It was noticeable, but I'd say now, you get a foul ball and look at the ball and like try to look at it from the side, there isn't one. There is no seam. I think it's more aesthetics than anything at this point just to hold the ball together."

In July, the Blue Jays' Marcus Stroman was removed from a start because of a blister. Afterward, he told *USA Today*, "I feel like it's an epidemic that's happening across the big leagues now, a bunch of pitchers getting blisters, guys who have never had blisters before. So for MLB to turn their back to it, I think that's kind of crazy."

And it's not just McHugh and Price and Stroman. Also this season, high-profile starting pitchers Rich Hill and Noah Syndergaard and Taijuan Walker and Johnny Cueto have all missed time with blisters. Oh, and Jharel Cotton's not been immune either; he missed a few starts in late June and early July because of a blister on his thumb. Like almost everybody else, he blamed the baseball: "Yeah, I think that's the feeling around the league," Cotton said. "I feel sure that's why I got my blister. The seams are raised and tighter." A's reliever Liam Hendriks told me he was rummaging through a pile of baseballs, earlier this season, and one of them drew blood, the seams were so sharp.[*]

Later, Brandon McCarthy will relate his own experience with 2017 baseballs. "Just going back and grabbing balls from 2013 and '14," he says, "and comparing them to these baseballs, the old balls used to feel like cue balls, and now they felt like high-school balls with the huge seams. That's what felt the most different to me. It was like someone did a pretty good impression of a baseball, but didn't get it all right."

So you've got Verlander saying the seams are lower than they used to be, and Cotton and McCarthy saying they're higher than they used to be. Oh, and Sean Doolittle said that when a batted ball gets back to him on the mound, "more often than not it's lopsided; you can see where it got hit."

Yes, this is classic *anecdata*. Still, it's almost as if the baseballs are not manufactured and/or stored with great precision. That's what the pitchers seem to think, anyway.

Historically, there have always been complaints about the baseballs when home runs or blisters have spiked. For the obvious reason. Sometimes even when the spike is just temporary. But these spikes are real. We already know the spike in home runs is fantastically real. And it turns out the spike in blisters is real too.

In July, the Ringer's Ben Lindbergh published a study of blisters and concluded that yes, blisters have become a bigger issue in recent seasons. Well, in this season and last season, anyway. Granted, 40 percent of the time missed because of blisters was accounted for by just two pitchers: Rich Hill and Aaron Sanchez.

---

[*] When I spoke to Cotton some months later, he largely disavowed his comments about the baseballs. "I've had blisters in the minor leagues too," he said. "For me, I think it's about change in climate, going from dry air to moist air. So I have to keep my fingers dry."

"It's possible that the blister spike has nothing to do with the ball," Lindbergh wrote. "It could be a fluke or a product of other developments, such as altered grips or the trends toward higher velocities and fewer fastballs."

It might indeed have nothing to do with the baseballs themselves. A year before Lindbergh wrote about *the blister spike*, Vice Sports' Eric Nusbaum wrote about blisters and cited a few experts—that is, ex-pitchers like Nolan Ryan and Mike Marshall—who argued that the traditional prescription to *toughen the skin* is actually counterproductive. Instead of soaking the worrisome digit in pickle brine or dry rice or urine (yes, really), pitchers should be aiming for *softer* skin. In fact, before each start, Ryan would actually pull out a scalpel and carve a few layers of skin from his fingers.

Similarly, it's theorized that while the application of various drying substances like pine tar and Firm Grip and sunscreen or some combination thereof helps pitchers grip the ball *and* improve their spin rates, it also results in greater friction and a higher risk of blisters. Which, even if true, would still be a risk worth taking for the great majority of pitchers, just as they push their pitch speeds to the limits despite knowing those speeds mean a higher risk of serious arm injuries.

If I were running the Players Association, I would scare up a few bucks and commission a study, since there's obviously a workplace safety issue here. But the union's never been much on safety, so we probably shouldn't hold our breath. Unless all the blisters *are* a fluke, we can only expect more of them, because the baseballs aren't changing anytime soon (that we know about) and the pitchers aren't going to suddenly start throwing softer, or gripping the baseballs differently, or cutting back on their wipeout sliders and curveballs.

McHugh's replacement, with Ryon Healy leading off and the Astros ahead 5–3, is Michael Feliz, a tremendous strikeout pitcher who could probably walk through Houston's busiest shopping mall without being recognized by a single soul. It's Feliz's first outing since going on the disabled list in early August with "right shoulder discomfort." (Whatever that means.)

How tremendous a strikeout pitcher is Feliz? Well, that sort of depends on your perspective.

Since arriving in the majors a couple of years ago, Feliz has struck out roughly a third of the batters he's faced. If he'd struck out so many in an earlier era, he would have been famous. In 1982, literally *nobody* struck out hitters so often. Among American League pitchers with at least fifty innings that season, only five struck out more than 20 percent of the batters they faced. Mariners closer Bill Caudill led the way at 29 percent, just a tick above future Hall of Famer Goose Gossage; another Hall of Famer, Rollie Fingers, was also in that small group.

These days? Hey, 33 percent is a lot. It's not the *most*, as it would have been in 1982. In 1992, it would have ranked second (behind high-octane, rage-fueled Rob Dibble). In 2002, it would have ranked second (behind steroids-fueled Eric Gagne). But in 2017, Michael Feliz can strike out a third of the batters he faces, and it's just barely worth mentioning.*

In this inning, Feliz will throw a dozen pitches: ten fastballs and two sliders, with the fastballs all around 95 miles per hour. And as impressive as 95 might sound, as impressive as it once *was*, 95's no longer much of a calling card; in fact, Feliz's fastball is far less impressive than his strikeout rate.

This season, Feliz will finish with forty-eight innings in the majors. Among relief pitchers with at least forty innings, Feliz's 96.2 average fastball speed will rank just thirty-second.

Again: Still a lot! Just not what it once was.

What's different about Feliz isn't his solid (but hardly unique) fastball or his outstanding (but hardly historic) strikeout rate; what's different about Feliz is that those qualities have not led to much success, even though he's coupled his tremendous strikeout rate with a perfectly acceptable walk rate. Somehow, Feliz will end this season with an unsightly 5.13 career ERA.

---

* Actually, this might be the first time anyone has mentioned it.

That said, Feliz's career numbers will also include only 121 innings, which is *not* a large sample size. Most people would guess it's plenty, especially as it's spread over two full seasons (and just a tiny bit of another). But 121 innings is *not* enough for all the luck to even out, and reasonably modern metrics suggest that Feliz has suffered from more than his fair share of poor luck.

Year in and year out, the great majority of pitchers will give up something like a .300 batting average on balls in play; that is, all batted balls that aren't home runs. There are a few exceptions to the rule, including knuckleball pitchers and Mariano Rivera pitchers. But there's no reason to believe Feliz is an exception. And yet he's somehow allowed a .340 batting average on balls in play. He's *also* given up more home runs per fly ball than we would expect. If we assume that's also due, at least somewhat, to bad luck, then we might figure Feliz's career ERA should begin not with a 5, but rather with a 3.

This "theory" (for lack of a better word) first burst upon the scene—the sabermetrics scene, that is, which at the time was quite small—back around the turn of the century, when a bright young fellow named Voros McCracken noticed there wasn't much year-to-year consistency between the batting averages allowed, just on batted balls in play, by major-league pitchers. At that time, Planet Earth's best pitcher was probably Pedro Martinez. Well, from 1998 through 2001, Martinez's alloweds looked like this: .270, .323, .236, and .307.

People tend to think that a pitcher's luck evens out over the course of the long season. But quite often, it does not. And that's more true now, when pitchers don't throw nearly as many innings as they used to. This is why nobody in baseball really cares about ERA anymore. Thanks to PITCHf/x and Statcast, analysts today hardly bother with raw walks and strikeouts and fly balls; they look at all the little pieces that *make* the walks and strikeouts and fly balls: the direction and the velocity with which the ball leaves the bat, the exact location of the strikeout pitch, and how likely it is to get called again, etc.

Feliz's third pitch to Ryon Healy is—as both you and Healy probably guessed—a 95-mile-an-hour fastball, and Healy whacks a line drive right over Feliz's head, into center field for a leadoff single.

It should be said (yes, again) that 95 just isn't what it once was. This year, hitters will face 110,529 fastballs measured as 95 miles an hour or more. That's an increase of 124 *percent* from 2011. But the more faster fastballs the hitters see, the better they seem to hit them. The fastest fastballs are *still* the most effective pitches, but they've become *less* effective, relatively speaking. In fact, the difference between 95+ fastballs and all other pitches has shrunk to near insignificance.

Which is hardly to suggest that pitchers shouldn't keep throwing them. Because the hitters are even better against *sub*-95 fastballs. As you would expect.

After throwing Bruce Maxwell four straight fastballs—again, all four right around 95; changing speeds on the fastball is largely a lost art, perhaps because so many pitchers throw at least two distinct *types* of fastballs—Feliz throws a slider that gets a lot of the plate. Maxwell puts a good swing on the pitch, but center fielder Maybin retreats to the warning track in dead center field and waits for the ball, 387 feet away, Healy retreating to his base.

Feliz goes right back to the fastball against Matt Chapman, who homered two innings ago. Chapman's late on the first heater, slicing a foul ball that bounces in the A's bullpen down the right-field line—the Coliseum's one of the very few stadiums where the bullpens are still on the actual playing field—before skipping into the stands. But he's not late on the second one; despite being jammed slightly inside, Chapman shoots a single into right center, with Healy scooting all the way to third base. As Ray Fosse says, "When you're that strong, you can muscle a ball into the outfield."

"Here's Boog Powell," Glen Kuiper says, next to Fosse. "Ninety-six miles an hour, Powell takes outside. We've seen a little bit lately, Ray, with Boog Powell, is pitchers really challenging him with fastballs. And Feliz has a good one; we'll see if he does that."

Boog Powell, all seventy inches of him, hardly has taken a traditional path to this moment.

As a twentieth-round draft pick in 2012, Powell began his pro career as a long shot; in fact, of the thirty twentieth-round picks that year, Powell and Jharel Cotton—selected by the Dodgers, seven picks after Powell—are the only two who have reached the major leagues.[*]

In his third pro season, Powell was an All-Star in the Midwest League. Shortly afterward, he drew a fifty-game suspension after testing positive for amphetamine. The following winter, the A's traded Powell to the Rays in a five-player deal designed to bolster Oakland's short-term chances of winning. After a decent 2015 season split between Double- and Triple-A, Powell was on the move again; this time to the Seattle Mariners in a trade that included six players.

Last year, Powell wasn't doing terribly well with the Mariners' Triple-A farm club in Tacoma when, in late June, he drew an *eighty-game* suspension after "testing positive for a banned performance-enhancing substance"; specifically, an anabolic steroid called dehydrochlormethyltestosterone.

So to that point, Powell had played in 358 minor-league games, and been suspended for 130 games. This is not an enviable record. In the wake of his second suspension, Powell released a statement, via the Major League Baseball Players Association—Powell was on the Mariners' forty-man major-league roster, so automatically a union member—that included the following: "While I realize this has become a common refrain among athletes faced with such discipline, the truth is I do not know how this substance could possibly have been in my system. . . . I have already taken proactive steps to look into this situation, and will not rest until there is a full explanation for this result which will vindicate me."

Now, this isn't the place to suggest that Powell was less than

---

[*] Time's running out for the rest of them, although we continue to root for pitcher Brock Dykxhoorn, chosen by the Reds but now toiling in the Astros' farm system.

truthful, but one bit there is perfectly accurate: declarations of innocence are common, if not quite universal. I will suggest that Powell's O.J.-esque vow to find the truth is perhaps just a bit too much, even for the most powerful union in America. Especially since almost nobody's ever vindicated. Powell has continued to maintain his innocence, and certainly seems sincere. But it's unlikely that we'll ever know more than we know now, unless Powell someday admits his guilt. (That has happened, if rarely, with other players.)

Hey, it took until the end of the fourth inning for performance-enhancing drugs to come up! Good for Baseball!

We do have to mention that yes, even though the (so-called!) Steroids Era ended in 2006, when the Players Association agreed to a drug policy with some real teeth, players do, in fact, continue to use illegal sports drugs, banned by Baseball's Collective Bargaining Agreement. There's no drug policy in the world that could cut usage to zero. Athletes are too competitive, the stakes too high.

It does seem likely that drug use has dropped significantly since 2006, largely because the testing is fairly rigorous, the penalties fairly severe. First it's 80 games, then 162 (plus any postseason games), and finally it's a "lifetime" suspension. After more than a decade, only one player—Mets relief pitcher Jenrry Mejia has failed three tests and drawn the lifetime suspension.[*]

The 2006 policy was essentially in place until 2015, when it was toughened some; it's this one that Powell fell afoul of. And while it's occasionally said, especially in the wake of busts, that the policy *doesn't work*, one might argue the opposite, that the busts mean the policy *is* working. Absent failed tests, a rational observer would have to assume the testing simply doesn't work, since we

---

[*] Technically, Mejia may apply for reinstatement and return to the majors as early as 2018, but in fact he won't apply until next July, and be granted reinstatement until 2019. Powell's amphetamine bust doesn't count against him, by the way, because that fell under a separate program for minor leaguers; a program, by the way, that includes testing for marijuana.

can't expect players to stop using sports drugs. Last year, seven players drew first-time suspensions (including one player who had his suspension dropped from eighty games to fifty, after actually winning an appeal in which he successfully argued that he'd failed a drug test because of something in his cold medicine). Mejia got popped for the third time, and thirty-eight-year-old outfielder Marlon Byrd's career essentially ended when he failed a second test, drawing a 162-game suspension.

This year, only two major leaguers will draw suspensions for failing a drug test; one of them was Astros pitcher David Paulino, a fine (and huge) prospect who made six starts for the big club before his suspension in late June.

Is the drug policy working? Again, that depends on your definition. But it sure seems that many fewer players are using drugs, which makes the players' lives (and work) a bit less complicated (and maybe even safer). It also makes the owners' lives easier, because they don't have to worry about their employees getting hauled before Congress and embarrassing themselves. Yes, the players gave up a fair chunk of their privacy and they have to pee into a lot of cups. But drugs haven't been a big story lately, really not since Alex Rodriguez retired, and everyone in Baseball seems pretty happy about that.

Meanwhile, back in the Coliseum, Feliz does *not* challenge Boog Powell with another fastball. Instead he tosses one of the slowest sliders you'll see, just 78 miles an hour. Powell chops a hard grounder to Altuve, who flips the ball to Correa, who forces out Chapman at second base before firing on to first base to complete the inning-ending double play.

Score: Astros 5, Athletics 3
Win Probability: Astros 75%

Visitors Fifth

Strikeouts are boring. Besides that, they're fascist. Throw some ground balls. It's more democratic.

—*BULL DURHAM* (1988)

Having thrown eighty-one pitches already, Cotton returns to center stage for the top of the fifth. With that pitch count, Cotton's highly unlikely to pitch beyond the fifth. In his whole career, he's never pitched beyond the seventh. Of course, these days only the *best* starting pitchers are expected to do that, and so manager Bob Melvin's only realistic hope is that Cotton keeps the game within reach at 5–3, and with four more shots for the home team to score a few runs.

Thirty years ago, Roger Clemens started thirty-six games for the Red Sox, and completed fully half of them; that same season, nine other major leaguers completed at least a dozen of their starts. This season, Cleveland's Corey Kluber and Minnesota's Ervin Santana will lead the majors with five complete games apiece. Perhaps more strikingly, six pitchers will tie for second place with only two. The Astros and A's will *combine* for two complete games: one apiece for (bearded) Dallas Keuchel and (mustachioed) Daniel Mengden.

All of which is considered okay. In this age of deep and specialized bullpens, there's usually no falloff in talent when shifting from the starting pitcher to a likely parade of relief pitchers.

Especially when you consider the dramatic drop in performance for starting pitchers as the game goes along.

It's now fashionable to talk about the "third time through the order" penalty for starters. But in one sense, that's a misrepresentation. Because there's also a second-time penalty, which is *essentially the same.* But we don't hear much about the second time through the order because there's not much that managers can do about it. Unless bullpen tactics are *radically* reimagined, managers simply can't get their starters out of the game after just two or three innings. However, they *can* engage their bullpens after five or six innings; with eight-man bullpens and liberal roster rules, managers don't really expect or *want* their starters going more than six innings. Again, except for the best, most durable starters. Cotton's never pitched in the eighth inning; McHugh's done it just ten times in 107 career starts (and just twice since 2015).

Ted Williams was way ahead of the curve. Way back when, he said, "It's simple arithmetic: You figure to face a pitcher at least three to four times in a game. The more information you log the first time up, the better your chances the next three. The more you make him pitch, the more information you get."*

And of course the Astros aren't the sort of hitters who make things easier for an enemy starting pitcher. As the A's television crew points out during this half inning, one amazing thing about the Astros this season is that while they rank first in the American League in a number of important hitting categories—runs, hits, doubles, batting average, and (most important) both on-base and slugging percentage, along with third in home runs—they've also struck out less often than every other team in the league. Finishing

---

* Williams was also preaching an uppercut swing *decades* before all the cool kids started doing it. Back then, they would say "Ted's nuts. Only Ted can hit like that. The rest of us are Bobby Doerr." Well, now almost everybody's hitting like that. Or at least trying.

a season with the most home runs *and* the fewest strikeouts is a rare feat, done just once in this century, and only six times since World War II (the last of them was the 2003 Atlanta Braves).

The Astros *will* finish the season with fewer strikeouts than any other team in the American League. By quite a lot. They will not lead the league in home runs, ultimately falling three homers short of the Yankees.

But what really distinguishes the Astros, in terms of team building, is that just two years ago they LED THE LEAGUE IN STRIKE-OUTS. And that was a good team!

In 2015, when the Astros made their Great Leap Forward—from 70-92 one season to 86-76 and a postseason berth the next—they featured the prototypical, *modern* Three True Outcomes offense: second in home runs, fifth in walks . . . and first/worst in strike-outs. All the things that don't involve the fielders at all, the Astros did lots of.

Now, even today hardly anyone will argue that strikeouts are A Good Thing . . . but hardly anybody except the old-timers will argue that they're A Particularly Bad Thing either. And more than a few will even suggest that strikeouts might be A Necessary Thing: a small, practically insignificant nuisance on the way to more home runs and walks.

But if Three True Outcomes is Modern Baseball . . . or rather, if *accepting* Three True Outcomes is Modern Baseball, then maybe *rejecting* one or another of those outcomes is Postmodern Baseball. On their way to first place this season, the Red Sox will finish sixth in the league in scoring, but somehow dead last in home runs for the first time since 1993 (which then seemed a huge fluke, as the traditionally power-happy Fenwayers hadn't trailed the rest of the American League in homers since the 1930s).

The Astros' transformation from strikeout-heavy to contact-happy might seem surprising, especially considering its dramatic degree. But if you believed in the numbers, this progression was actually quite predictable. Last winter, FanGraphs' Jeff Sullivan wrote, "As the Astros have built a better order, there's also been a rather significant side effect. I can't tell you whether it's been intentional, or whether it's been a coincidence. But if you can believe it, the Astros are going to make contact. In fact, they project to be very nearly the best contact-hitting lineup in the game."

Just last year, the Astros' non-pitchers struck out 23.4 percent of the time, fourth worst in the majors. But this year, they *projected* to strike out just 17.7 percent of the time. That would have been the largest decline in strikeout percentage since at least 1950. By quite a lot.

So what actually happened? This season, the Astros will actually beat their projection by a smidge: 17.3 percent strikeout rate. Best in the majors.

So *how* did that happen? Almost exactly as you might guess.

Actually, I shouldn't assume how you might guess. You *might* guess the organization waved some sort of magical hitting wand. Or just told their hitters to stop swinging at so many crappy pitches.

But, no. It's the other thing you might guess. They replaced a bunch of high-strikeout guys with medium- or low-strikeout guys. Brian McCann strikes out less often than Jason Castro did. Alex Bregman and Yuli Gurriel are both contact hitters, playing a lot more this season than last. High-strikeout guys Colby Rasmus and Carlos Gomez are both gone. Et cetera.

Just to be clear about this: you *can* win, scoring plenty of runs, while striking out plenty. The Astros scored (and won) in 2015. This season, the contending Brewers and wild card-winning Diamondbacks will finish with the highest and sixth-highest team strikeout percentages, respectively. It can be done. But if you can avoid striking out *without* sacrificing power and on-base percentage, well of course that's preferred.

Something else that's preferred? Having Jose Altuve and Carlos Correa in your lineup. Altuve leads off the fifth inning with a ground-out, but Correa drives a high changeup into center field for a single.

Having said all those nice things about the Astros, they *have* struck out 927 times this season. Extrapolated to the end of the season, they'll finish with 1,080 strikeouts, which would have been middle of the American League pack in 2001, the last time Houston finished in first place. Meanwhile, the Athletics will wind up with nearly 1,500 strikeouts this season. In 2001, only two teams cleared 1,100 strikeouts (and then, just barely).

From the mid-1960s through the mid-'90s, the strikeout rate essentially held steady—aside from an odd downturn in the late '70s—at around 15 percent of plate appearances, give or take a percentage point or so. But for the next twenty years, the rate edged toward 20 percent. Finally, three years ago fully one-fifth of all plate appearances ended in strikeouts. Last year it was 21 percent; this year, nearly 22 percent.

And there's simply no reason to think this trend is going to reverse itself anytime soon. So ultimately the owners and the players will need to answer this question: Do baseball fans really want to spend most of their time waiting for strikeouts and home runs? Or do they still want to see runners stealing bases, hitters hustling for doubles and triples, and fielders making great plays? Do baseball fans still want to see baseball?

Everything except homers and strikeouts is dying. Sure, we all die eventually. And it's a slow death. But this feels more like some sort of chronic, slow-moving terminal cancer than a natural aging process.

With Correa aboard and Reddick coming up, Cotton sure could use one of those strikeouts. Well, that or a double-play grounder. But this just doesn't seem to be Jharel Cotton's year. With the count 1 and 1, he throws a high changeup, nearly the same pitch that Correa drove into center field. Reddick takes a whack, but fouls the pitch straight back.

Cotton's next move is one of the oldest tricks in the book. *He swung at a high changeup? I'll throw him a fastball but even higher, and he'll probably chase it.*

Behind the plate, Maxwell sets a high target. Cotton throws even higher, shoulder high, at least half a foot above the zone. And Red-dick *tomahawks* the baseball down the right-field line, plenty fair and plenty deep for a two-run homer.[*]

According to Statcast, the 109th home run in Reddick's career came on a pitch four feet four inches off the ground, *easily* the highest pitch among those 109 homers. What's more, it's the 9th-highest pitch turned into a round-tripper in the last decade. If it weren't for Jharel Cotton's bad luck this season, he would have hardly any luck at all.

Gurriel's next, with his team now holding a big four-run lead. Cotton muscles up and throws 95, one of his two or three fastest pitches all evening, and Gurriel chops the ball to shortstop, where Semien makes the easy play. Which brings up Marwin Gonzalez.

Until somewhat recently, teams had relatively little use for a player like Marwin Gonzalez. Or perhaps it's more accurate to say that until recently, there seemed relatively little need to *create* play-ers like Marwin Gonzalez.[†]

---

[*] I had to use the word *tomahawk* because that's literally what all four (English-language) broadcast teams said: He *tomahawked* it. What a swing like Reddick's has to do with a tomahawk, I can't really figure. But I guess you know it when you see it.

[†] By the way, it's not as if the emergence of Gonzalez was ever part of some grand plan. "The night I was hired," Luhnow told me in an e-mail message, "I immedi-ately went into a meeting with the baseball operations folks to review their Rule 5 list. The group wanted to take Rhiner Cruz number one. but didn't feel passion-ately about any other player in the second round. I suggested we take Marwin (I knew the Astros needed middle infielders) with our second pick. As we were getting ready for the R5 draft, the Red Sox asked if they could swap picks with us (they picked behind us in the second round). They were worried a team would take the player they wanted before they picked. We figured Marwin would be safe until their second round pick so we agreed and then swapped players afterwards. Clear as mud, right? The Marwin pick was my first decision as a GM and I was about two hours into the job." (And Rhiner Cruz, the player the Astros *really* wanted in the Rule 5 draft? In two seasons with the Astros, he went 1–3 with a 5.31 ERA. (Youneverknow. You just don't.)

Baseball has never really agreed on the right word for players like Gonzalez. In the old days, if you could (and did) play two or three different infield positions, they'd call you a utility infielder. If you played more than one outfield position—basically, if you were fast enough to play center field or had enough arm for right field, but weren't locked into just one of those spots—you were an outfielder. Just an outfielder.

And for the most part, never the twain would meet.

Sure, back in the 1930s, Bucky Walters might be a third baseman one year, and one of the National League's best starting pitchers two or three years later. Future Hall of Famer Bob Lemon might be an Opening Day center fielder one year, a fine pitcher the next. Johnny Lindell was a star outfielder for the Yankees during World War II . . . and a knuckleball pitcher in the National League a few years later. Before the 1970s, and perhaps this is related to the introduction of the designated hitter in '73, the dividing line between pitchers and hitters just wasn't what it's become. These days, if someone's going to switch, a hitter will become a pitcher and it will happen in the low minors. As it did with minor-league catcher Kenley Jansen, now one of MLB's great relief pitchers.[*]

But managers have been significantly more flexible with their *fielders*. What's new today is *not* the use of a player in various roles, both infield and outfield. In 1966, Twins rookie César Tovar started seventy-three games at second base, twenty-seven at shortstop, seventeen in center field, and four in left field. The next year he played a lot less second and short, but added third base to his portfolio while playing in 164 games and leading the majors in plate appearances. Tovar was just a league-average hitter on a second-place team, but the writers were so impressed with

---

[*] The one notable exception to both rules is Rick Ankiel, who washed out as a pitcher in the majors with Steve Blass Disease, and returned as a pretty good hitter and center fielder.

his versatility, he finished seventh in the league's Most Valuable Player voting.[*]

Tovar would remain an everyday utility player for another four seasons. But he was sui generis; there had never been anyone like him, and for a long time he would remain the only one.

Then Tony Phillips came along. When Phillips broke in with the A's in 1982, he was a shortstop. The next year he was a shortstop and a second baseman, with a few innings at third base. Phillips was obviously versatile, or perhaps just not good enough with the glove to earn an everyday job at one position. He was your ordinary, average, run-of-the-mill utility infielder.

Until 1986. White Sox manager Tony La Russa got fired by the White Sox in June, and in July was scooped up by the Athletics. By then, Phillips had been installed as the A's regular second baseman, and La Russa left him alone. Phillips remained mostly a second baseman in 1987 too.

Now's when I have to mention José Oquendo. Even though I would rather ignore him. He gets in the way of the story. But I can't ignore him, because it's actually the St. Louis Cardinals, managed by Whitey Herzog—like La Russa, ticketed for the Hall of Fame— who first took up Tovar's legacy. In '87, Oquendo started at least one game at every position except pitcher and catcher . . . and even finished one game pitching.[†]

It wasn't until '88 that La Russa took full advantage of Phillips's versatility; that season, both Phillips and Oquendo saw plenty of action all over the field. In 1989, Oquendo took over at second base for the Cardinals, while Phillips continued his peripatetic ways.

---

[*] One voter—a local voter who basically admitted he hadn't been paying much attention—actually listed Tovar first, preventing Carl Yastrzemski from winning unanimously.

[†] Herzog tells a story about running into George Steinbrenner in an airport. "How the hell can you win a World Series with José Oquendo playing right field," Steinbrenner said, "and I can't win with Dave Winfield?"

In 1990, he kept playing everywhere, except now with the Tigers; meanwhile, La Russa found new super-utility options in Lance Blankenship and Scott Brosius. And later he found more of them while managing the Cardinals.

Since then, though, finding room for these guys has gotten both harder *and* more beneficial. And it was sorta La Russa's fault.

Well into the twenty-first century, every manager would figure on this sort of active roster: ten or eleven pitchers, including five starters; two or three catchers; plus another twelve or thirteen guys. But in 2017, almost every manager prefers at least *twelve* pitchers. Sometimes thirteen or even, in the case of a doubleheader that permits a temporary twenty-six-man roster, *fourteen pitchers*. And while La Russa never actually invented anything, he did a great deal to popularize both the one-inning closer and the LOOGY (lefty one-out guy). And such specialization only begat more specialization, which goes a long way toward explaining today's crowded bullpens.

Which in turn means less room for bench players: utility infielders, fifth outfielders, platoon players, and pinch-hitting and -running specialists. There was a time, within living memory for most of us, when a player in the National League could make a pretty good living *just* as a pinch-hitter. In the last five years of his career, Lenny Harris played in 482 games, but started only 61 of those in the field. In his last two seasons, 2004 and 2005, he got into 162 games and played defense in just 21 of those.[*]

That was with the Marlins. Coincidentally, this season the nearest thing to Another Lenny Harris is another Marlin: forty-three-year-old Ichiro Suzuki, who will wind up playing in 136 of Miami's 162 games, but start only 46 of them. So there are still a few specialists. The Braves are getting fine service from a twenty-seven-year-old journeyman named Lane Adams, who pinch-hit a

---

[*] Back in the 1970s, for a few years the A's actually carried players whose *only* job was pinch-running. Sometimes two of them at the same time.

ton during the summer. In fact, in the National League there's still plenty of pinch-hitting. But that's because of all the pitching changes, and *not* because there are players on the bench, living off their bats.

Thanks to today's overstuffed bullpens, there just isn't much room on the roster for the (non-pitching) specialists. If you're not in the lineup most of the time, you need to be able to do at least a couple of things reasonably well, and the more the better. Which is where Marwin Gonzalez and his Super-Utility Friends come in.[*]

If you've got a player who's at least semicompetent at two or three infield positions *and* can handle the outfield chores without embarrassing himself . . . well, you've just made the manager's job quite a lot easier.

Look, these days the manager is *going to carry a dozen pitchers.* Maybe a baker's dozen. Forty years ago, a *professional hitter*—which is to say, a veteran who couldn't really play the field, but could, as the saying went, "roll out of bed in January and hit a line drive"—was almost every manager's favorite security blanket. Or second favorite, after a multi-innings relief ace. Today? Their favorite security blanket—and we know this is true because literally every manager must have one, even in the face of all that is logical and holy—is that eighth pitcher in the bullpen, who will likely as not be back in Triple-A within a week or two, replaced by yet another pitcher from Triple-A, no better than the young man he replaced, or the one *he* replaced.

In 1982, the Seattle Mariners used fifteen pitchers on their way

---

[*] There's even a next level: the relief pitcher who can also hit and/or play defense in a pinch. The Brewers actually gave this a shot in 2003, when erstwhile college superstar Brooks Kieschnick batted .300 (with seven homers) in seventy at-bats *and* pitched in forty-two games. But his hitting cratered the next season, which ended that experiment. Since then, there haven't been any two-way players for more than a moment. Granted, that's expected to change in 2018 with the arrival of Japan's Shohei Ohtani. . . .

to a 74-88 record. In 2017, the Mariners will use forty pitchers to go 78-84.

Meanwhile, the Astros will eventually use "only" twenty-seven pitchers this season; the A's, twenty-eight. So yes, the Mariners, because of injuries and transaction-happy general manager Jerry Dipoto, are outliers. But every manager and/or general manager today is addicted to hard-throwing relief pitchers, easily summoned from the minors and just as easily banished, or consigned with a minor (or phantom) injury to the disabled list, after a shaky outing or two. Actually, relievers are often demoted (or DL'd) simply because they threw a ton of pitches—well, a relative ton—in their last outing, leaving them unavailable for the next game, which in turn leaves the manager with only (egads!) six or seven arms in the bullpen.

A manager's second-favorite security blanket might be the super-utility player. Except there aren't enough of them to go around. Granted, you can simply *create* one. Few (if any) of the guys filling the role now were groomed for the job in the minors. All of them, or almost all of them, arrived in the majors as something specific, but didn't hit or field well enough to nail down an everyday job.

But now there's a new, potent generation of super-utility players. Where once it was just Tovar, then Phillips, and (briefly) Oquendo and a bunch of guys who couldn't hit and usually didn't last long, the *new* super-utility guys can actually hit too.

In 2006, Ben Zobrist reached the majors with the Rays. By 2008, he was still a shortstop: an (almost) twenty-seven-year-old shortstop with only eighty-three major-league games in his ledger. Which is to say, history suggested that Zobrist's professional baseball career was hanging by a fairly thin thread.

After the 2007 season, in which they finished in last place for the ninth time in their ten years of existence, the Rays traded incumbent shortstop Brendan Harris—a pretty good hitter and pretty lousy fielder—to the Twins for another shortstop: Jason Bartlett, a pretty good fielder, pretty lousy hitter. This *might* have been a real opportunity for Zobrist, at shortstop. But instead, the Rays went defense-first, and (a) zoomed all the way to first place, while (b) Zobrist played a little shortstop, a little left field, and a little bit of just about everything else.

In 2009, Zobrist came out of nowhere to finish eighth in the American League's Most Valuable Player voting. The meaningful numbers actually suggested a far higher finish; as usual, the voters were far more impressed by high batting averages and RBIs than by on-base percentage and fielding value. In fact, the (meaningful) numbers suggest that from 2009 through '14, Zobrist was one of the four or five most valuable players in all of Major League Baseball. And that's *without* awarding bonus points for his versatility; in those years he played 653 games in the middle of the infield, 385 in the outfield, and 20 more at the infield corners, just to show off. And with just a little bit of (so far, nonanalytical) extra credit, you can make a reasonable case for Zobrist as THE best, or at least most valuable, player in the game for those six years.[*]

Rays manager Joe Maddon obviously wasn't the only manager who saw the value in a super-utility player. But he might have been the first since La Russa to make a real habit of them. Even while using Zobrist everywhere, he did the same with Sean Rodríguez, a much inferior hitter. And upon taking the reins as Cubs manager in 2015, Maddon used eventual Rookie of the Year (and the next year, MVP) Kris Bryant everywhere, and did the same with veteran outfielder Chris Coghlan. In 2016, Maddon got Zobrist back. This

---

[*] Back in 2000, Baseball Prospectus's Keith Woolner published a list of "Baseball's Hilbert Problems"—key questions for future research—and one of them was quantifying the value of positional flexibility. "Because roster spots are scarce," Woolner wrote, "a team gets value from a player's ability to play multiple positions, but we do not yet have an understanding of how much value there is to having a Mark Loretta or Jose Hernandez on your roster." We still don't have that understanding, at least not publicly. Woolner might—since 2007 he's been running the Cleveland Indians' small analytics shop.

year, he dialed back Bryant's peregrinations . . . but has replaced them with those of Ian Happ, a Rookie of the Year candidate—and like Bryant, a recent first-round draft pick—who will start twenty-eight games at second base and sixty in the outfield.

Before this season, Marwin Gonzalez has never been close to César Tovar or Tony Phillips or Ben Zobrist or Kris Bryant. He was more in the mold of Willie Bloomquist or (now) Milwaukee's Hernán Pérez: long on versatility, short on run production. Still worth keeping around, because he was both versatile and cheap. But he didn't hit, or play good defense anywhere, and his almost everyday action in 2016 was not, it seemed, something the Astros should want to see again in 2017.

But something funny's happened on the way to first place: Marwin Gonzalez turned into a good hitter. By one measure—adjusted on-base plus slugging percentage, an imperfect shorthand for general production—Gonzalez will actually be the American League's fourth-best hitter this season. His only betters? All-World Mike Trout, MVP candidate Aaron Judge, and MVP candidate Jose Altuve.

Which isn't to suggest that Gonzalez belongs in that class. Or is the new Ben Zobrist (although he might be close). And Gonzalez's performance is hardly a miracle. But it's exceptionally uncommon for a below-average hitter to become, at twenty-eight, among the game's most productive hitters.

Of course, you don't get from 84-78 one year to 100-some wins the next year without some happy surprises—surprises you simply could not have reasonably expected, no matter how smart you are—and Gonzalez's big season is just one of the Astros', along with Yuli Gurriel's production and Josh Reddick's best season at the non-tender age of thirty.

There will be fewer happy surprises on the pitching side, with Brad Peacock's 13-2 record, 3.00 ERA, and out-of-character strikeout rate the only modest shocker there.

But the real key for the Astros this season? Nobody has been terrible. Beltrán could have been better, and workman Mike Fiers will lead the pitching staff with twenty-eight starts, with ace Dallas Keuchel managing only twenty-three. But otherwise just about everything will go as planned, *or better*. At least on the position-player side of the equation. Which is a fine recipe for winning a division title. If usually quite overoptimistic.

If Gonzalez did ten years ago what he's done this year, the smart set would largely have waved away his future. After all, history is littered with wildly out-of-character "career years," not expected and never to be repeated. But in 2017, things aren't so simple. In 2017, the easy dissemination of both verbal and statistical information makes it at least somewhat easier to distinguish a legitimate "breakthrough season"—that is, an actual, sustainable improvement in talent—from a flash-in-the-pan, unlikely-to-be-repeated performance.

In Gonzalez's case, the only obvious difference in his underlying performance this season has been his avowed willingness to wait for better pitches to hit. For the sake of our story, it would be fantastic if sabermetrics played some obvious role. Or if, at the very least, the Astros' front office had somehow seen this coming.

But how could they have? If they couldn't read J. D. Martinez's palms or tea leaves, how could they have read Marwin Gonzalez's? How could they have guessed that on a roster stacked with fine hitters, Gonzalez will wind up leading the club this season with 90 runs batted in?[*]

Zobrist and Bryant and Happ and now Gonzalez are probably the most famous of the current super-utility players who can also

––––––––––––––––

[*] How has Gonzalez done it? He's credited most of his improvement to his willingness to learn from both Carlos Correa and Jose Altuve, the latter being Gonzalez's best friend. Certainly, Gonzalez has been more selective at the plate this season. The numbers also suggest that he's been fairly lucky, especially with his batting average.

hit. What we're supposed to call these guys, we still don't seem to know. Dan O'Dowd, a longtime MLB executive who now works as an analyst for the MLB Network, favors "everyday versatile player." Perhaps a bit wordy, though. If we're looking for a namesake, the line forms not behind Ben Zobrist—which I mention because at least one wag has named this job "Zobrist"—but rather behind César Tovar or Tony Phillips. Because Tovar and Phillips were Ben Zobrist before Ben Zobrist was even a gleam in Joe Maddon's eye.[*]

But here, Cotton finally gets another strikeout, fanning Gonzalez with his fastest fastball of the whole game: 95.6 miles an hour. Cotton's ninety-seventh pitch, a good one, is almost certainly his last.

Score: Astros 7, Athletics 3
Win Probability: Astros 88%

---

[*] Meanwhile, the A's are developing their own version. Rookie Chad Pinder won't get into this game, but this season he'll start thirty-four games in the outfield, eighteen at shortstop, and thirteen at second base. And Pinder, a second-round draft pick four years ago, can hit some too. Somewhere, the two Tonys are smiling.

Home Fifth

Hell, if the game was half as complicated as some of these writers make out it is, a lot of us boys from the farm would never have been able to make a living at it.

—BUCKY WALTERS (1909–1991)

Tony Sipp, now tasked with preserving the Astros' 7–3 lead, most assuredly does *not* explain Postmodern Baseball.

First, there's Sipp's draft history. Within the space of four years, he was a 28th-, 33rd-, and 45th-round draft pick: high school, junior college, and four-year college. Now, very few 45th-round draft picks reach the majors; of the 228 45th-rounders drafted *since* Sipp was the 1,333rd player selected in 2004, only seven have since reached the major leagues.*

In fact, the forty-fifth round of the amateur draft was ultimately deemed so inconsequential that today it doesn't exist. Today there are only forty rounds. If you're not deemed worthy of being chosen

---

* The most notable of the seven: ambidextrous pitcher Pat Venditte, who pitched for the A's two years ago after spending forever in the minor leagues, and Cardinals outfielder Stephen Piscotty, who didn't sign a pro contract at the time, and three years later was the thirty-sixth player chosen in the entire draft. Teams will often take a late-round flyer on a player who's considered unsignable, or nearly so. Because occasionally he will sign.

among the first 1,200-some high school and college players, you sign for peanuts or you go back to school or you hook up with an indy-league team somewhere. Or you find something else to do with your summers.

But upon being drafted, Sipp spurned the Indians; instead he played in the amateur Cape Cod League, the top summer showcase for college players, with designs on enhancing his value. It worked; he was so impressive in the Cape League, the Indians ultimately offered him $130,000 to sign. Which might well have been a record signing bonus for a forty-fifth-round draftee.

Sipp, who's today built more like a small-college linebacker than a professional left-handed pitcher, did sign in time to make ten starts for the Indians' minor-league club in the New York-Penn League, and showed enough to rank as the franchise's number twenty-two prospect before the next season. According to *Baseball America,* "Sipp profiles as a short reliever and has two pitches he can put hitters away with."

Oddly, while that was still the case a few years later, they weren't the same two pitches. Early in his pro career, Sipp's key offerings were a low-90s fastball and a slider, with a changeup that needed plenty of work. But the slider never really became a high-quality pitch in the majors; meanwhile, as Manny Acta, Sipp's manager in Cleveland for three seasons, told me, "When he first came up, he was blessed with the arm, the athleticism. Then he learned at the big-league level. He came up with a split-fingered fastball that allowed him to be more than just a situational left-hander."[*]

Now, if a pitcher throws in the nineties (Sipp does!) with a slider and an effective splitter, you might expect a great deal. Either a

---

[*] A friend observes, "This is one of the greatest (if low-key) things about Postmodern Baseball. In a world made more and more predictable through analysis, pitchers can just learn a new pitch and essentially reinvent themselves. It's among our last delights."

wipeout reliever *or* one of those situational lefties, routinely summoned from the bullpen to face the other team's tough left-handed hitters. Every manager wants one of those, and these days nearly every manager has one. Bob Melvin's is Danny Coulombe (whom, with a little luck, we'll soon meet more formally).

A. J. Hinch does not have one. Over the course of his career, Sipp has been no more effective against left-handed hitters than righties. A Dominican rookie named Reymin Guduan has gotten a few trials this season, but (so far) has a 5.54 ERA in seventeen outings. The Astros traded for veteran lefty Francisco Liriano at the July 31 trade deadline, but he's posted a 5.59 ERA in thirteen games.

Meanwhile, with the exception of 2014 and '15 with the Astros, when Sipp combined for a 2.66 ERA and posted the two best strikeout-to-walk ratios of his career—after which, by the way, he cashed in with a three-year, $18 million contract—Sipp has walked too many hitters *and* given up too many home runs for anyone to rate him a premier reliever. This season, he gave up seven homers in only thirty-five innings before hitting the disabled list in early August, with "right calf soreness." And while I won't suggest that his right calf *wasn't* sore, or that his sore right calf didn't hurt his pitching, I will mention in passing that when a team wants to give a veteran pitcher a break because he's struggling, it's not difficult to come up with a minor injury that will give him a chance to rest a bit, without the embarrassment of a demotion to the minor leagues. Because hardly any major leaguer is ever *100 percent*, physically.

So this is Sipp's first appearance in the majors since July 31— he did make a couple of rehab outings in the minors before recently rejoining the big club—and first retiring Semien on an easy grounder, then Joyce on a called strikeout are good signs.

Sipp doesn't fare quite so well against Jed Lowrie, who rockets the second pitch he sees, a low fastball, well into center field. Cameron Maybin does make the catch, but the ball does travel 387 feet. Not as far as the four home runs we've seen in the game already, but farther than (spoiler alert) three more we'll see later.

With Lowrie's long, loud third out, the A's "win expectancy" stands at just 7.2 percent, according to the FanGraphs website, which generates a running graph for every major-league game. Because people like numbers—people with internet connections and favorite sports teams *especially* like numbers—the Win Expectancy charts have become popular, at least among the cognoscenti. It's potentially a pretty good "storytelling stat," if you're desperate for something like that. In fact, top-notch analyst (and now Major League Baseball Advanced Media staffer) Tom Tango has called Win Expectancy *the ultimate story statistic.*[*]

Well, except usually it's not really much fun to drop a percentage into the middle of a story. Win Expectancy works well visually, when the line on the graph reverses itself a few times, or makes a huge jump (or fall) right at the end.

But if you're not FanGraphs or FiveThirtyEight, how often do you drop a graph into the middle of a story?

What's more, Win Expectancy leaves out much. As FanGraphs' glossary notes, "WE is the long-run average, however, so you need to remember that a 40% chance of winning is based on average players. If Miguel Cabrera is at the plate against Aaron Crow, the true odds favor the Tigers more than WE graph indicates."

Aaron Crow hasn't pitched in the majors since 2014. If you don't remember him, feel free to substitute Seth Maness or Nate Jones or Al Alburquerque. You can also swap in Jose Altuve for Cabrera if you want.

In the context of this game—the Astros have the better lineup, and the better bullpen—one might reasonably knock a percentage point or two off the A's *true* chance of winning this game. Either way,

---

[*] Win Expectancy, along with its cousin, Win Probability Added, has probably helped kill the sacrifice bunt for non-pitchers, since the actual numbers suggest that bunting doesn't improve your chances of winning, but actually lowers them a smidgen.

based purely on what we know, the home team now has roughly a 1 in 20 chance of winning this game.

Is this a thing worth knowing, if you're just a fan watching the game? I think for most fans, it probably is not. You might rather *not* know. Especially if you're a fan of the team that's losing. We know that fans tend to change the channel or go home if their team's almost certainly going to lose. I can understand how Win Expectancy would serve as a fine story stat. But only after the fact, and only in games with a big change, or changes. It's a tremendous *comeback* stat. Again: after the fact.

So? We're perfectly free to ignore Win Expectancy when it's not interesting, right? We are. I have greatly enjoyed entire seasons of baseball without seeing or hearing or reading about a single WE graph. At least until October, when curiosity does sometimes push me toward the (alas, context-free) percentages. And broadcasters, hardly interested in losing viewers and listeners, have no (good) reason to mention Win Expectancy during a game. They're far more likely to say something like, "Gee, if we can just get a few guys on base and somebody hits one out, things could get real interesting." Which of course happens less often, even in today's game, than they want us to think.

Win Expectancy, then, is the perfect Postmodern Baseball statistic: it's there when you want it—when it's interesting or useful, however rarely that might be—but the rest of the time it's not there.

I wish we could say the same about the new Statcast numbers that have so quickly weaseled their way into the broadcasts. Especially the national broadcasts; so far, only a few local broadcasts have incorporated the Statcast data (although the Astros' TV crew seems to be among the enthusiasts).

As Keith Hernandez writes, "I wonder what [Yogi Berra] and some of the other old-timers would say if they heard some of the broadcasters in the game today. Too many of them emphasize all these crazy stats, like 'exit velocity,' 'trajectory angles,' or, and this is my favorite, 'percentage rate of someone making a catch.' 'His probable rate of making that play was seventy-six percent!' Give me a break. Who cares how many miles per hour the ball traveled once it left the bat, or how high the ball traveled in degrees, or how many seconds it took to leave the ballpark?"

Hernandez does possess some self-awareness, also writing, "Am I dating myself? Am I a dinosaur? I guess to a degree I am. . . ."

He does have a point, though. What too many broadcasters don't seem to understand is that the new, user-friendly Statcast-driven numbers are interesting *only at the extremes* (and of course there's also the little issue of suggesting to listeners, however implicitly, that catch probability is anything close to precise).

When Altuve homered back in the first inning, Geoff Blum intoned, "Altuve pummels it, to the tune of 106 off the barrel, estimated 415 feet." When Chapman homered in the second, Blum said, "One hundred and three miles an hour off the bat," with an onscreen graphic listing that number, along with **"26 DEGREE LAUNCH ANGLE."**

Okay: 415 feet. We know something about 415. We know something about 415 because for as long as they've been painting numbers on outfield walls, we've had some context for outfield distances. It was obvious to me, as a kid, that 400 feet was a long ways from the plate. Because if you hit the ball 400 feet, usually it would be a home run. Hell, you could hit the ball only 330 feet and get a home run. Even fewer feet in Boston! But you kinda knew. Because *the numbers were right there on the wall.*

Launch angle, though? Exit velocity? We have no context, and only a Very Chosen Few of us will *ever* have any meaningful context. For two reasons. One theoretically solvable, one probably not.

The first reason is that the broadcasters are making absolutely no effort to provide any context, and are unlikely to. Exit velocity 103: Is that a lot? No idea! We're simply given the information, and information should not be given unless it's somehow useful and it's not useful without context and we're practically never given any context. Too much trouble, probably.

But broadcasters can learn.

The second, bigger reason is the numbers themselves. Baseball statistics work when they describe something we care about and when we can, given a reasonable chance, tell the difference between something that's impressive or interesting, and something that is not.

A three hundred-foot home run in the old Polo Grounds? Interesting perhaps, but hardly impressive. A five-hundred-foot home run? Hell yeah. On both counts.

These are things we know, without even really having to be taught. Four hundred feet is a long drive, usually plenty enough for a home run. Four hundred and fifty feet, that's one hell of a blast. And five hundred feet? Now we're in Babe Ruth–Josh Gibson–Mickey Mantle–Mark McGwire–Giancarlo Stanton–Aaron Judge territory, and the views are spectacular. Five hundred feet, friend, is something you're gonna tell the grandkids about. All those powerful feet come with their own, ready-made context. Based on a century's worth of experience and stories and memories.

Exactly none of which can be said about launch angle or exit velocity. When Billy Broadcaster says Joe Shlabotnik's home run resulted from a 24-degree launch angle and 97.4 exit velocity . . . so, what? We don't know what those numbers mean, and I suspect this is *not* because the numbers are new; I suspect that we'll never know. Again, except for the extremes. For example, if a pitcher gives up a home run with a low exit velocity, that's worth knowing. We can feel sorry for him! When it comes to launch angles, it's probably enough to know the most basic information: line drive, or fly ball, or somewhere in between. Which we don't need a number for. Sometimes words actually tell the best story. But sure, throw in the precise distance. Because we understand 415 feet.

It's not Statcast's fault, or MLBAM's fault, that we're seemingly on the verge of being inundated by meaningless, context-free information. Quite frankly, it's 100 percent the broadcasters' fault. The broadcasters who *still* seem obsessed with small sample sizes and

RBIs and fielding percentages have now skipped an entire generation of good, hard-won, contextualized knowledge, and for some reason seized upon exit velocity as a key objective in Statistics Scavenger Hunt.

But perhaps this was inevitable. Perhaps it's inevitable that in today's game, with its collective obsession with POWER, broadcasters will focus on a metric that's got *velocity* in its name.[*]

Essentially, the new Statcast data is wildly important for the evaluators and decision-makers in the front offices, and modestly useful for that subset of journalists and essayists who rely on, and have the head for, in-depth statistical analysis. But otherwise, the data are often just more meaningless dribs of information, good for filling airtime in the absence of genuinely insightful analysis, but not much else. And in some cases the numbers are crowding out evocative, lyrical prose and verbiage. Which were already in alarmingly short supply.[†]

Score: Astros 7, Athletics 3
Win Probability: Astros 92%

---

[*] Exit velocity's perhaps inevitable ubiquity might be connected to its vague kinship with fastball velocity, for which we do have plenty of context. "Hey, 103 exit velocity! That's faster than Noah Syndergaard throws!" So not exactly context-free; just misleading as hell.

[†] I would be doing you a disservice, Dear Reader, if I didn't mention MLB.com's tremendous page Baseball Savant, overseen by the tremendous Daren Willman, who takes the Statcast data that MLB does release and creates tremendously useful visuals and sortable tables. This book wouldn't be nearly the same without Statcast and Daren's great work.

Visitors Sixth

With young pitchers as well as veterans, there has been an epidemic of arm trouble in recent seasons, and surgical operations on ailing soupbones are becoming a baseball fashion.

—*BASEBALL MAGAZINE* (1940)

As expected, Jharel Cotton's out of the game. These days, there's little shame in lasting only five innings, but Bob Melvin didn't have much choice.

In his twenty-seven career starts, Cotton has thrown more than a hundred pitches just six times; his career high is 107. So at 97 in this game, there was nothing to be gained by sending him out for the sixth. Better to let a fresh arm take over, to protect Cotton and (ideally) keep the scoreboard from getting out of hand.

We should pause for a moment and consider those words: *protect Cotton*. Because there was a time, not so long ago really, when ninety-seven pitches wouldn't have been enough pitches to even notice. Sure, a manager might have removed a starter after five innings, just because he'd given up seven runs. But ninety-seven pitches? Hardly a trifle. Today: klaxons.

What's happened? Yes, today's pitchers generally work harder *per pitch*. So they tire sooner. But it's not just that; probably is not mostly that.

Twenty seasons ago, in 1997, there were 374 games in which

the starter threw at least 120 pitches. There were 74 with at least 130 pitches. Randy Johnson alone racked up eleven of those 130-plus starts. In five games, he reached 140 pitches. It was nothing for Roger Clemens and Pedro Martinez to throw more than 120 pitches, sometimes more than 130.

In 2,430 games this season, not a single pitcher will throw 130 pitches. This season, there will be exactly eighteen starts in which the starting pitcher threw even 120 pitches.

Randy Johnson and Roger Clemens and Pedro Martinez were immensely talented, but they weren't any more talented than to-day's pitchers. And yet, nobody's allowed to come anywhere *near* the workloads of those erstwhile aces.

So at this point, it seems that 130 is a Threshold of Calamity; no matter how well even the greatest pitcher is pitching, he simply will not be permitted to reach that number.*

What's happened is that essentially everyone in professional baseball has become tremendously risk averse, even in the absence of any real evidence that adhering closely to pitch-count guidelines is keeping pitchers healthy. The real magic number, by the way, isn't 130 or 120. It's 100. Once a starting pitcher gets close to 100 pitches, the manager starts looking for reasons to get him out of the game.

If one hundred seems as if it's been pulled from a hat, that's because it has been. Roughly twenty years ago, two things happened: *USA Today* began publishing pitch counts in box scores, and *Baseball Prospectus*—both the annual book and the website—began promoting something called Pitcher Abuse Points, which (arbitrarily) didn't begin counting until one hundred. Toss in some high-profile pitchers suffering serious injuries after racking up high pitch counts, and a general consensus—okay, groupthink—

---

* There's no reason to think the Threshold won't soon be 120 pitches; in the first three months of the 2018 season, only six pitchers will throw that number.

developed, and the result was a steady ratcheting down of cultur-
ally permissible pitch counts.

It's probably true that some pitchers shouldn't be throwing more
than 100 or 110 or 120 or 130 pitches in a game. But all pitchers?
One of the truly strange things about Postmodern Baseball is
that with all the data allowing every single pitcher to be classified
uniquely, in this particular respect they're all treated almost iden-
tically. Managers start getting nervous at 100 pitches not because
they're concerned about their pitcher, but because they're concerned about the heat they'll get from their bosses, from the media,
and from the pitchers' agents if they let the guy throw much more
than 100. Oh, and if somebody throws 120 pitches and gets hurt?
Turn out the lights, party's over.

Pitch counts aren't a tool; they're a crutch and a club, and rank
among the most obvious ways in which Baseball still falls well
short of eliminating the human element. Because it's actually the
human element—and *not* some pinhead's spreadsheet—that keeps
even the strongest, most durable hurlers from throwing much
more than 110 pitches.

Speaking of strongest, Cotton's replacement, with Carlos Beltrán
due to lead off the top of the sixth, is a large right-handed power
pitcher named Raul Alcántara: yet another Player Who Explains
Postmodern Baseball.

A Dominican native, Alcántara signed a pro contract with the
Red Sox when he was just sixteen, as so many Dominicans do. At
eighteen, following a rookie pro season in the Dominican Summer
League, he earned a promotion to the Lowell Spinners in the New
York-Penn League.[*]

Just imagine. You've spent the first seventeen years of your life
in the Dominican Republic, and suddenly you're a Lowell Spinner.

---

[*] Lowell is in neither New York nor Pennsylvania. But then, the Iowa Cubs play
in the Pacific Coast League; geography and professional baseball have a strange,
often counterfactual relationship.

But at least Alcántara probably had someone to talk to. There were four other Dominican Spinners that summer, and even more Venezuelans.

And then just as suddenly, you're a mere throw-in when your organization trades for a couple of major-league players; in this case, the Red Sox traded Alcántara, a minor-league outfielder named Miles Head, and a young major-league outfielder named Josh Reddick to the A's for a Proven Closer™ and a youngish fourth outfielder named Ryan Sweeney.

Shockingly, the Proven Closer™ (Andrew Bailey, if you must know) flamed out with the Red Sox. (If you've skipped ahead to later in the book for some reason, this news should not be shocking.) Meanwhile, Reddick wound up hitting thirty-two homers and winning a Gold Glove in his first season with Oakland. So the A's won that trade. Even without considering Miles Head. Or Alcántara; did I mention he was just a throw-in? Because nobody reasonably expects an eighteen-year-old pitcher in the New York-Penn League to someday become even decent in the majors for a season or two. That's how hard it is.

Alcántara did move up the A's minor-league ladder, establishing himself as a real prospect four years ago, walking only twenty-seven Class A batters in 156 innings.

Three years ago, he made three starts in Double-A, his elbow ligament snapped, and the throw-in was done for the season. Tommy John surgery. Which wound up being just one of roughly 150 Tommy John surgeries performed on professional pitchers in 2014. Sounds like an epidemic! And in fact the explosion in Tommy John surgeries has been described, many times, as exactly that. From 2014 through this month, more than *five hundred* professional pitchers have undergone the surgery (and been sidelined for a season or more). Of the 921 pitchers who will appear in the major leagues this season, fully 183 of them (give or take) will have at least one TJS in their medicals: essentially a fifth of them. Why so many? Pitchers are working out more than they used to, and now specifically training to throw harder. But you can't train an ulnar collateral ligament to be stronger. "Everything gets bigger," A's scout Jim Coffman says, "but that UCL tendon doesn't."

In this game alone, three of Oakland's pitchers—Alcántara, Cotton, and Danny Coulombe, whom we'll meet soon—have had an elbow ligament replaced with a compatible, ideally stronger ligament; maybe one taken from their wrist, maybe one harvested from a cadaver.

The good news is that Tommy John surgery works. Pretty well, anyway. The success rate isn't 100 percent, and the popular notion that pitchers typically come back *stronger* after the surgery is an insidious myth; there are even some sad stories about parents, dollar signs in their eyes, pushing their teenaged sons toward *elective* Tommy John surgery.

More good news, though: catastrophic *shoulder* injuries—specifically, rotator-cuff injuries—which were once fairly common, and destroyed the careers of many tremendous pitchers, have practically disappeared.*

Most pitchers *do* pitch again after TJS—somewhere between 80 and 90 percent of the major leaguers make it *back* to the majors—and Cotton, Alcántara, and Coulombe have all bounced back nicely from their surgeries.†

---

* It's difficult to understand *how* they've practically disappeared, but the most popular theory is a simple one: better shoulder exercises, or "prehab" (to use a modern term for an old idea). If only someone had told Kevin Appier, Johan Santana, Kerry Wood, and far too many other premier starting pitchers. Oddly, another shoulder-area injury has recently appeared: thoracic outlet syndrome, which has recently presented in stars Matt Harvey, Josh Beckett, Phil Hughes, and others. Surgery's an option, but not a good one. More good news! Doctors are no longer prescribing the removal of teeth for pitchers with sore arms, which was common well into the 1950s.

† There have also been dozens of pitchers with *two* Tommy John surgeries. While roughly two-thirds have come back to pitch professionally, most have *not*

When Alcántara returned to the mound, he did take a small step backward in the A's system. But by 2016, that seemed just a minor setback when Alcántara pitched in Double-A and Triple-A and then, a year and three days ago tonight, made his major-league debut with a start against the Angels.

That didn't go so well—he gave up five runs in three innings—and things didn't improve much later, as Alcántara finished the season with a 7.25 ERA in his five starts with the A's. This spring, he pitched well enough to earn the number five starter role . . . which lasted for exactly one start, in which he gave up eight runs in two innings. After a couple of relief outings—one fine, one disastrous—Alcántara, out of minor-league options, was "designated for assignment."

Minor-league options are part of a complicated process, but essentially you can send a player back to the minor leagues during only three, or sometimes four seasons, before he must be exposed to the other teams via waivers. At that point, any one of the other twenty-nine MLB teams could have claimed Alcántara; when none did, the A's sent him back to the minors. He spent June and most of July on the disabled list with a minor elbow injury; upon his return to the mound with Triple-A Nashville, Alcántara was pitching exclusively as a relief pitcher. As someone in the booth says, "The feeling was, and the reports from down there, there was an uptick in the fastball, pitching in relief, and that he gained a couple miles an hour."

Hey, no kidding!

In Leonard Koppett's 2004 book, *The Thinking Fan's Guide to Baseball*—updating his 1991 book, which updated his 1967 book—

_____

returned to their previous performance levels. In 2018, Jonny Venters will become the first pitcher to make it back to the majors after a *third* TJS (there was almost a fourth, but instead of replacing the already transplanted ligament, it was successfully reattached).

he included a chapter, "Where Did the Hitters Go?" Of course, the hitters didn't go anywhere; what bothered Koppett was that most of the high batting averages of his youth were gone. But when enumerating the various causes of the observed change, Koppett argued that relief pitching was the largest factor. "The hitter is affected adversely in three ways," he wrote. "First, the starters don't have to pace themselves, because they know (and the manager assures them) that relief will be available if needed, so they can throw 'as hard as they can as long as they can.' Second, the relief pitcher who comes into the game in the seventh, eighth, or ninth is fresh, so the hitter doesn't get a crack at a tired pitcher. Third, if the situation is crucial at the time of the pitching change, the relief pitcher is often chosen precisely because he is particularly tough for the particular hitter."

Koppett wasn't really *wrong* about any of that, except for this: Starters still have to pace themselves, because while throwing 100 pitches might not be the same as throwing 120 pitches, it's still a lot more than 20 or 30. So no, the great majority of starters do *not* throw as hard as they can for as long as they can. Research shows that if you do unleash a starting pitcher for just an inning or so, he'll typically add roughly 2 miles an hour to his fastball.

So now Alcántara, relieved of any need to pace himself, throws *hard*, sitting around 96 with both his four-seam fastball *and* his two-seamer, the sinking fastball. Which is rare. Historically, anyway, if you throw both fastballs there's a notable (and noticeable) difference between the two pitches, speedwise. But with Alcántara and others like him, the important difference isn't the speed, but the location: up in the zone with the four-seamer, down in the zone with the two-seamer. And here, he starts off Carlos Beltrán with a low sinker that Beltrán takes for ball one. Changing speeds with the fastball might be a lost art, but changing *movement* is not, as most pitchers, or at least most starting pitchers, throw at least two of the three fastballs: four-seamer, sinker, and cutter. Most relievers, on the other hand, focus on just one of those, and maybe Alcántara will, in time.

Both Alcántara and Beltrán are trying their best, because that's what players do, at least until *all* reasonable hope is lost. Pitchers, especially. Earned run averages are fragile things. But a team with a four-run lead at this point in the game is going to win nine times out of ten. Without even considering that one of these teams—as it happens, the one with the four-run lead—is significantly, measurably better than the other. At least some of the fans have to already be considering the best time for their escape from a stadium that was mostly deserted when Jharel Cotton threw his first pitch.

But of course the players must push on. Just in case.

Alcántara follows up with three pitches low in the zone, two of which Beltrán fouls off. With the count 1 and 2, Beltrán gets a sinker in the middle of the strike zone, usually a perfectly hittable pitch. Except maybe not at 97 miles an hour, and maybe not in Beltrán's forty-first year on earth. He pulls a routine grounder to second baseman Lowrie for the inning's first out.

Essentially, you're not going to get much attention from the scouts as a young pitcher unless you throw at least 90; typically, a bit more than that. Ultimately, most young starting pitchers either can't handle the workload *or* can't come up with a reliable third pitch, which is generally deemed necessary if one's going to survive for five or six innings against top-flight professional hitters. But when that low-90s fastball becomes a mid-90s fastball? With a slightly improved curveball or slider or changeup besides? Now you've got the makings of a Postmodern relief pitcher. For which there's a great need, in these Postmodern times.

In 1985, the fourth-place A's used eleven relief pitchers.

In 2017, the fifth-place A's will use seventeen relief pitchers. The fourth-place Rangers will use twenty-two relief pitchers. The third-place Mariners will use twenty-three.

Relief pitchers, we're talking about. Remember the Mariners and their forty pitchers this season? Given the modern thirteen-man pitching staff, that's *three whole rosters of pitchers*: your thirteen major leaguers, your thirteen Triple-A pitchers, *and* your thirteen Double-A pitchers.

Obviously, that's a simplistic way of looking at the numbers. Pitching staffs are exceptionally fluid, and a Class A pitcher one day might actually be good enough for Triple-A or even the major leagues a month or two later. All you gotta do is throw reasonably hard (which these days means around 95) and throw some non-obvious strikes, and these days there are hundreds of professional pitchers who can do those things. And nearly all of them will pitch in the major leagues this season, because somehow the supply can never quite meet the demand. Perhaps because so many of them are getting hurt, and perhaps so many of them are getting hurt because the game now demands that they push themselves not only to their natural limits but beyond. You can build up muscles and all of them do; you can't beef up ligaments.

Alcántara starts Brian McCann with a sinker, just as he did Beltrán. Same result: ball one. Alcántara's next pitch is a four-seamer right through the zone, but McCann just misses, and the result is a batted ball that's classified by Statcast as a screaming liner but looks like a routine play for Joyce in right field. Alcántara also needs only two pitches to dispatch Maybin, on a soft grounder to third base. Fast *and* efficient: what a concept.

Score: Astros 7, Athletics 3
Win Probability: Astros 90%

Home Sixth

Too many pitchers, that's all, there are just too many pitchers. Ten or twelve on a team. Don't see how any of them get enough work. Four starting pitchers and one relief man ought to be enough.

—CY YOUNG (1867–1955)

Whether because of the loaded bullpen or the idea (maybe true!) that relief pitchers are delicate, A. J. Hinch has summoned yet another reinforcement from the bullpen. Yes, even though Tony Sipp threw only eleven pitches in the fifth, after Michael Feliz threw only a dozen in the fourth. Hinch's quick hook is probably because the bullpen's full *and* he's already thinking about October; this is the time to see who's got what in the tank, especially someone like Sipp who so recently wasn't healthy enough to pitch.

With the entrance of right-hander Mike Fiers to face Khris Davis here in the sixth inning, the Astros still leading 7–3, one is reminded just how *deep* the Astros have become, at least when it comes to (theoretically) MLB-quality starting pitchers. I'm also reminded that were I focusing on just nine players in this book, Davis might be one of them.

Though Khris Davis's skills as a hitter—scads of home runs and strikeouts, smattering of walks—are not particularly rare, he is exceptionally rare in another way: he's an outfielder with the yips. Rarer still, this summer he essentially outed himself on the internet, with a distinctly personal essay. No, not as gay; Davis admitted that he's an outfielder whose brain gets in the way of his throwing arm, with uncomfortable frequency.

Traditional sports journalism gets harder and harder all the time, and not just because of newspapers going out of business and social media occupying so much space and league-controlled websites doing their best to crowd out everyone else. As athletes earn ever more money, and realize they might control their own stories, at least to some degree, they're less and less interested in talking to reporters. Especially the high-paid veterans, who have all said it before. In fact, sometimes you hear rumblings that one of these years, reporters simply won't be allowed in the locker rooms any more at all. The players see the clubhouse as their personal sanctums, especially as they've become tremendously more posh, customized to accommodate the players' many needs (and desires). In the newer *spring-training* ballparks, the locker rooms would have been considered palatial in major-league ballparks just a decade or so ago.

So with managers already submitting to formal press conferences following each game, are players far behind? Maybe the team will toss out a star performer or two, so the beat writers have *something* for their stories? Especially when the players now have so many ways to express themselves when they want, how they want?

Twitter went live in July 2006. Facebook became available to almost everyone a couple of months later. Early on, the inherent possibilities of social media seemed to scare the living hell out of Baseball's p.r. people. Just imagine what John Rocker would have done! Or what players might say during a serious labor dispute! We can't have these guys running around loose and *expressing themselves.*

But of course when it turned out *everyone* would be on social media, whether Twitter or Facebook or (later) Instagram, or maybe all three, by golly it became apparent that regulating players' use of social media was simply impractical. Maybe even counterproductive. And for the most part, everything's worked out beautifully. So today's players are largely free to say whatever they like, which—let's be honest—typically isn't terribly interesting, with the exception of a few brave and thoughtful souls like ex-A's pitchers Brandon McCarthy and (now-retired) Dan Haren.*

Which isn't to say things don't occasionally go terribly wrong. Curt Schilling and Chipper Jones have both cost themselves fans—and Schilling, at least a few Hall of Fame votes—with intemperate social-media posts. But at least those came after their playing careers. In 2016, a backup catcher named Steve Clevenger essentially destroyed his career with a few moments of indiscriminate (but discriminatory) tweeting.

In the wake of Black Lives Matter–sponsored protests in Charlotte, North Carolina, along with Colin Kaepernick's decision to kneel during National Anthem ceremonies prior to NFL games, Clevenger—who grew up in Baltimore, and went to college in Florida and Louisiana—posted these rhetorical gems: *Black people beating whites when a thug got shot holding a gun by a black officer haha shit cracks me up. Keep kneeling for the Anthem!*

(followed moments later by . . .)

BLM is pathetic once again! Obama you are pathetic once again! Everyone involved should be locked behind bars like animals!

Clevenger posted his sentiments on a Thursday morning, before a doctor's appointment. By the time he was out of the exam room . . . well, when you post something offensive enough, it doesn't take long for the words to get around.†

---

* Is it coincidental that *many* of the most interesting players and ex-players on social media used to play for Billy Beane's A's? In addition to McCarthy and Haren, there's also Brett Anderson, Brad Ziegler, Eric Byrnes, Sean Doolittle, and more. Nope, probably not a coincidence.

† Perhaps history's best example is a young woman named Justine Sacco, who made a lame joke on Twitter just before an overseas flight in 2013, and upon landing found she'd become a national pariah. Sacco had 170 Twitter followers.

That very same evening, Clevenger issued an incredibly contrite, wonderfully articulate apology via FOX Sports' Ken Rosenthal's Facebook page, which was almost certainly composed by
Clevenger's agent (then an occasional contributor at the Baseball Prospectus website). Since, you know, not many professional athletes are likely to write, within the space of a few
hours, "I do believe that supporting First Amendment rights
and supporting local law enforcement are not mutually exclu-
sive" *and* "Everyone involved should be locked behind bars like
animals!"

So that was Thursday. Friday, the Mariners suspended Clevenger without pay for the rest of the season. Which, this being
September, was almost over. Clevenger had been on the disabled
list since late June, earning the MLB minimum salary. He did
not appeal, and his suspension cost him roughly $34,000.

In *USA Today*, Bob Nightengale wrote, "Unofficially, he will
never again wear the Mariners' uniform. . . . Clevenger may indeed play again, but it's not going to be in this country."

So much for second chances, huh? But Nightengale was probably right. If there's a third rail in Baseball, it's race. You can say
you "don't agree with" someone being gay—as then Mets second
baseman Daniel Murphy did about Billy Bean, now MLB's vice
president of Social Responsibility and Inclusion, two years ago—
but naked odes to racism like Clevenger's cross the line. Not just
now either. All the way back in 2000, John Rocker earned a two-
week suspension for his wildly prejudiced words in *Sports Illustrated*. Hell, all the way back in 1938, Yankees outfielder Jake
Powell said some sickening things about African-Americans in a
radio interview, and was suspended by Commissioner Kenesaw
Landis for ten days, for making "an uncomplimentary reference
to a portion of the population." So public sensitivity to public
insensitivity isn't new. Even in staid old Major League Baseball. The difference today is that social media makes it so much

easier to express hatred, in your own words, whenever the mood strikes.*

Last winter Clevenger got nary a nibble from any of the thirty major-league clubs, many of which must have been looking, at the very least, for organizational depth at Clevenger's position. In February, he granted his first post-Facebook interview to Yahoo's Jeff Passan, and said all the right things, from "I am sorry for it. I can only ask for forgiveness" to "I've spent all off-season trying to become a better person. Learn different cultures. The history of the United States."

Turned out, Nightengale was not precisely right.

This July, Clevenger did sign a contract with a team in this country: the Lancaster Barnstormers in the independent Atlantic League. Playing mostly with and against other guys in their late twenties and early thirties, Clevenger ranked among the worst hitters on his team. So even if an MLB organization was charitably inclined toward him *and* desperate for help behind the plate, his performance this summer simply didn't merit a shot at redemption.

All of which does lead to an uncomfortable question for the Mariners, and by extension, Major League Baseball: Would they have cut ties with Clevenger if he were a significantly better player? That's somewhat hard to imagine.

As it's always been. The standards have changed, in Baseball as in society. But the basic rule remains the same: the bigger the star, the more you can get away with, the sooner you'll be forgiven. Just ask Mel Gibson.

Back in May, Toronto's Kevin Pillar called Atlanta relief pitcher Jason Motte a faggot. Motte's married to a woman, and they've got a

---

* Our story has a surprising twist: Daniel Murphy and Billy Bean have since become friends.

couple of kids. Pillar didn't mean it literally. He was angry, because he struck out when Motte quick-pitched him. So Pillar yelled at Motte, both teams' benches cleared, and the Blue Jays suspended Pillar for two games without pay.

Just a month ago, Oakland's Matt Joyce drew his own two-game suspension for making an "anti-gay slur" against a fan in Anaheim, during a game against the Angels. If possible, Joyce seemed even more contrite than Pillar, saying the next day, "I'd like to apologize to the fans, the Oakland A's, the Bay Area—the community has been awesome to me—and to MLB, and especially obviously to the LGBTQ community, who I have a lot of respect for. I really hope people can find it in their hearts to forgive me and not be too quick to judge me on one incident."

Pillar and Joyce are both among their teams' better players, so of course they were missed while absent. But inaction by the league would have been a bad look. And between the suspensions and what seemed like genuine contriteness, both have continued their careers with little or no blowback.

Maybe there won't be any for Khris Davis either.

Three years ago, the Players' Tribune website launched. Its mission statement was clear: *Provide athletes with a platform to connect directly with their fans in their own words.*

Ironically, the site was founded by Derek Jeter, who was somewhat famous, as a player, for *never doing or saying anything interesting.* In his own words or anyone else's.*

Just a month ago, Khris Davis's byline appeared for the first time (and probably the last, as most Players' Tribune contributors seem to tell just one story before retiring as essayists) under the headline, "The Creature."

---

* Oddly, upon becoming a minority owner and the public face of the Miami Marlins this winter, Jeter will say all sorts of interesting things, most of which don't play well in the sporting press or with the few remaining Marlins fans.

"I've never been able to talk about it publicly," Davis wrote, "so there are very few people who know that this is something I deal with. Until now, maybe out of embarrassment, or even pride, this wasn't something I wanted to bring out into the open."

What's *it*? Davis's Creature first showed up in 2009, shortly after he signed out of college with the Milwaukee Brewers. Essentially, the moment Davis became a professional baseball player, he "developed this strange fear of overthrowing the cutoff man—of messing up and costing my team runs with my throws."

What's more interesting about Davis's essay is that he has revealed his malady before anyone seems to have noticed it. Which isn't to say *opponents* didn't know; they've been taking advantage of Davis's throwing for years. But the *reason* for Davis's throwing problems had been previously unknown to the public, and perhaps also to people in Baseball. So he's made himself vulnerable: to enemy fans who now have extra fodder for their jeers, *and* to enemy players who might now be a bit more willing to challenge Davis's arm.

I wonder, though. Players can be oddly charitable when they know a player is struggling with the mental side of the game. Tell them an outfielder has a peashooter throwing arm, and they'll run on him all day long. But tell them an outfielder has the yips? I'm not so sure. In 2011, then Red Sox pitcher Jon Lester developed a case of the yips so severe that by April 2013, he simply gave up, making not even a single pickoff throw from the middle of that month through the end of 2014. Not one! Runners did take advantage. Lester went to the A's in the summer of '14, and in the A.L. Wild Card Game that fall, the Royals stole seven bases on their way to a crushing (for the A's) loss in twelve innings.

That winter, Lester signed with the Cubs. In spring training, they tried all sorts of things, but he still couldn't throw to the bases with any consistency. Finally, Cubs manager Joe Maddon had an epiphany: Lester wasn't going to have an epiphany. "No," Maddon later said. "That doesn't happen. That's not what happens when you're thirty years old." So Maddon came up with some work-arounds, and Lester played a key role for the Cubs when they won the World Series last fall. Still, why not bunt against Lester two or three or four times every game, and make him prove he can throw you out? Why not try to rattle him so badly that he struggles not just with throws to first base, but also with throwing pitches where he wants them?

In today's game, showing a physical vulnerability is like blood in the water. The sharks will attack. But showing emotional vulnerability is safe, or at least safer than it used to be. Because the players are, by and large, at least a little kinder than they used to be.

Still, Khris Davis turns thirty this winter. An epiphany seems unlikely. And without an epiphany or something like it, runners will continue to take *some* advantage of Davis's arm/psyche, and so he'll continue to be a real liability in the outfield (in addition to the arm, he's also got limited range afield). Which means his long-term future in the majors, if he has one—if he's not another Chris Carter—is probably as a designated hitter. Not that there's anything wrong with that.

Fiers works carefully to the dangerous Davis, who nevertheless rifles Fiers's third straight two-seam fastball into left field for a leadoff single. Fiers is even more careful with the even more dangerous Matt Olson; not one of his three pitches so much as grazes the strike zone. But Olson still drives a low changeup toward right field . . . except it's intercepted by Gurriel, who snares the ball before stepping on first base to retire Davis too. They always tell baserunners to "make the line drive go through," but sometimes that just isn't realistic.

Fiers's relief outing is essentially a one-off (he'll start a game five days hence, then get shut down for the rest of the season), and he's essentially pitched himself out of the Astros' postseason plans by giving up thirty-two home runs in 153 innings. Even in 2017, that's simply too many home runs.*

But the Astros couldn't have figured on Fiers's struggles, before the season. For one thing, if they had any *real* inkling, he wouldn't have opened the season in the rotation. For another, Fiers had been perfectly decent since coming over from the Brewers in a late-July trade back in 2015. That summer he tossed the franchise's first official no-hitter in quite some time, and in 2016 he was, if nothing else, good for five or six decent innings every five or six days. It was perfectly reasonable for management to figure Fiers would do roughly as well this year. He just didn't. Which wound up leaving a hole in the rotation, despite a number of other fairly experienced candidates (and there were even more, younger options: fine prospects who were given opportunities during the summer but did poorly).

Granted, Mike Fiers is just one man. But he hasn't been the Astros' only underperforming starter; essentially all of them have been disappointing in one way or another. Which makes this team's lofty place in the standings all the more impressive.

Leaving aside wins and losses, the most obvious difference between contenders and noncontenders—and this is a fairly recent thing—is that contenders are typically hyperaggressive during the summer months about trying to get better *right now*, while noncontenders, and especially ill-heeled noncontenders like the A's, are generally aggressive about trying to get better in future seasons . . . at the obvious expense of getting worse in the short term.

Over this season's first four months, Oakland's best hitter was

---

* Maybe after the game, Fiers and Cotton and Sipp will steal away to a dive bar in Jack London Square and spend the wee hours commiserating about big hitters and bouncy baseballs. Hey, a fella can dream a little.

first baseman Yonder Alonso; their best pitcher, Sonny Gray. On the last day of July, the A's traded Gray to the Yankees for three prospects. A week later, they traded thirty-year-old Alonso for twenty-four-year-old, minimum-wage outfielder Boog Powell. Technically this was after the so-called "trade deadline." But deals are made after July; it's just a little more complicated.

And as sometimes happens, probably a lot more often than you would think, Powell has actually played better than Alonso since the trade. The good news for the Mariners is that even if they'd kept Powell, they still (as we'll learn in a few more weeks) would miss the playoffs. The bad news, and the bad news is way, way worse than the good news is good, is that the M's essentially *gave away* a cost-controlled (i.e., cheap), potentially useful player for the next six years. Because Alonso isn't in their post-2017 plans.

Sure, there have always been deadline deals, contenders trading young players for veteran help down the stretch. Back in the 1950s, the Yankees seemed to trade for Enos "Country" Slaughter, a grizzled outfielder who'd been a star back in the '40s, just about every summer. But the annual trade-deadline drama didn't get serious until the 1990s, when franchises began routinely making (a) personnel decisions based largely on salary considerations, and (b) no real bones about giving up on a season in July. Maybe the next two or three seasons.

This Astros regime hasn't made one of those giving-up, salary-dump deals since Luhnow's first year. When he took over after the 2011 season, the Astros had just one productive hitter under contract: thirty-five-year-old Carlos Lee. In 2012, Lee would be playing the last season of his six-year, $100 million contract. When Luhnow did finally unload him, Lee's numbers were among the worst of his career, the Astros were well on their way to a hundred losses, and they simply had no business giving at-bats to a player like Lee. At whatever salary. So on the Fourth of July, Lee was dispatched to the Marlins, who were then hanging around the fringes of the wild-card chase.

What happened next? Lee and the Marlins collapsed down the stretch, and neither of the young players the Astros got in the deal ever really developed. It was, purely in terms of what happened on the field, a nothing deal. As many are. Perhaps most, statistically speaking (which is to say, leaving aside the always considerable concerns about team chemistry).

A few weeks later, the Astros traded Wandy Rodriguez, their only high-priced pitcher, to the contending Pirates for three young players. Two of them have since washed out of professional baseball (in the U.S. at least). But the third, outfielder Robbie Grossman, did eventually become a pretty good major leaguer.

With the Minnesota Twins.

After the Astros flat-out released him.

Deals like these can go every which way. In 1993, the Padres traded (future) borderline Hall of Fame first baseman Fred Mc-Griff to the Braves. McGriff wasn't just a short-term "rental"; he was signed through 1995, and the Braves gave up a lot to get him: three young players, all of them with real promise. McGriff would play tremendously well the rest of the season, and the Braves simply wouldn't have reached the postseason without him. Meanwhile, none of those fine prospects really panned out in San Diego.*

For more than two years now, the Astros haven't been in the trade market with the aim of dumping dollars and collecting prospects; they've been in the market to win, now.

Some teams, like the A's most years lately, enter the season on the fence; they don't know if they'll be competitive or not, so are content to open the season with a few holes. If things are going well in the middle of the summer, they can fill the holes with trades, or

---

* The Braves ultimately won 104 games and needed every one of them, as the Giants won 103. This was the last season before realignment and wild cards, so you had the (now) odd spectacles of Atlanta and San Francisco both playing in the National League "West"—ah, that pesky baseball geography again—and a 103-win team missing the playoffs.

promote from within. If things don't, they can get an early start on next season.

But that's not the Astros. Teams like the Astros generally don't enter the season with holes, including the number six and seven starters. Used to be, you might hope to open spring training with three or four good starting pitchers, and fill the last slot or two during spring training, with no real expectation that your number five man would last long. But today? Today the number five guy still isn't going to make it all the way through the season . . . but the number one guy probably won't either.

In 1997, sixty-six major leaguers started at least thirty games; that is, sixty-six starting pitchers managed to avoid the disabled list, or almost avoid it, and take the mound for practically every fifth game. For a manager, that's the gold standard. Because it's one less headache in a long season loaded with headaches, a new one almost every day.

In 2017, forty-six major leaguers will start at least thirty games.

Hey, maybe it's an anomaly! After all, just last year, sixty-two guys started at least thirty games.

But maybe it's not.

This is the first year of the 10-day disabled list, which replaces the old 15-day disabled list. Now, the logic of the change seems inescapable: Why lose the services of a fine player for fifteen days, when he's healthy enough to play after ten or eleven or twelve? Don't we *want* to see the best players, you know, playing?

For sure! But the rules about disabled lists and the rules about minor-league promotions and demotions are intertwined, and the *practical* impact of shortening the required time on the disabled list is more rest for almost everyone, and correspondingly more pitchers.

As ESPN.com's Sam Miller wrote this spring, "Now a club could look ahead at the schedule, see an off-day and 'disable' the fifth starter, skipping his spot in the rotation and using that roster space to call up an extra reliever from Triple-A. By the time the fifth

starter is needed again, the 10 days would be up, and the extra reliever could be sent back down."

So that's one way to do it, and of course it's done. Another, as
Sam points out, is simply to give a starting pitcher a bit of extra rest
by "disabling" him with a minor injury, and slotting another starter
into his rotation slot for a week or two. On the assumption—which
might well be backed up by data—that some, or perhaps even all
pitchers, are more valuable over the course of twenty-five starts
than thirty.*

Beginning next season, each team will have four additional off
days during the regular season. As Joel Sherman will write (next
spring) in the *New York Post*, "The modern front office sees approximately 1,450 innings that need to be covered in a season and if
someone offers 115 of those innings in, say, 20 starts, but would be
worse if pushed to more, then so be it."

For many decades, a pitcher needed an inning per (scheduled)
team game to qualify for his league's ERA title. So since 1962, not
counting strike-marred seasons, that's been 162 innings. This season, only fifty-eight pitchers will qualify: almost exactly two per
team. Remember, every team this season will supposedly be hum-
ming along with five-man pitching rotations, same as it's been
since the 1970s.

In 1987, seventy-eight pitchers threw at least 162 innings. There
were only twenty-six teams then, which works out to exactly three
ERA qualifiers per team. So by that measure, anyway, teams
have lost a third of their "regular" starting pitchers since thirty
years ago. There are other measures of course, but all of them tell
us the same thing: generally speaking, starting pitchers are being

---

* By the way, it's hardly difficult for a perfectly honorable doctor to justify a DL
stint for a pitcher. As one front-office analyst told me, "They're all hurt, all the
time. So how are you going to argue that not pitching for ten days isn't going to
make you healthier?"

asked to do far less than they were asked to do thirty years ago (let alone forty or fifty). And with the new roster rules, it's now easier to ask them to do less. Easier *and* smarter, probably.

So these days, five starting pitchers just aren't enough. Not nearly enough. Of course, you can always find a guy to go out there and give it his best try. But if you're really trying to win the season, you enter the season with *more* than a rotationful of rotation-worthy starters.

The Astros opened this season with at least seven pitchers on the forty-man roster who looked good enough to start for *most* major-league clubs, from 2015 American League Cy Young Award winner Dallas Keuchel—who did fall off quite a bit in 2016—to Joe Musgrove, who pitched creditably last year as a twenty-three-year-old rookie.

In the event, those seven—Keuchel, Fiers, Musgrove, and McHugh, plus Charlie Morton, Brad Peacock, and Lance McCullers (at twenty-three the youngest of the group)—will wind up starting 146 of the Astros' 162 games.

But with two outs in the bottom of the sixth, when Glen Kuiper says of the Astros, "They really right now have seven starters," he is *not* referring to the aforementioned septet. Because Musgrove, thanks to a 6.12 earned run average, earned a demotion from the rotation to the bullpen back in the middle of July. Musgrove would make eight, actually.

So, seven? Yes. Seven. While the Astros held a nearly insurmountable lead as August met September, and their six non-Musgrove starters remained impressive in their number, they weren't so impressive in their *numbers*. Good enough to win the West, yes—thanks to a great deal of help from all their friends with the big sticks—but hardly impressive relative to their likely competition in the fiery cauldron of (with luck) a deep postseason run.

As things stood on the last day of August, the Astros simply didn't have their own Clayton Kershaw or Max Scherzer.

Actually, nobody except the Dodgers and Nationals has their

own Kershaw or Scherzer. But the Astros also didn't have their own Corey Kluber (Indians) or Chris Sale (Red Sox) or Carlos Carrasco (Indians again) or Luis Severino (Yankees) or Stephen Strasburg (Nationals again). It wasn't that the Astros couldn't win without a Grade A+ starting pitcher; they'd been winning without one for five months. Or at least since Dallas Keuchel hit the disabled list in early June. But they'd been winning, in part, because of their *depth* of starting pitching, and that depth becomes considerably less important in October, when you can get through a series with only four starting pitchers. Or three.

But you want at least one of those three or four to scare people. And with Keuchel struggling in August upon his return from the disabled list, the Astros didn't have even one scary starter.

Until the very last minute in August. And that last-minute matters. A lot. Because if you trade for a player *after* August, he's ineligible for the postseason. No exceptions. And as well as the Astros played for the first five months of this season—best record in the American League, fourth-best run differential in the majors, all those impressive hitters in the lineup—they still craved the *scary guy*.

And if you're still wondering about baseball's inherent unpredictability, about the enduring beauty and existence of the short hops, there's this: when the Astros finally got their scary guy, at the very last minute, they got one who less than two months earlier hadn't been scary at all.

From 2009 through '13, Detroit Tigers ace Justin Verlander looked like a future Hall of Famer. In 2014 and '15, Verlander looked more like an old pitcher on his way down, suffering from a "sports hernia" that just kept lingering. He did bounce back with a nice 2016. But then he bounced back down in the first half of this season; after a disastrous start in early July against the Indians—knocked out in the fourth inning, seven runs allowed on nine hits and three walks—Verlander's ERA stood at 4.96. This, combined with a contract that guarantees him $28 million in both 2018 and '19, seemed to make him practically untradeable. Which was a real problem for the Tigers, who this season became fully engaged in a long-term rebuilding effort (part of which included trading J. D. Martinez to the Diamondbacks). Would the Tigers really be stuck paying an obviously, painfully declining Verlander roughly a million dollars per game for another two whole seasons?

Considering his ERA and unimpressive peripherals, it sure looked like they might.

And then Verlander fixed himself. As *Bleacher Report*'s Danny Knobler learned: "It was a small adjustment, Verlander said, a mechanical tweak so small he had missed it all those other times he looked at the video. One day, he saw it, and he fixed it."

Verlander pitched better in his next five starts, heading into that July 31 deadline. But he certainly wasn't great. And this once-brilliant pitcher, famous for throwing harder in the ninth inning than in the first inning, still hadn't thrown a single pitch in the *eighth* all season. So the Tigers still couldn't find any takers for that big contract.

Then: August, in which Verlander struck out fifty hitters in forty-two innings, while walking only eight. He also went eight innings in two of his starts, and seven in two others. He wasn't throwing any harder; he was simply throwing *better.* And with the still-improving version of Verlander having passed through revocable waivers early in August, unclaimed by any of the other twenty-nine teams—all the contenders still scared off by that $56 million—Verlander was still sitting there in late August, presumably available to anyone willing to (a) eat the contract, or (b) eat *some* of the contract *and* send young talent to Detroit.

When the Astros didn't do much at the July 31 deadline, it didn't go over well internally. In today's baseball culture, you're *supposed to do something.* Even if you've got a big lead, as the Astros did. And especially considering they did *nothing* at the deadline last year, despite being in the thick of the wild-card chase. "I'm not going to lie," Dallas Keuchel told reporters this time around, "disappointment is a little bit of an understatement."

Another thing that didn't go well: August, in which the Astros somehow went 11-17, easily their worst monthly record of the season. Toss in the fact that Keuchel wasn't pitching well after his long disabled-list stint, McCullers didn't pitch all month, Fiers was struggling, and Musgrove had pitched his way out of the rotation . . . well, the postseason still seemed a sure thing, but a deep postseason *run* seemed anything but.

Which is why, less than two hours before the midnight deadline on the last day of August, Jeff Luhnow called Tigers general manager Al Avila. By eleven or so, they had a deal hammered out. But they still needed to check medical reports, get ownership's approval, and convince Verlander to waive his no-trade rights. During that hour, Verlander wavered; a phone call from Keuchel just might have helped convince him to approve the deal. And so just a minute or two before midnight, Verlander was on the phone with Major League Baseball in Manhattan, making his decision official. Luhnow didn't know for sure that everything got wrapped up until fifteen minutes after the deadline.

But the Astros got their scary guy. All it cost them was three of their top prospects, plus around $5 million in salary this season and $20 million in both 2018 and '19 (the Tigers remain on the hook for the other $16 million, their price for the long-term rights to those three young players).

And the early results? So far, so good. Verlander made his Astros debut three nights ago in Seattle and gave up just one run, striking out seven Mariners in six innings. He might not still be the scary guy who throws 95 in the first inning and 98 in the ninth. But he is the scariest guy the Astros have. Scarier than Dallas Keuchel's beard, even.*

---

* Later this fall, Tom Verducci will write, "The joke among the quants in the organization was that Verlander was the first guy to actually ask for more than the reams of information they already were crunching."

So with Verlander's arrival and McCullers's return from the disabled list this week, there's just no room in the rotation for the slumping Mike Fiers. Which is how he's come to make his third relief outing in the last three seasons.

With the bases now empty, Fiers falls behind Ryon Healy, three balls and no strikes. But Healy takes a fastball down the middle for a strike, then shoots a hot grounder to Semien at shortstop. This is the major leagues. Healy's out at first base. Even though Fiers retired the side in order (so to speak), this half inning exemplifies his struggles over the last six weeks.[*]

Score: Astros 7, Athletics 3
Win Probability: Astros 94%

---

[*] He'll pitch just once more in 2017. Five nights from now, Fiers will start against the Angels in Anaheim, filling in for Lance McCullers. In the first inning, he'll give up a home run to Luis Valbuena, an ex-Astros teammate. Valbuena's a habitual bat flipper, but for some reason Fiers takes offense this time. In the fourth inning, he'll throw a fastball near Valbuena's head. There aren't any consequences then; Fiers does get yanked from the game a few hitters later, having surrendered seven runs. The next day, MLB suspends Fiers for five games, and even after his suspension, he won't get into another game before being left off the Astros' postseason rosters.

Visitors Seventh

The ball is round but it comes in a square box.

—LATINO BASEBALL PROVERB

Having thrown only nine pitches in the sixth inning, Alcántara's back on the mound for the seventh. His first pitch to George Springer is pure heat, 95 miles an hour through the middle of the strike zone, and Springer's mighty swing meets nothing but air. Alcántara's second pitch is supposed to be more of the same, except this time down. Down, and inside.

Well, Alcántara gets it inside. But it's inside and *up*, so far off target that Springer's struck flush on his left elbow by another mid-90s fastball.

Which might be catastrophic for him and his team. Except the missile caroms harmlessly off Springer's elbow pad, which he nonchalantly flings aside before trotting to first base, none the worse for wear. Meanwhile, Alcántara had turned toward the outfield and rested his hands on his knees, a sort of remorseful cringe that anyone within a hundred yards could recognize.

The Astros' next four hitters are Altuve, Correa, Reddick, and Gurriel. Which means Alcántara, a native of the Dominican Republic, will face, if he lasts long enough, a native of Venezuela, a native of Puerto Rico, a native of Georgia, and a native of Cuba. Jharel Cotton was born in the U.S. Virgin Islands. And later in the game, a native of Australia will pitch for the A's. Internationally speaking, just about the only thing missing from this game is an Asian player.

Which we could have had! Earlier this season, Japanese native Norichiki Aoki was usually in the Astros' lineup when a right-handed pitcher started for the other team. But while Aoki did what he might reasonably have been expected to do, what he did—hitting and fielding approximately as a league-average hitter and out-fielder does—wasn't something the star-studded Astros particularly needed. Especially with the emergence of both Jake Marisnick and (especially) Marwin Gonzalez as solid hitters. So at the July 31 trade deadline, Aoki *and* outfield prospect Teoscar Hernández were swapped to the Blue Jays for veteran lefty Francisco Liriano, who'd been starting for Toronto but went straight into the Astros' bullpen.*

It's easy to miss, because of the gradual nature of the transformation. But when you sit down and start looking at the numbers, you realize that the paramount accomplishment of ex-Commissioner Selig's long tenure wasn't adding a couple of franchises or growing revenues or shepherding MLB into the Internet Age or adding wild cards to the postseason format. No, Selig's biggest success was largely achieving his avowed goal of *globalizing* the game.

In Game 1 of the 1954 World Series, twenty-eight players got into the box score. Exactly one of them—Indians shortstop Bobby Avila, from Mexico—was born outside the continental United States. One.

In Game 3, Puerto Rico native Rubén Gómez started on the mound for the Giants; he and Avila were the only two players in the entire World Series born outside the forty-eight U.S. states.

There were, in the 1950s, a smattering of major leaguers born in Mexico, Puerto Rico, and Cuba. Just a smattering, and of course all

---

* This trade hasn't worked out so well for the Astros, as Liriano struggles in his new role, and will pitch just briefly and semi-effectively in the postseason (granted, there will be one semi-shining moment in the most biggest of big games, because baseball's always got a few surprises like that).

of them faced language and cultural barriers along the way. There were also a fair number of players who got their start in the Negro Leagues, both before and after the initial integration (in 1946) of Organized Baseball, when Jackie Robinson and a few others joined the Brooklyn Dodgers' farm system (of course the next year Jackie integrated the majors in the Dodgers' first game of the season).

Oddly, today there are very few Mexican players in the major leagues. Or Mexican hitters, anyway. In 2017, fifteen Mexican-born players will appear in the major leagues, and *fourteen* of them will be pitchers. The lone hitter will be a twenty-six-year-old rookie named Christian Villanueva, who will debut with the Padres about a week from now and make a big impression with four homers in only thirty-two at-bats by season's end. The last Mexican hitting star was Vinny Castilla, who averaged thirty home runs per season from 1995 through '99.

But those fourteen Mexican-born pitchers? Only four of them will pitch more than sixty-four innings in 2017, and all four of *them* actually went to high school in California or Texas. For whatever reasons, the pipeline of baseball players from Mexico to the majors—the one that produced Castilla and Avila and Fernando Valenzuela—seems to have gone largely dry.*

By contrast, easily the greatest change in the demographics of Major League Baseball over the last few decades has been the surge of players from the Dominican Republic, Venezuela, and (just recently) northeast Asia.

When Arnold Hano wrote *A Day in the Bleachers* in 1954 and '55, not a single Dominican player had yet appeared in the majors.

---

* The most notable Mexican-born player this season is Blue Jays closer Roberto Osuna, a prodigy who's ranked among the game's top relief pitchers since arriving in the majors two years ago, shortly after his twentieth birthday. The paucity of major leaguers from Mexico, with its rich baseball history and 120 million citizens, is striking. Just last year, Major League Baseball opened an office in Mexico City, and there's been talk about the city someday hosting an MLB franchise.

In 1956, Ozzie Virgil, whose family moved to the Bronx when he was thirteen, became the first Dominican-born player in the major leagues. In 1958, Felipe Alou, born and raised in the Dominican, arrived in the majors; two years later, Felipe's little brother Matty and future Hall of Fame pitcher Juan Marichal both joined Felipe with the San Francisco Giants. Since then, the island nation—well, half an island, to be precise—has by *far* been the most productive non-U.S. source for major leaguers. Through the end of this season, 707 Dominicans will have graced the majors, including superstars Marichal, Pedro Martinez, Albert Pujols, Vladimir Guerrero, Robinson Canó, David Ortiz, and Sammy Sosa.

By 1954, it would have been difficult for Hano to imagine the major-league landscape without the great U.S.-born black players, particularly Jackie Robinson and Willie Mays.

By 1967, when Leonard Koppett's *The Thinking Man's Guide to Baseball* was first published, *most* of the superstars were U.S.-born blacks. Which Koppett didn't even mention, perhaps because it was so obvious. But one might wonder why Koppett didn't mention the recent influx of players from the Dominican Republic. Not only was Marichal among the game's top pitchers; in '66, the top three finishers in the National League batting race were all Dominicans: Matty Alou (.342), big brother Felipe (.327), and Rico Carty (.326). Still, Marichal would remain the only true Dominican superstar for some years.

By 1985, though? When Dan Okrent's *Nine Innings* was published that year, the Dominican Republic was well established as a baseball factory. In 1985, twelve major leaguers hailed from (or were said to hail from) the city of San Pedro de Macoris alone, which today ranks as the nation's fourth- or fifth-largest city, with around two hundred thousand citizens. (Of those twelve, four were everyday shortstops, which is how the city came to be known as *the cradle of shortstops*.)

MLB hadn't seen anything yet. This year, 152 Dominican-born players will play in the majors. And the stereotype of the skinny

Dominican shortstop is long gone. This year, fifteen Dominicans will hit at least twenty home runs, with Nelson Cruz, Edwin Encarnación, Marcell Ozuna, and Gary Sánchez all ranking among the game's top power hitters.

But wait. For a moment, forget the superstars. One of the most interesting numbers in this book should be that number: 152.

In 2017, fully 11 percent of all the major leaguers were born in a country with roughly the same population as Josh Reddick's home state of Georgia.*

Meanwhile, Puerto Rico has comparatively fallen off the map. Notably, we've got Carlos Correa and Carlos Beltrán on the Astros, along with stars Francisco Lindor, Yadier Molina, and Javier Baez. But otherwise the bucket's fairly small, without a single star pitcher, despite a legacy that includes Roberto Clemente, Roberto Alomar, and Ivan Rodriguez. This year, only twenty-eight major leaguers will hail from Puerto Rico; that's 2 percent, while the U.S. territory has a population roughly a third that of the Dominican Republic.

As youth participation in the United States has dropped, the talent gap has obviously been filled, and filled quite nicely, by foreign-born players. And it's not just the Dominican Republic and Venezuela and Mexico and Cuba, the traditional Spanish-speaking baseball factories. This season, seven major leaguers will hail from Panama—in the tradition of Rod Carew and Mariano Rivera—along with six from Colombia and three from Nicaragua.

But there are also four major leaguers from Brazil, and five from Curaçao—including stars Kenley Jansen, Andrelton Simmons, and Jonathan Schoop—and ten from Canada, including All-World hitter Joey Votto.

That's just this side of the Pacific. From the other side, we're blessed with eight natives of Japan, seven from South Korea, five

---

* Also in 2017, 3.4 percent of all the major leaguers were actually born in Georgia.

from Taiwan, and three from Australia (including Alcántara's bully-mate Liam Hendriks).

In 1982, there were zero major leaguers from the other side of the Pacific. For that matter, there were none from Curaçao or Brazil or Colombia either.

Even as the population of major-league players has both expanded—officially, there will be 1,358 major leaguers this season, compared to only 932 in 1982—*and* diversified, with players from eighteen countries this season, plus a few territories and dependencies, one demographic has dropped dramatically: U.S.-born black players.

I'm going to stop here, and carefully explain that term: *U.S.-born black players.*

Every spring when the Opening Day rosters are announced, there's a rush of stories about the relative paucity—relative to the 1970s and '80s, especially—of "African-American" or "black" players in the major leagues.

Ken Rosenthal ranks among the smartest, most respected national baseball writers, and here's a snippet of his column on the issue, from last spring: "I contacted all 30 clubs, asking them to disclose the number of African-American pitchers in their respective farm systems. I also asked each to reveal the number of African-American catchers in its organization, knowing that such players were in rarer supply."

The thirty clubs knew what he meant by "African-American," and every club sent him the lists. Which were short. Or empty. There were fifty-four African-American pitchers, or roughly two per organization. There were five catchers. Five, in all the minor leagues. And while that number seems scarcely believable, we have no reason to doubt its essential accuracy.

But here's why I put "African-American" in quotes. Even while acknowledging that today practically everyone uses "African-American" (or "black") to mean U.S.-born African-American players, I would still like to make a few points about this. For the sake of clarity.

First, it's impossible to precisely define "African-American." Hell, when baseball started, we didn't even know what "white" meant; it took some years for the Italians to attain that lofty status. Now, the malleability and imprecision of labels should be self-evident once you think about it for a couple of minutes; nevertheless, it seems largely forgotten or ignored. Today, shortstop Ian Desmond and pitching brothers Joe and Tyson Ross and catcher Russell Martin are categorized as African-American. But Desmond's and Martin's and the Ross brothers' mothers are "white." As is Derek Jeter's. Giancarlo Stanton's father is white; his mother, of African-American and Puerto Rican descent. So does someone actually go ask these guys for their preferred labels? Probably not.

Or a bit closer to home, there's Bruce Maxwell. His mother self-identifies as white, but Maxwell—with a black father, plus two Native American grandmothers—does self-identify as African-American.

Self-identifying or not, all these men *are* black or African-American, in this important sense: If they had been in Jackie Robinson's place on Opening Day in 1947, *they* would have been credited with breaking Major League Baseball's color line. Before 1947, Roy Campanella—with a black mother and an Italian-American father—got his professional start in the Negro Leagues. He didn't have a choice. Felipe Alou, who became in 1956 the first player to go straight from the Dominican Republic to Organized Baseball, was the son of a black father and a white mother; he too would have been prohibited from the majors before integration.

Researcher (and author, and friend) Mark Armour has gone back to 1947 and categorized literally *every* major leaguer as either white, African-American, Latino, or Asian. His definition of African-American: "As my study was intended to estimate the effects of lifting the color barrier, I used skin color as the determining factor, because this is how Organized Baseball itself defined the issue prior to [Jackie] Robinson (and even for many years thereafter). As there are more than 11,000 players, disagreements on a few of these are not going to change our conclusion."

Mark is not precisely right about (reputedly "white") Organized

Baseball; for example, there were almost certainly Native American players in the major leagues with darker skin than at least a few players who were *not* permitted to play Organized Baseball, because of their presumed heritage. If a player might "pass" as white (or Indian) but was known to have a black parent, he certainly would have been barred from O.B. No, it wasn't just about skin color.

So while Mark classifies Grady Sizemore—who starred for Cleveland just a few years ago—as white, Sizemore's black father certainly would have left him on the wrong side of the color barrier before 1946. Oh, and by the way? The same goes for George Springer: black father, white mother. If you could just look at Springer and correctly identify the ethnicity of his parents . . . well, your powers are special. But again, if he'd been around eighty years ago, he would have been consigned to the Negro Leagues.

Bottom line, though? A few (mostly modern) quibbles aside, we've got enough players, and few enough tough calls, that Mark's numbers are essentially accurate enough for analysis. If we insist on analyzing. As we seem to do, every spring.

In 1962, the percentage of U.S.-born blacks in Major League Baseball topped 10 percent for the first time. Of course, those 10 percent included many of the game's biggest, greatest stars: Willie Mays, Hank Aaron, and Frank Robinson, to name just a few.

In 1968, the figure topped 15 percent; in 1975, 18 percent.

From 1973 through 1994, the percentage held steady, always around 17 or 18 percent.

Now let's skip ahead to 2016 . . .

6.7 percent.

Which, understandably, is upsetting to some folks. For *decades*, many of Baseball's Greatest Players were U.S.-born black players. For *decades*, Baseball has congratulated itself, with big flashing lights and seventy-six trombones and more ceremonies than anyone can count, for the trail blazed by Jackie Robinson and his fellow pioneers.

For decades, Baseball used the great U.S.-born black players as both a public-relations gimmick and a recruiting tool. But the gimmick's wearing thin, and the recruiting tool doesn't seem to be working. At all. And hasn't for some time.

All this has led to a fair amount of hand-wringing. Understandably. But everything boils down to a couple of questions: *How did we get here?* and *What can be done about it?* Oh, and one more: "It's hard to talk about this," outfielder-turned-analyst Doug Glanville points out, "without asking what it *should* look like."

None of these questions are easily answered. Sometimes, though, Occam's razor is too quickly ignored. I've often read that the biggest reason for the observed lack of participation by American black kids is money. The counterargument is all those (mostly) poor Dominican kids who certainly can't afford the latest and greatest carbon-fiber bats and shiny baseball shoes. But the simple truth is that in the Dominican Republic and elsewhere, kids play baseball for *fun*, generally with no adults around, until they're at least half grown. In many places, that is the most obvious, publicly visible path to a way out and financial comfort.

The path in the U.S. is simply different. There's very little adult-free baseball here. Instead there are hypercompetitive leagues and Top 20 prospect lists for second-graders, and "travel teams" that drive (or fly!) hundreds of miles to compete against similarly skilled children. And if your parents can't afford the high costs associated with such competition? You're probably stuck playing against relatively weak competition, unable to afford private coaching, falling behind your peers, and eventually losing interest.

All of that's a generalization, of course. But if you're not from a middle-class home in a middle-class neighborhood, at least, you might well get left behind.*

---

* Which flips the traditional model on its head, by the way. Even now, the best basketball and football players generally hail from inner cities and rural areas, where sports are still seen as a way up and out. Much as baseball used to be seen in the United States, and still is in Latin America.

Now, all that's assuming you would have played baseball in the first place. I've often read that so few black players get drafted because teams today are focusing on college players more than they used to, and that black players are less likely to get offered scholarships. Perhaps. But there seem to be plenty of football and basketball players on scholarship; granted, the baseball scholarships tend to be half scholarships, and there are never enough to go around. But if you're eighteen with a high school degree and you can play baseball, really play baseball, seems unlikely there's not a college somewhere for you.

Anyway, in this summer's amateur draft, twenty-four of the first fifty players chosen were from either high schools or junior/community colleges.*

It's a fact that in the U.S., playing at the highest levels of amateur, pre-college competition has become ridiculously expensive, and that there almost *have* to be talented young baseball players, black *and* white *and* Hispanic, who are currently priced out of top competition before they have a chance to be drafted, or offered a college scholarship, or simply encouraged to pursue a baseball career. But, you know . . . at least *some* of the things we might say about teenagers playing baseball, we might also say about teenagers playing basketball or football or soccer, too.

The one thing that's almost always missing from these discussions?

Agency.

Which is a fancy word for people making decisions for their own reasons, some of them unfathomable and at the same time perfectly reasonable, and difficult to blame on other people. And to (very roughly) paraphrase black scholar Gerald Early, "If there are

---

* In an encouraging moment for Baseball, the top *two* picks in the draft were African American . . . at least if you count Royce Lewis, whose mother is white, and father black. And it seems everyone does.

more black doctors and more black lawyers but fewer black baseball players, maybe that's all right?"

Which is a fancy way of saying that maybe a lot of young black athletes in the U.S. aren't playing baseball because they prefer playing (or doing) something else. For whatever reasons, and yes there are no doubt plenty of them, black kids in America usually choose basketball or football over baseball. Which just wasn't true in the 1950s and '60s. That is the fundamental, undeniable difference that leads directly to the precipitous decline in the number of U.S.-born black major leaguers.

What's to be done about it? Well, again: to some large degree *it's not up to Baseball*. Nobody gets to wave a wand or a wallet and suddenly all the best young athletes wanna be Andrew McCutchen instead of Stephen Curry or Cam Newton.

But Baseball does seem compelled, if only for the sake of public relations, to at least try.

And Baseball *is* trying. Baseball's sorta trying.

Reviving Baseball in Inner Cities (RBI) has been around since 1989, when it began in Los Angeles with grants from the city and the Amateur Athletic Union. Two years later, Major League Baseball took over. In 2017, RBI's website claimed that "RBI programs have been started in more than 200 cities worldwide," and "MLB and its clubs have designated more than $30 million of resources to the RBI program."

Oh. Well.

In more than twenty-five years, Baseball has spent more than $30 million. Which, and I'm not sure how to put this kindly, doesn't seem like a lot. This season, Yankees left-hander CC Sabathia will start twenty-seven games and earn $25 million.

It's just unrealistic to think $30 million spread over all those years is going to accomplish much of anything. Or even $60 million, or $90 million. Unless all those millions are spent in one year, and then again every year for a bunch more years. But over nearly thirty years, ostensibly in efforts to change the hearts and minds of hundreds of thousands of American kids? To convince them not just to play baseball, but also become lifelong fans? "It's too good of a cause to be a lost cause," longtime Dodgers executive Fred Claire says. "I think Baseball can do a better job. You can't change society, but you can be a part of that change."

At least until the very recent past, it's mostly been public relations; well, that and labor relations, as there are U.S.-born black major leaguers who care deeply about this issue and want to see Baseball doing something. Sure, you could argue that the union itself could be doing a great deal more than it does. But . . . well, you know. The union's not in business to give away money.

None of which is to say the percentages are stuck in place forever. Human endeavors are hardly so stable. It's hardly clear that football will remain a popular youth sport for much longer; according to a recent study, only 3 percent of children aged six to twelve played tackle football, with another 3 percent playing flag football. If those percentages drop *much* further, high schools in great swaths of America might have trouble finding enough teenagers to form more than symbolic teams.

It's also not clear that professional basketball will seem like a viable career path for young athletes who don't figure on winding up taller than six feet two or so, while we know there's still plenty of room for "short" baseball players at the very highest level. In baseball, you can stand five and a half feet tall and earn millions.

What's more, it does seem that Major League Baseball is doing more than just throwing a few bucks at this thing for the good public relations. "They're doing a great job of getting the younger kids to play on some level," longtime baseball executive Bill Bavasi says. "Next thing is to help the fourteen- and fifteen-year-olds choose baseball instead of football. But there are programs making it affordable. All this is not lost on the commissioner." And this year there *has* been an uptick in youth participation, thanks largely to a new $30 million initiative, launched two years ago by MLB and the United States Conference of Mayors, with the idea of just getting kids *familiar* with baseball (and softball). It's early, but so far the numbers are encouraging, as more kids *are* getting familiar.

Still, it's easy to overstate the opportunity here, for Baseball. Not with just black kids; with all kids. While baseball might seem a more viable, or at least healthier career path than football or basketball, what about soccer? And lacrosse? And, heaven forfend, e-sports? We simply cannot predict with any accuracy what the sports landscape will look like in ten or fifteen years, and especially when it comes to athletes who haven't been born yet. We might guess that a great deal will depend on the justifiable fear of concussions. But beyond that, who can say? If youth football is profoundly affected, x number of kids are likely to play soccer or baseball instead. It's just impossible to estimate x with any confidence.

Perhaps all we can say with confidence is that Baseball appears to be trying, but should try harder. Especially considering how many dollars they could throw at the problem, if they truly wanted to solve it. Especially considering how few U.S.-born blacks are managing teams, or serving as special assistants to general managers. Let alone actually running front offices, or even departments of front offices.

As Doug Glanville also points out, for some years blacks were told that if they wanted to manage, they had to put in their time in the minor leagues, or perhaps as base coaches. But now? "What's been so frustrating," Glanville says, "is that as soon as the pipeline filled up, the rules changed for managers; now it's special assistants, bench coaches."

Then there's the stunning lack of diversity in front offices. These days, it's not just that you'll find hardly any diversity at the upper reaches of baseball management; it's that there's increasingly little room for anyone at the top who's not white *and* the product of an elite university. Twenty years ago, Billy Beane could bemoan the network of ex-players who seemed to run the game; as an ex-player himself, Beane perhaps had more credibility than an outsider. So the A's and the Red Sox hired a bunch of Ivy League wizards, which seemed like . . . well, a sort of diversity, anyway.*

Today? Today at least half the franchises in Major League Baseball are run by graduates of Ivy League schools, or elite universities like Amherst and Georgetown. Today only two clubs are run by ex-players: the A's and the Mariners (ex-pitcher Jerry Dipoto, who rarely *sounds* like an ex-pitcher). Next spring, author Dan Levitt will write, "This trend will likely continue for many years, until someone tries a new route, is successful, and another model for leading front offices emerges."†

One wonders how *many* years. In 1972, Jackie Robinson, frustrated with the almost complete lack of African-American representation anywhere but on the actual field of play, wrote, "I cannot stand and sing the anthem. I cannot stand and salute the flag; I know that I am a black man in a white man's world."

Today of course, Robinson is lionized. But if he were alive today, would he feel much differently about the "progress" made by Major League Baseball? If today he refused to stand for the anthem, would every major leaguer wear his number for one game every spring? These are rhetorical questions, but you probably know the correct answers.

After Altuve drives a double over the right fielder's head, pushing Springer to third base, manager Melvin orders the A's infield-

---

* Next spring, at the annual SABR Analytics Conference in Phoenix, MLB Network's Brian Kenny will joke about MLB's voluminous Ivy League hires: "It's good, because those guys need a break."

† A few years ago, a scout told Howard Bryant, "First they tell you you have to play the game. Then they tell you you have to work in the minors and scout to learn the business of the game. And now, once you get all that experience, once you think you're ready, once you've put your time in, then they tell you you have to have a [expletive] Ivy League degree to be a general manager. I'll never get a call now. Not even for an interview. You got to know the [expletive] Ivy League handshake now."

ers to move in some. With his club already losing by four runs, the idea is to keep Springer on third base in the event of a ground ball. It's hard to say whether or not it's a smart percentage move; you might save a run, but you might also lose a couple of runs, as a player's batting average goes up when the infielders are drawn closer and have less time to react if the ball comes their way.

When you can throw like Alcántara, the infield's often irrelevant, and now he rockets three straight fastballs past Correa: first 95, then a couple of 97s. Which brings up Josh Reddick, who's already walked, doubled, and homered tonight. Melvin orders an intentional walk . . . but unlike in every other season before 2017, Melvin's pitcher doesn't actually have to throw any pitches.

The "automatic" intentional walk was introduced just this season, as part of Baseball's ongoing, if fitful, efforts to address "pace of play" issues. There's now (apparently) serious talk about enforcing rules limiting pitchers' time between pitches; in fact, the clocks are already in place in stadiums, but to this point they've essentially been ignored, due largely to objections from the players' union.

So this season, for the first time ever, the intentional walk can easily pass without notice. Because instead of the manager giving some signal to his catcher, followed by four pitches delivered (usually) way high and outside—and so practically impossible to hit— *now* a manager need merely make a signal to the umpire . . . and off trots the batter to first base, having witnessed not a single pitch.

The point of course is to quicken *the pace of play.*

The old intentional walks took around one minute apiece. Now, one minute of dead time: that's not nothing. Except these days there just aren't many of those particular dead minutes to kill.*

The A's will finish this season having issued only seventeen intentional walks all season; the Astros, also seventeen. By contrast,

---

* Wait, can you kill something that's dead already? You can. I saw it on *The Walking Dead.* (I saw it once. Once was enough.)

in 2002—the year of Moneyball—A's manager Art Howe ordered forty-five intentional walks (much, we might imagine, to Billy Beane's chagrin).*

In 2016, there were only 932 intentional walks all season. In 2017, there will be only 970. (With their seventeen intentional walks apiece, the A's and Astros will tie for second fewest in the majors, with Terry Francona's first-place Indians issuing fifteen. In the National League, Bud Black's Rockies will finish last with only twenty.)

So, let's see . . . 970 minutes spread over six months is 162 minutes per month, or 40 minutes per week, or 6 minutes per day. Not for every team, or every game. For all of Major League Baseball. Which seems like . . . not a lot?

In fact, it really is not a lot. It's hardly a smidgen.

But you gotta start somewhere. Baseball has gotten slower. Yes, also longer. But no longer than a football game, and lately even basketball games are seeming interminable. But few observers seem terribly concerned about baseball games that run three hours—as this one will, with another six minutes just for fun—because, after all, the longer the game goes, the more beer and hot dogs you can sell, and all that programming space on the regional sports network won't fill itself.

Pace, though? There *is* a feeling, or maybe it's better described as an argument, or a plea, that when the game slows down, that's when someone at home is going to change the channel. Or fall asleep. That's when someone who's actually in the ballpark looks at their watch and wonders if they want to spend three-plus hours here again, anytime soon.

No, six minutes per day doesn't really help. But again, you have

---

* Seventy-eight that season for Houston, but that figure isn't directly comparable, because the Astros were still in the National League, where intentional walks are naturally more popular because number eight hitters are routinely walked with two outs and the pitcher coming up next.

to start somewhere. The most obvious way to speed up the pace would be shorter commercial breaks. They used to be shorter, and still there was enough time for the teams to switch places on the field, for the pitcher to get his warm-up tosses. Now, you *could* (reasonably, I think) argue that cutting thirty seconds of advertisements between each half inning would (a) bring in lower revenue in the short term, but (b) bring in *more* revenue in the long term, with a slightly quicker game leading to slightly higher ratings, and (thus) ad rates.*

So far, it doesn't seem that anyone's much appreciated those extra six minutes. It also doesn't seem that anyone's much missed the four-pitch intentional walks. Yes, the *prospect* of the new rule deeply offended some sensibilities. At least one journalist blamed the rule on those damned millennials.

And yes, we should at least acknowledge the occasional excitement (yes, excitement) of the intentional walk. Just a year ago, for example, the Yankees' Gary Sánchez reached out and turned an intended intentional ball into a sacrifice fly. Susan Slusser, who's been covering the A's for the *San Francisco Chronicle* since 1999, fondly recalls seeing Giants first baseman Will Clark spoil an intentional walk with a base hit. And most famously, in the 1972 World Series, Cincinnati's Johnny Bench struck out looking on a *fake* intentional walk by A's relief ace Rollie Fingers.

If you appreciate the improbable—and if you don't, how did you make it this far into the book?—you probably composed a brief, but heartfelt eulogy when Commissioner Manfred killed the intentional walk. Realistically, though? You could watch every one of your team's games for five years and never see an intentional walk

---

* Back in spring training this year, Commissioner Manfred floated the idea of shorter commercial breaks. But then, Commissioner Manfred floats a lot of things. Most of them never leave port. More to the point, shorter commercial breaks, as we'll see later, really would not speed up or shorten the proceedings. As odd as that might seem.

go awry. Especially now, when the tactic is generally eschewed; and even when it's not, the pitchers and catchers are more skilled and careful than ever.

Still, such a fundamental exception to the game's fundamental rules—you know, four balls for a walk, three strikes yer out, etc.—is defensible *only* if it's part of something larger. And in 2017, it's really not. The commercial breaks are the same, and there's a pitch clock but . . . just in the minor leagues, with the aim of helping umpires enforce the long-standing rule, minors *and* majors, that a pitcher must deliver a pitch within . . . well, you're probably not going to believe this, but within twelve seconds. It's right there in the book, Rule 5.07(c): *When the bases are unoccupied, the pitcher shall deliver the ball to the batter within 12 seconds after he receives the ball. Each time the pitcher delays the game by violating this rule, the umpire shall call "Ball."*

You wanna guess how many times a major-league umpire has enforced Rule 5.07(c) in 2017? Okay, so I don't know. But if the number isn't zero, it's very, very, very close to zero. It's difficult for umpires to hurry along the pitchers, and it's difficult for umpires to hurry along the hitters. As long-time umpire Dale Scott told me, "All we could do was write up the chronic violators, and then the league will send them a letter, and then maybe they'll fine them. But the union takes the teeth out of everything. The fines aren't large enough to deter anything, and MLB didn't want ejections."

When that keeps happening, year after year, can you blame the umpires for giving up on enforcing the rules? "It was just a lot of frustration for everybody," Scott said, "Park Avenue"—that is, Major League Baseball—"and the umpires."

So, to sum up: In 2017, there's not a pitch clock in the majors, or any other meaningful efforts to discourage or prohibit pitchers or hitters from lollygagging, and *certainly* no plan at all to cut down even a little on all the pitching changes.

Bill James thinks all these measures, or half measures, even if implemented, would make little difference. "The essence of the problem," Bill will write in a few weeks, "is that there are many, many, many things which *can* be done inside of a baseball game to waste time, and it is always in someone's interest to do these things. Pitchers can stand on the mound without pitching. Catchers can visit the mound. Pitchers can throw to first. Managers can change pitchers. If you limit pitching changes they will start changing outfielders in the middle of the game, or holding up the inning to move the outfielders around. Batters can ask for time and step out between pitches. Base runners can ask for a sliding glove. Batters can change bats. Networks can sell more commercials between innings."

More Bill: "Baseball is trying to address a *general* problem with remedies targeting one issue or another. This is never going to work, because there will always be something else that can pop up that will waste even more time than whatever you were trying to stamp out before. I'm glad they are *trying* to fix the problem, but it is never going to work. It's like swatting mosquitoes. There will always be more mosquitoes."

As Bill often does, he's got a radical proposal: a $200 million "reward fund for quickly played games." Bill doesn't say exactly where that $200 million would go, but the point is to create real financial incentives for speeding up the games.

Which might work! Except it's almost certainly far too radical for the old fuddy-duddies who run Baseball. The biggest issue, I think—I mean, once you get past the *what in the hell is he talking about* factor—would be the various parties' unwillingness to loosen their collective grips on the disbursement of that $200 million. Oh, and by the way? I'm also not convinced that $200 million would be enough. Or maybe the figure doesn't even matter, because Baseball wouldn't consider *any* meaningful figure, whether $200 million or $100 million or even something less impressive.

Anyway, I think Bill is wrong. Or wrong enough.

Most especially, Bill is largely wrong when he says Baseball is trying to address a *general* problem with remedies targeting one issue or another. Baseball hasn't actually made any real commitment to such remedies. Go back and look at that list of ways to waste time. None of them have actually been addressed in meaningful ways. And you can't even include intentional walks, because the point of them was never to waste time; it just worked out that way.

So let's actually try some real remedies first, and then—if, as Bill predicts, that doesn't work—we can talk about getting a little nuts. Meanwhile, I would guess it's more like Whac-A-Mole than swatting mosquitoes: if you're good enough, you might actually beat the game. At worst, you can battle them pesky varmints to a draw for a while.

Ultimately, it all comes back to the pitcher. He's the one with the ball in his hand. Unless he's got a really good excuse, he simply must deliver the next pitch within a reasonable number of seconds. If he doesn't do that, it's a ball. If he does but the batter's not ready, tough shit for the batter. Essentially, it comes down to reasonably clear rules and the umpires' willingness to enforce them.

Because when it comes to the pitch clock in the minor leagues, nearly everyone who's been quoted on the subject says essentially the same thing: Before you know it, you've forgotten it's even there. This was just one of the changes in Double- and Triple-A a few years ago, designed to speed things up, but it's the clock that seems to have made the biggest difference. In 2015, the first year of the clocks, Triple-A game times dropped by twelve minutes.

That said, it's far from clear if *just* a pitch clock would have the same impact in the majors. Because it turns out *most* of the dead time between pitches comes with runners on base, when the pitch clock's turned off, because of the time required to mind those runners. Considering that research shows most pitchers, in the absence of baserunners, *already* deliver the next pitch within twenty seconds, the time saved might be negligible, or less than we'd expect.

Or maybe it's not really so much about the time at all. Automatic intentional walks, as we've seen, make little difference in anything. Except maybe perception. With every supposed remedy, at least Baseball can say, "Hey, get off our back! Can't you see that we're doing *something*?"

There is literally not a human being on earth who could discern the few minutes per week "saved" by junking those four-pitch intentional walks, just as there's not a human who could notice, with their eyes, the difference between a .250 hitter and a .300 hitter. But *tell* someone a guy's a .300 hitter, and they'll figure they saw it all along.*

Same thing with pace of play. It's not all just psychology and persuasion. Some, though. If Baseball keeps *saying* they're concerned about it, and actually does throw in a few time-saving wrinkles, most fans might well believe the pace has picked up. More than it actually has. And so everyone wins, a little.

This is just the fifteenth time all season that Melvin's called for an intentional walk, a tactic that's become wildly unpopular since Bill James pointed out, way back in the 1980s, that teams typically give up more runs *with* the intentional walk than without. Which is a pretty strong argument against doing it. But it still *occasionally* makes sense, and this might be one of those occasions. Or maybe this is just post facto analysis; as the Astros' radio team sadly notes, "the intentional walk pays off for Melvin and the A's" when Yuli Gurriel grounds into a routine 5-4-3 double play—third baseman to second baseman to first baseman—to end the inning.

Score: Astros 7, Athletics 3
Win Probability: Astros 93%

---

* Over the course of a whole season, as Crash Davis relates so vividly in *Bull Durham*, the difference between .250 and .300 is roughly one hit per week.

Home Seventh

We are all agreed that your theory is crazy. The question that divides us is whether it is crazy enough to have a chance of being correct.

—NIELS BOHR (1885–1962)

There have already been a few brief mentions in the various broadcasts, but in the opening of this half inning, with Fiers back to the hill, the Oakland TV crew really focuses on the hurricane (Harvey) that so recently flooded much of Houston for some days, and necessitated the relocation of three Astros games from Houston to St. Petersburg, home of the Tampa Bay Rays (for the rest of this season, the Astros are wearing Houston-centric "Strong" patches near their hearts). And just today, MLB announced that with Category 5 Hurricane Irma looming, three Rays-Yankees games scheduled for next week in St. Petersburg will instead be played at Citi Field, home of the Mets.

On the list of climate change's deleterious effects, the impact on professional sports must rank very near the bottom. Maybe *the* bottom. But there will be an impact, and within professional sports it will feel serious.

Hell, it feels serious today if you live in Houston. Or if you're Jharel Cotton or Carlos Beltrán or Carlos Correa. Just yesterday, Irma devastated St. Thomas, where Cotton grew up. While his parents huddled in a closet, the roof of their house was swept away by the winds. Later, Cotton will recall Bob Melvin telling him to go ahead and check on his parents between innings tonight, so he caught as much news on TV as he could. "My dad called," Cotton said, "and said, 'Can you call someone to come and help us?' It was a terrible day.

"That's not why I didn't pitch so well," he says. "I just got beat. The Astros are just a really good team, and I knew all the time I would talk to my parents after the game."

Before Irma swept across St. Thomas, she grazed Puerto Rico, leaving a million residents without electricity. So Correa and Beltrán's minds must be wandering far from Oakland tonight too.*

Ten years ago, *Sports Illustrated* ran a cover story on the long-term impact of climate change on the world of sports. Referring to baseball's seasonal traditions, Bill McKibben said, "It's the last of the semipagan calendars we keep, and a lot of it is going to disappear. All that Bart Giamatti stuff has a different valence if we're not going to Florida for spring training, but to St. Paul."

McKibben's prediction hasn't come true yet. Which doesn't mean it won't.

Meanwhile, the Oakland A's are one of only two franchises in the majors with serious short-term ballpark issues (the Tampa Bay Rays are the other). Safe from hurricanes, yes, but the Coliseum isn't immune to aging or apathy.

The Coliseum has been the Athletics' home since they arrived from Kansas City in 1968, and only four current ballparks are older. All four of *those*—Fenway Park, Wrigley Field, Dodger Stadium, and

---

* In less than two weeks, Hurricane Maria will crash into both Puerto Rico and the Dominican Republic. Another Category 5 storm, even stronger than Irma, Maria will be described as history's worst natural disaster in both Puerto Rico and Dominica. And St. Thomas isn't spared; many of the roofs that Irma didn't snatch, Maria will. Beltrán will ultimately donate a million dollars to relief efforts in his home territory.

Angels Stadium—have been modernized at great cost, and all but perhaps Angels Stadium figure to endure for decades longer. The Coliseum, on the other hand, has been an albatross for some time.

In the late 1970s, with owner Charlie Finley having essentially given up, at least two A's games drew fewer than a thousand fans. But thanks in part to Finley's antimarketing acumen, attendance had never been good, even when the club was winning three straight World Series; back in '73, third baseman Sal Bando said, "Look how drab this place is. All gray cement. Players call it the Oakland Mausoleum."

But the real problem, in the long term, wasn't Charlie Finley. The real problem was football. More than any other franchise and stadium, the A's and the Coliseum have been linked for half a century to football. Even with the Oakland Raiders moving to Las Vegas in 2019 or '20—this, following a thirteen-year stint in Los Angeles in the 1980s and '90s—the Coliseum will remain, until the day it's brought down with dynamite, more than anything else a *football stadium*.

From their lofty perch behind the plate, and with Bruce Maxwell leading off the inning against Fiers, the A's television crew offers this appraisal of their view . . .

RAY FOSSE: The structure in center field has changed the dynamics of where the ball travels, considerably.
GLEN KUIPER: It's a structure all right.
FOSSE: HUGE structure.
KUIPER: It's a massive structure that stares right at us, every home game. Never blinks.

Nope. Never blinks. And never hosts any baseball fans either. In 2006, the A's covered the upper-deck seats all the way around the stadium with giant dark-green tarpaulins (some of which you can see on the cover of this book), reducing capacity for baseball games to just thirty-five-thousand-some visitors. This season, though, the tarps were stripped from the upper decks *except* Mt. Davis. So still, it never blinks.

Like most of the stadiums built in the fifteen or twenty years after baseball-only Dodger Stadium, the Coliseum was designed for baseball *and* football (along with whatever else promoters could squeeze in). Really the only exception was Kansas City, where Jackson County voters somehow agreed to finance the massive Truman Sports Complex, with dedicated buildings for both the Royals and the Chiefs, surrounded by parking lots stretching to the horizon. Everybody else in the late 1960s and '70s got multipurpose, "cookie-cutter" stadiums. Although in fact that's a bit of a misnomer, as they did *not* all look alike. Most because some were fully enclosed—with seating all the way around—and some were not. The Coliseum was not enclosed, which meant (a) the fans were afforded a reasonably nice view of Oakland's hills beyond the outfield, and (b) the stadium held only fifty-five thousand seats for football games. That relatively low capacity contributed to the Raiders leaving for Los Angeles, fifteen years after taking up residence in the Coliseum.[*]

Oakland—or more accurately, the City of Oakland, plus Alameda County—lured the Raiders back by adding roughly twenty thousand seats, with a new upper deck beyond the outfield walls. Those seats, dubbed "Mt. Davis" in honor (or dishonor) of Raiders owner Al Davis, turned the stadium into a "concrete ashtray" of sorts . . . just as most major-league franchises were escaping such places. For that reason and (certainly) others, the A's have struggled badly to attract fans to the Coliseum. From 1988 through '90, when they won three straight division titles, the A's averaged 2.6 million attendance per season. When they went to the playoffs four straight times, from

---

[*] In 1960 and '61 the Oakland Raiders actually played their home games not in Oakland, but in two San Francisco stadiums.

2000 through 2003—these of course were the *Moneyball* teams Michael Lewis wrote about, especially 2002 and 2003—the A's averaged only 2 million per season. And from 2012 through '14, when they again reached the playoffs every year, the A's averaged only 1.8 million per season. Which is obviously a disturbing trend.

It's not *all* the Coliseum's fault. Baseball fans do seem less thrilled by cheap, relatively anonymous players than by expensive, relatively famous ones. Even when the cheap guys are playing just as well.

Either way, the A's attendance is now a long-running issue. Since 2005, they've sold 2 million tickets just once: in 2014, when they won ninety-nine games and *just* squeaked over 2 million in their last home game. Typically the A's finish second worst in attendance in all the major leagues, ahead of only the Tampa Bay Rays (who have stadium issues of their own, with a sterile domed facility that's inconveniently sited for most of their fans).*

Again, the Coliseum is *not* the oldest ballpark in the majors, and in a strange historical twist it's just the third oldest in California. But Dodger Stadium has always been baseball-only, still looking as fresh today as fifty years ago. And the Angels' Anaheim Stadium, once the home of the Los Angeles Rams football team, was extensively remodeled before the 1998 baseball season, becoming a baseball-only venue with around forty-five thousand seats. Kansas City's ballpark, which opened in 1973, got a $250 million facelift a few years ago. And hundreds of millions of dollars have been spent renovating both Fenway Park and Wrigley Field in recent years.

So essentially the A's have the *only* home that's both "old" *and* comes with no hope of some meaningful renovation/modernization. With the Coliseum, what you see is almost exactly what the A's have been getting for fifty years, and will keep getting for at least a few more.

---

* Aside: When we reference official "attendance" we're indulging in an MLB-mandated fiction. The reported figures are simply tickets sold, *not* actually people, you know, attending the game.

This isn't the place for a treatise on the A's efforts to find a new home. You could write a whole book, except it would be so sad that nobody would read it. Suffice to say, it's not easy to get things built in Oakland. But the A's keep plugging away.*

It's been said that when (if?) the A's and Rays finally procure their new homes, MLB might seriously consider expansion for the first time since the late 1990s. When we say "it's been said that," we mean that it's been said by the commissioner. Who said in July, "I think for us to expand, we need to be resolved in Tampa and Oakland in terms of their stadium situations."

What's the connection? Well, a cynic—which is to say, anyone who's ever paid a shred of attention to how sports owners conduct their affairs—might guess that MLB prefers cities like Montreal, Portland, and Charlotte to remain fallow, as leverage for the magnates in Oakland and St. Petersburg whilst they continue their seemingly forever efforts to extort—er, convince local politicians and voters that profitable businesses owned by billionaires and staffed by millionaires deserve public dollars.

While the A's first plans obviously hit a roadblock, the ballpark village does seem to be the next step in stadium evolution. First there were the steel-and-concrete palaces of the early twentieth century, then the multipurpose, (often) artificially turfed stadiums of the 1970s, then the "retro" stadiums of the 1990s, and now the ballpark villages.

The new paradigm is probably the Braves' new home in Atlanta (or rather, near Atlanta).

---

* Just three days after tonight's game, the A's will unveil, with great fanfare, plans for a new "ballpark village"—which is a fancy name for a new stadium surrounded by various businesses, all of them supposedly generating income for the baseball team and tax revenues for the local authorities—a few miles away from the Coliseum, on property currently owned by a local community college. A few weeks later, the college's teachers' union will, with great enthusiasm, vote against the proposal, essentially killing it.

In 1997, the Braves took up residence in Turner Field, slightly repurposed after serving as the central venue for the 1996 Summer Olympics. But despite resting only a mile from the heart of downtown Atlanta, Turner Field was not particularly well sited: traffic was ugly, the surrounding neighborhood ill suited for development (or parking lots). So after only twenty seasons, the Braves left for suburban Cobb County, where the new facility sits on a giant plot of land and will ultimately be surrounded by restaurants, bars, shops, offices, hotel rooms, and (of course) parking lots. The extrastadium development, projected to cost the Braves $400 million, is called the Battery Atlanta.*

When the first wave of retro stadiums were being built in the 1990s, modeled (if just cosmetically) on the classic old ballparks (which featured, just being frank about this, no legroom and obstructed views and medieval sanitation facilities), there was some consensus that these new palaces would endure for many decades, perhaps as long as the old ones had: a half century, maybe more. After all, they were made of brick! And everyone just adored them!

We forget our history so easily.

Much the same was actually said about the multipurpose, borderline-Brutalist buildings built in the 1960s and '70s, which were almost unanimously hailed as huge improvements on the old-fashioned yards they replaced. Seriously. Yes, I know that by the 1980s people were complaining about them. But go back and check the archives. At the time, people loved the damn things.

Ultimately, *some* of the 1990s stadiums will survive for many decades, just as (for various mostly accidental reasons) Fenway Park and Wrigley Field and Dodger Stadium soldier on. But the survivors will be accidents of history, and not some natural, evolutionary end point.

---

* Just as the New York Giants and New York Jets don't play in New York and the Los Angeles Angels don't play in Los Angeles—nowhere *near* Los Angeles!—the Battery Atlanta isn't actually in Atlanta. Nor are the Atlanta Braves.

And just as the Braves have left their 1990s stadium, the Texas Rangers will soon leave theirs; in 2020, they'll move across the street to a new home with a retractable roof (which will rarely be retracted, sorry to say) and surrounded by a shopping mall, a hotel, and (you guessed it) a "ballpark village." Meanwhile, just in the last few weeks, the Arizona Diamondbacks and Maricopa County—the county owns and maintains Chase Field, the Diamondbacks' retractably roofed, fully air-conditioned home—have been embroiled in a public dispute over who should pay for maintenance that's projected to cost $200 million over the next decade. Some reports even suggested that MLB might force the Diamondbacks to leave Phoenix rather than pony up much of the dough. Presumably in favor of one of the city's prosperous suburbs, which themselves have ponied up for new, enormously expensive homes for football's Arizona Cardinals and hockey's Arizona Coyotes, not to mention a number of posh spring-training complexes for many baseball teams.*

Tired of all the good news? Let's talk more about climate change! And rising sea levels! Because the question isn't if the water's coming. Because, you know: the water's coming already. With the inevitable melting of the ice sheets and glaciers in Greenland and Antarctica, the water will keep coming for as many years as it matters to anyone now alive. But in the relatively short term, estimates for the actual numbers fall within a wide range. Suffice to say, it seems unlikely that any stadium in a low-lying area—Safeco Field in Seattle, AT&T Park in San Francisco, anywhere the A's are likely to be playing, and essentially the entire state of Florida—will last nearly as long as Fenway Park . . . which itself sits a couple of blocks from the edge of a coastal wetland, just twenty feet above sea level.

Today's sea level. Another decade or two, all bets are off.

---

* Next May, the Diamondbacks will hammer out an agreement with friendly local politicians, allowing them to leave Phoenix with no penalty before 2023, as long as they remain in Maricopa County, or pay a small fee if they leave after 2022.

In the short term, the A's will keep playing in a dry Coliseum—well, usually dry; every so often, an ancient pipe explodes and everything's soaked in a healthy dose of sewage—and so the fans will continue to stay away, and the franchise will continue to carry a relatively low payroll, regardless of ownership's personal wealth (which of course is considerable). And it should be said that a new stadium, even when publicly financed, is hardly a panacea for every financial ill. The Marlins spent like they were poor before the locals gave them a shiny new postmodern ballpark. And now after too. A new ballpark confers a real competitive advantage only if it's usually filled with lots of people spending lots of money, and you can't really know if that will happen until you try it.

The A's *do* seem to have history on their side. When they had good ownership, good teams, *and* famous players—superstars, we used to call them—in the late 1980s, they did attract droves of passionate spectators. Since then, the Bay Area—and yes, even the relatively middle-class East Bay—has only become more populous and moneyed. Which might explain why the A's are *still* in Oakland rather than (say) Portland or Vancouver or Sacramento (where the A's top farm team occasionally attracts more customers than the big club, eighty-five miles away).

But there's simply nothing new happening for the A's, anytime soon. If ever.

Meanwhile, it's hard to imagine that Bruce Maxwell's terribly concerned about the Athletics' future digs, let alone catastrophic climate change. The A's still trail the Astros by four runs, but you gotta start somewhere. Maxwell doesn't have much power; he'll finish this season with thirty-one home runs in nearly two thousand professional at-bats. But Maxwell *is* a reasonably patient hitter, and his patience really pays off here.

Fiers's first pitch is an inside curveball that *might* have caught just the tiniest sliver of the strike zone. But Maxwell doesn't offer, and the umpire's arm doesn't move. Fiers's second pitch is a high fastball that *might* have caught just the tiniest sliver of the corner of the zone, up and away. But Maxwell doesn't offer; the umpire's arm doesn't move.

From Fiers's perspective, these might seem like two perfect pitches: strikes, but practically unhittable. Except they're not strikes. Because Maxwell didn't swing at them and the umpire didn't call them. Which must be debited, to some small, almost impossibly small and perhaps unfair degree, against catcher Brian McCann.

When people think about the new data and the old, institutional knowledge—or the old opinions, if you prefer—they (or we) usually assume that the new stuff blows up the old stuff. While that has always been (and remains) an oversimplification, it's also probably true, at least as often as not.

And then there's pitch framing.

For a long while, it's been *theorized* that a close pitch was more likely to be called a strike by the umpire if the catcher *received* or *presented* the pitch/catch in a particular way. With smooth being better than jerky. This has been taught for many decades to professional catchers.

In 1982—yes, the very same year in which Dan Okrent visited them—the Milwaukee Brewers actually published, for the general public, their organizational manual—essentially their "way" of teaching and playing baseball. And the Brewers were clear about the techniques for getting the close call—or as they (and perhaps they alone) called such pitches: *stri-balls*. "Every pitch in or near the strike zone should be caught with a minimum of body movement. We tell our catchers to shrink the strike zone with their hands. We liken it to picking fruit off a tree. The ball should be caught with very smooth hand action."

But the Brewers weren't the first to give up their organizational semisecrets. Way back in 1954, Dodgers executive Al Campanis penned, for the mass market, *The Dodger Way to Play Baseball*. Within, he wrote:

> *The good receiver often makes many doubtful strikes pitches by catching the ball properly. This is not done by jerking or pulling*

the ball over the plate. Instead it is done by bringing all close pitches toward the belt buckle if they are just inside or outside of home plate. . . . The entire action must be smooth if the umpire is to be deceived. Deception in this case is quite ethical and a part of the game, as the call is based on the umpire's judgment and not on whether a thing is right or wrong.

This was, in fact, the standard technique taught to catchers for decades: bring every borderline pitch, as smoothly as possible, *to the belt buckle.*

In the 1990s, catcher-turned-broadcaster Tim McCarver routinely espoused the game-changing importance of pitch framing, and I didn't buy it. For one thing, why wouldn't the umpires simply watch the baseball and ignore the catcher? And second, *where is the data?* There was no data.

Sure, some catchers, year in, year out, would give up fewer runs than their teammates, even if you accounted for the different number of innings thrown by a team's pitchers with different catchers behind the plate. But why? Without granular data, we could only guess. Maybe the best receivers called pitchers better, or were better psychologists, or were better at buttering up the umpires. Or maybe Campanis and the Brewers and McCarver were right, and the best catchers were getting more called strikes on the borderline pitches.

But maybe was all that nerds (like me) could say.

Until 2008, or thereabouts.

In 2008, clever fellows on the internet began looking at PITCH-f/x data—the product of specialized cameras, by then installed in almost every stadium—and were able to see *precisely* the travels of almost every pitched baseball from the pitcher's hand until it met the batter's bat or the catcher's mitt.

Analysts' first thought seems to have been, "Hey, let's figure out which umpires are terrible!"

But once you've done that—and by the way, MLB was doing

the same thing, and incorporating the results into their internal evaluations*—the next step is obvious, at least in retrospect: see if some catchers get significantly more close calls than others.

The first public pass at this was made by Dan Turkenkopf, then writing for the website Beyond the Box Score. Turkenkopf, along with the rest of us—well, maybe not Tim McCarver—was dumbfounded by what he found: the difference between the top-rated catcher and the bottom-rated was 250 runs per 120 games. That difference was so massive, Turkenkopf wrote, "that I have to think there's something wrong in the analysis."

He was right. There was something wrong. But this is how science works, and Turkenkopf and others would just keep working the problem. Eventually, a sort of consensus did emerge: pitch framing is real, and it's fantastically important. Or can be. Turtenkopf placed the value of an "extra" strike at 0.13 runs . . . and over the course of a season, enough 0.13s turn into real runs, and those real runs turn into real wins.

"Once you train yourself to see it," Ben Lindbergh wrote a few years ago in Grantland, "it's almost impossible to stop seeing it. Baseball is often described as a chess match between batter and pitcher. But it's more like a chess match between batter and pitcher in which, once in a while, the catcher grabs the board and moves someone's piece."

We can quibble (and smart folks still do) about the degree, and *will* quibble until the robot umpires arrive, but there really is a big difference between the best pitch framers and the worst. No, not 250 runs difference. More like 25, give or take. But when comparing two players, 25 runs is immense. Twenty-five runs is the difference between a superstar and a fine everyday player, or the difference between a fine everyday player and someone who

---

* Postseason umpire assignments are officially merit based, at least in part, but the "in part" often seems a terribly obvious caveat.

has trouble staying in the lineup, or even in the major leagues at all.*

In other seasons, McCann has been rated as one of the top framers in the majors; these last couple of years, though, not so much. Why wouldn't pitch framing, which might seem an acquired skill the least vulnerable to advancing years, hold steady for many years? Well, there's some evidence that catchers typically suffer a mild but significant decline in their framing talents upon reaching their middle thirties (McCann turned thirty-three last winter). It's also possible that the variables involved—the pitchers involved, the different pitches they throw, the catcher's home ballpark—play hell with the idea of attributing framing runs to catchers.

Except all the careful methods suggest that framing *is* a measurable, repeatable skill. And so as longtime coach and manager John McLaren says, "Everybody's all-in on this deal. I know the Diamondbacks signed Jeff Mathis"—$2 million this season, $2 million next season—"because of his pitch framing." Indeed, there's no other way to explain the continuing employment of Mathis, who's enjoyed a long career in the majors despite being one of the worst hitters in living memory. As longtime catcher (and now Cubs staffer) John Baker says, "Once things have a dollar sign, we're all going to focus on what gives measurable value." And now framing pitches does essentially come with both measurable value and those dollars.

If you believe the numbers, both McCann and Maxwell have *seemed* roughly average this season, in terms of those often pivotal stri-balls.

Fiers seems to have little control over his third pitch, another fastball, this time well outside the strike zone. He does get a borderline call with his fourth pitch, a sinker on the outside edge of

---

* The *Baseball Prospectus* website's version of "framing runs" does suggest that the difference between the best and worst pitch framers might actually be something like fifty runs. This seems an outlier, but does point to the uncertainty that remains, at least among the publicly available metrics.

the zone. It's not clear that this pitch caught more of the plate than his first or second offerings, but umpires have a (probably) subconscious bias *against* deciding the outcomes of plate appearances. In 2016, a study of the previous five seasons demonstrated that the effective strike zone becomes measurably *smaller* when the count is 0 and 2, and measurably *larger* when it's 3 and 0.

As it was here.

But the umpire's (subconscious) generosity finally does Fiers no good, as his fifth pitch, yet another two-seamer, is a few inches outside and Maxwell trots down to first base with a well-earned free pass.

Next up is Chapman, who (like Maxwell, and a million other Oakland Athletics before him) seems content to wait out the pitcher, looking at four straight pitches: two balls, two strikes. Fiers's fifth pitch is a curveball: "12 to 6" as they say, meaning it carves a vertical path as it arcs toward the plate. This one does *not* penetrate the strike zone. It's not supposed to; it's supposed to start high but end low, enticing Chapman to swing over the top, and strike out or dribble a ground ball somewhere. But instead he goes below the zone with the barrel of his bat, and lines a single into left field.

And with that, Fiers's twenty-first pitch, A. J. Hinch has seen plenty and walks to the mound to change pitchers, summoning from the bullpen Luke Gregerson, who presents a fine object lesson in the myth of the Proven Closer™, and perhaps the fungibility of relief pitchers, generally (but that's a story for another inning).

Gregerson's first hitter is Boog Powell, who chops the second pitch he sees over a leaping Gurriel. Altuve corrals the ball at the end of the outfield grass; meanwhile, Powell and Gurriel and Gregerson are all sprinting toward first base. Gurriel and Gregerson both arrive in time to receive Altuve's throw, which beats Powell to the base.*

---

* Powell slides headfirst, by the way, which this time is foolish. It's nearly always foolish, unless your manager's a big fan of eyewash.

But Gurriel, preoccupied with catching the baseball, can only feel around for the base with his foot, and misses. So the bases are loaded for leadoff man Marcus Semien. Just a few minutes ago, the A's seemed practically finished. Now, as Royals broadcaster Fred White used to say all the time, you can dream a little.

Semien falls behind 1 and 2 after his checked swing is ruled an actual swing by the first-base umpire. Semien's skeptical about the call. So is Ray Fosse. "That's a hold up," Fosse says. "That's not a swing." Even Astros broadcaster Geoff Blum says, upon seeing the replay, "That's checking your swing."

For whatever reason, umpires in recent years have become more aggressive about calling strikes on checked swings. Perhaps because hitters swing so aggressively that it's simply become more difficult to tell how *far* they swung. Granted, usually the umpires are right; usually when they rule swing, a reasonable standard has been met. But Semien's got a good beef with this call, in such a critical spot. And Semien must realize he's in the hole now, especially considering he's gone hitless in four career at-bats against Gregerson, striking out three times.

But Gregerson, despite throwing as hard as ever this season, just hasn't had the same *stuff*. At least if you believe the numbers, which show his slider as a below-average pitch in 2017, and his fastball just fair. Gregerson's 1-and-2 fastball is an inch or three outside; at just 90 miles an hour, it doesn't fool Semien.

For Gregerson's next offering, McCann calls a slider and sets up behind the outer half of the plate; they want Semien to chase a bad pitch, just as right-handed batters have been doing for most of Gregerson's career.

But Gregerson misses his spot. Misses badly.

There's long been a myth floating around that major-league pitchers are nearly perfect; that they routinely throw the ball almost exactly where they want to throw it.

Did I mention that's a myth? Major-league pitchers are probably better than any *other* pitchers at hitting their targets . . . and still they miss all the time. Sometimes when a pitcher will seem to have pitched a really good game except maybe for giving up a decisive home run, after the game he'll say, "Well, I just made one mistake, and he hit it." Usually he made a few mistakes and got away with all but one of them. Because the hitters aren't perfect either. Most "mistake" pitches don't get walloped over the fence, and most of them probably aren't even hit hard. This time, Gregerson's not so lucky.

Typically, when a pitcher's trying to throw a slider away from the hitter, he misses *farther* away. Not this time! This time, Gregerson's slider loops right through the middle of the strike zone, and Semien wallops the ball into the left-field stands, 358 feet away for a game-tying grand slam. The A's now have seven runs, and all seven have come on home runs. That's Oakland Athletics baseball, circa 2017.

Rattled or not, Gregerson falls behind Joyce 2 and 0, both pitches well low. This forces Gregerson to serve up a hit-me fastball, and Joyce obliges with a screamer to deep center that Springer is just able to snag with a leap at the warning track.

With an exit velocity of 105.9 miles per hour, it's actually the A's hardest-hit ball of the entire game. By contrast, Semien's grand slam was just 95.7 miles an hour, the A's fourteenth-hardest. Exit velocity's a big deal. Obviously. But where you hit the ball is a big deal too. Obviously.

With his thirteenth pitch, Gregerson retires Lowrie on a relatively weak liner to center field, and finishes the inning when Khris Davis grounds out to shortstop. Still, everything is different now.

Score: Astros 7, Athletics 7
Win Probability: Even!

Visitors Eighth

Everything takes time. Bees have to move very fast to stay still.

—DAVID FOSTER WALLACE (1962–2008)

Now pitching in this (somewhat shockingly) tie game for the A's: lefty Danny Coulombe, who's notable for a couple of reasons. One, he's listed at just five feet ten (for which I can vouch, having stood right next to him). And two, he throws a bunch of different pitches. There have been some outstanding relief pitchers who threw three or four distinct offerings; Doug Jones and Jeff Montgomery, who starred in the 1980s and '90s, come to mind. But these days more than ever, the great majority of relievers enter the game throwing heat, plus one. Might be a slider or curveball or changeup, but usually it's just one. Or it might *just* be the fastball, like Mariano Rivera and now Kenley Jansen, with their cutters.

Coulombe, though, complements his low-90s fastballs—two- and four-seamers—with nearly equal amounts of curveballs and sliders. In fact, Coulombe will throw his curves and sliders roughly 70 percent of the time this season, and nobody else in the majors will come remotely close to that figure. He's just a completely different sort of cat.

"Yeah, I have four pitches," he says. "So I like to look at the scouting reports, like to know who's better against the slider, the curveball. So I know, when in doubt, I can go to this breaking ball."

Coulombe owes his slider to Scott Radinsky, his Triple-A pitching coach in the Dodgers organization (as well as the singer in some pretty good punk bands, including Pulley, who opened for Green Day on one tour). One of baseball's top lefty relievers in the 1990s with the White Sox and Dodgers, Radinsky told Coulombe, "Hey, if you wanna make it to the next level, you need a slider. What hitters are seeing is your curveball, with a hump, and your fastball, straight. You need something that's straight *and* moves."

So Coulombe picked up the slider. Almost exactly two years ago, the Dodgers needed to clear a space on their forty-man roster, and sold Coulombe's contract to the A's (the figures involved in these deals are never public these days, but in this case it was probably in the low six figures, at most, which turned out to be a real bargain).

After splitting last season between Oakland's Triple-A team and the big club, he's spent all of this season with the A's. Bob Melvin's only lefty reliever for much of this season, Coulombe has especially thrived against left-handed hitters. It's a tough way to make a living, because a few bad outings can ruin your earned run average for months. But there are never enough lefties, and if Coulombe stays healthy he should enjoy a long career. Even if he has to bounce around every year or two.

Being a lefty doesn't help against the Astros' leadoff man, though, because switch-hitter Marwin Gonzalez has historically hit lefties and righties equally well (or not well, before this season).

Back in the third inning, Gonzalez also batted with the bases empty, and the average amount of time between the six pitches he saw was twenty-four seconds. Which is notable because Gonzalez is literally the Pokiest Player in the Major Leagues.

Those twenty-four seconds per pitch in the third inning weren't anything special. But Gonzalez makes up for that now, in the eighth. Between the first five pitches he sees from the A's new pitcher, Gonzalez averages twenty-nine seconds, right in line with his MLB-slowest season's average. But after the fifth pitch, a curve in the dirt that bounces away from Maxwell, Gonzalez really out-does himself: forty-seven seconds until the sixth pitch.

Forty-seven!

So how do you kill forty-seven seconds?

Well, first you take a few steps away from the plate, and casually knock some imaginary mud from your shoes. Then you step back into the batter's box, but pull back your front foot and knead your bat's handle, give your helmet a slight adjustment, finally go into your stance . . . and call time-out when the pitcher takes too long to read the catcher's signs. Pull that front foot back again, knead the bat again, spit something yucky to the ground, adjust the helmet again, and finally step fully into the box and assume your stance.

"They may put a clock on the hitter," Ray Fosse jokes, up in the booth, "just for him next year."

There's a long tradition of hitters fooling around before finally settling into the batter's box—forty years ago there was Mike "Human Rain Delay" Hargrove, twenty years ago there was Nomar Garciaparra, and they were hardly alone—but the problem is that Gonzalez barely even stands out, because so many of his colleagues are nearly as slow.

After all that, finally Gonzalez slaps a grounder toward right field. But Jed Lowrie, with a dive that carries him to the outfield grass, snares the ball, springs to his feet, and throws to first base. After striding through the bag, Gonzalez throws out both of his hands in a *safe* call, but at the same time first-base umpire D. J. Reyburn is emphatically calling him out.

With the naked eye, it looks like Gonzalez might have a pretty good case. With the naked eye, we might expect to see the first official appeal in this game. But we don't, because the first instant replay makes it obvious that Gonzalez's left foot tromped on the base just a few milliseconds *after* the ball arrived in Matt Olson's big mitt.

Major League Baseball was actually the last of the four major sports to inject video review into the officiating process. And even then, Baseball hardly embraced the idea. From late in the 2008 season—oddly, the parties just couldn't hold off until the following spring, probably because everybody was worried about being embarrassed during the postseason—through 2013, review was permitted only for "boundary calls"; basically, home run or no home run. During that span, there were 387 reviews, with roughly a third of the initial calls reversed.

Also during that span, there were some stunningly bad calls, embarrassing calls, made on nonboundary plays. In 2010, first-base umpire Jim Joyce blew a call at first base that cost Detroit's Armando Galarraga a perfect game. The previous October in the American League Championship Series, veteran umpire Tim McClelland somehow didn't notice that a runner had been tagged out while standing *right in front of him*. And there were numerous other egregious decisions during postseason series in those years.

With so many cameras and so many angles and so much broadcast technology, it finally became indefensible for everyone in the world to know almost exactly what happened on the field . . . *except* for the men whose sole job was to know almost exactly what happened on the field.

Everything finally changed in 2014. Since then, managers can challenge everything.

Well, almost everything. Perhaps most notably, they can't challenge fair/foul when it's a question of where a ground ball passed from fair ground into foul ground (this situation will actually come up later in this game). They also can't challenge check-swing calls. In both instances, it's probably true that (a) umpires miss a significant percentage of the close ones, and (b) replay probably wouldn't help much, except in the few stadiums where it's possible to place a camera directly overhead.*

---

* Technically, that's not really true. It wouldn't be terribly difficult to rig technology that would precisely track the baseball's path, relative to first and third base. It also wouldn't be terribly difficult to devise a reasonably precise definition of

Essentially, here's how the system works:

1. Close call, usually on the bases.
2. Manager indicates he's *considering* an appeal.
3. Team staffer locked away in a small room quickly looks at available replay, calls the dugout with recommendation.

If the manager does challenge the call, the crew chief gets on the phone with Replay Central in Manhattan, where a team of officials, including actual umpires, can watch all the available video in super-slow motion on tremendous screens. Upon making their judgment, someone in New York relays the decision to the crew chief, who then tells the rest of us. The whole process isn't supposed to take more than ninety seconds, but the average is closer to two minutes.

Is two minutes too long? "Time is precious," Benjamin Disraeli wrote, "but truth is more precious than time." And when looking for explanations for Baseball's ever-longer games and ever-slowing pace, video review actually falls somewhere near the bottom of the list. This season, there will ultimately be 1,422 reviews in 2,430 games. So, roughly half the games don't even *have* a review (figuring many games have more than one). Sure, you can tack on a few seconds for all those times the game is held up for a few extra seconds while everyone waits to see if there will *be* a review. On the other hand, reviews obviate a fair number of manager-umpire kerfuffles, and those usually killed a lot more than two minutes!

You might argue that arguments actually made the games a bit more fun, along with a bit longer. I would probably agree with you; there was always a certain joy in seeing Earl Weaver kick dirt on an umpire's pants, or Lou Piniella tossing second base into the

---

a swing, and then connect that definition to some off-the-shelf technology. But none of this seems to be on anyone's agenda.

outfield. But we're talking about time, and pace, and there's just no reason to worry much about the effects of video review on time and pace.

There are *some* new stories in baseball. Using an Apple Watch to relay stolen signs, as the Red Sox did against the Yankees earlier this season? That's a new one. Getting fired because of racially charged social-media posts? That's a new one. Granted, even those stories are essentially just modern variations on old, even ancient ones. But there is at least a meaningful veneer of modernity about them. Most stories don't even have that, once you scratch lightly. Infield shifting? That's so nineteenth century. Games taking too long? Too-long games were considered a scourge a century ago. Not to mention nearly every year since then. In 1915, when the average game didn't last even two hours, Federal League president James Gilmore complained, "Something must be done to speed up play, as the public does not like to see unnecessary wrangling on the field and a slow, dragging game."

In 1984, the average major-league game lasted around two and a half hours. In 2017, it's more than three hours.* As recently as 2010, the average game lasted just two hours and fifty minutes, roughly in line with 2006 through '11. But in 2014 the games averaged more than three hours for the first time. And after a downtick in 2015, due to some half-hearted, grudgingly accepted time-saving measures . . . well, here we are. A new record in 2017. (Yay?)

But all this means is that the doomsayers were wrong, and have been wrong for a long time. As doomsayers usually are. Professional football and basketball didn't kill baseball. Youth soccer and video games didn't kill baseball. Television didn't kill baseball. Ever-

---

* The precise figures: 2:35 in 1984, and 3:05 this year. Figures are for nine-inning games. Including extra-inning games pushes the average by four or five minutes. (Extra-inning games aren't as common as you might guess, and most of them end pretty quickly.)

slower and ever-longer games haven't killed baseball. Baseball, it seems, might actually be unkillable.

But as popular and profitable as baseball is, couldn't it be *more* profitable and popular? Of course it could be. There's a reasonable argument to be made that baseball would be somewhat more popular and profitable if the games were 5 percent shorter, 10 percent quicker.

Okay, maybe not more profitable. There's a lot of money in all those commercial breaks during pitching changes. So, a Fair Question: Enough money to make up for all the viewers who tuned out because it didn't seem like anything was happening?

I don't know. Nobody knows. Surveys wouldn't really tell you a whole lot. What you would need is plenty of experimentation, and Baseball seems almost allergic to experiments. But the notion that surveys will guide baseball toward popularity is a chimera. As the author Mo Willems has observed, "You don't give people what they want. You give them what they don't yet know they want."

Even if you don't believe that the length and pace of today's games don't cost Baseball *some* fans—and particularly the young fans the business supposedly craves—don't you still have to believe there's *some* limit to how many hours the fans, or potential fans in the future, will tolerate?

What about three hours and twenty minutes? Three hours and thirty? More? You give the players and coaches and manager a minute here and another minute there, because you figure hey, what can it hurt? But those minutes keep piling up and then one day you wake up and realize you've got a problem. And especially in the postseason, when the players (and the commercials) really slow down the action, at the exact moment when the most prospective fans are watching. The value of baseball as a sort of pastoral anachronism is real, but perhaps more so in June when you're at the ballpark, and less so in October when the games don't begin until well after eight in the evening on the East Coast and you're watching on television and they're still playing at midnight.

Earlier this year, SB Nation's Grant Brisbee compared a 1984 game to a 2014 game, minute by minute. And while the commercial breaks were significantly shorter in 1984, the *playing breaks* were not. Often, the broadcast would come back from commercials well before everyone was ready to start playing again. Which was nice if you were a fan of Harry Caray or whomever, but didn't make the game itself go any quicker. Grant found that longer commercial breaks added around ten minutes to the 2014 game, which is a relatively small bit of the overall increase.

The biggest reasons for longer games and slower pace are more mid-inning pitching changes, and more pitchers and hitters farting around when they could be, you know, pitching and hitting. And among the hitters, among *all* the hitters, Marwin Gonzalez is your poster boy for farting around.

Carlos Beltrán's next. Like Gonzalez, Beltrán's a switch-hitter who's been equally effective, over the course of his career, from both sides of the plate. So again, no edge for Coulombe. Except for the fact that Beltrán, at forty, isn't nearly the hitter he once was. And to cap his fourth fruitless at-bat of the game, Beltrán chops a low curveball to shortstop Semien, who makes a pinpoint throw to first base for the out.

Which brings up McCann with nobody aboard. Finally a lefty hitter for Coulombe. So of course McCann, after barely checking his swing to gain a full count, then fouling off a low curveball to stay alive, drives a hanging curveball into center field for a single.

Exit, Danny Coulombe. Enter: Liam Hendriks, to face Cameron Maybin.

Also, exit Brian McCann. Enter: Jake Marisnick, pinch-running for McCann.

This is the obvious move by A. J. Hinch, as Marisnick's one of the two fastest Astros—probably just a tick slower than rookie Derek Fisher, according to Statcast—while McCann ranks among the very slowest players in all the major leagues. With three other catchers on the expanded September roster, there's no good rea-son *not* to pinch-run for him.[*]

With Marisnick aboard in a tie game, we're treated to a small chess game that you can follow even from the cheap seats. "I've come up against him a lot," Hendriks will later say of Marisnick. "I know that he runs well, and he runs a lot off *me*."[†]

Before throwing a pitch to Maybin, Hendriks pivots for a pick-off throw to first base. Once, twice, three times. Marisnick dives back safely once, twice, three times. But is that enough?

"If I go over once," Hendriks says, "it is what it is. If I go over twice or a third time, he might be leaning the wrong way. But as soon as I get into pitch mode, he's probably going. He's always a threat, and generally if you bring in a pinch-runner, he's going."

When Hendriks finally throws toward the plate—a fastball down the middle for a called strike—Marisnick does *not* go. He does alight for second on the next pitch, another fat fastball, and this time Maybin swings. But he makes just a bit of contact, with the ball caroming straight into catcher Bruce Maxwell's mask.

Maxwell immediately bends over but doesn't fall to his knees,

---

[*] This report on McCann's "speed" isn't just an opinion. We know he's one of the slowest men in the majors, without a shred of doubt. According to Statcast, the average MLB "sprint speed" is 27 feet per second. McCann's at just 23 feet per second. Now you might be thinking sure, but all catchers are slow. Almost all, yes. But there's been just one catcher (Wilson Ramos) this season *slower* than McCann. In fact, only three major leaguers have been slower: Ramos, plus creaky old designated hitters Albert Pujols and Victor Martinez. In related news, I'll bet there are a few players who don't exactly adore Statcast.

[†] Hendriks will finish this season having given up forty-five stolen bases in his career, with eight runners out trying and a couple picked off base. Overall, the MLB success rate for runners (not including pickoffs) is annually around 70 per-cent. But the great majority of righty relievers like Hendriks aren't much good at holding runners.

instead steadying himself with his glove on the ground before removing his helmet and blinking hard a few times.

"Another direct hit," Fosse says, with the benefit of experience. "He was coming up to throw, with Marisnick on the move and, wow. That ball was *crushed* off his mask."

Not so long ago, Maxwell probably would have just looked toward the dugout, shouted *I'm okay!* and everyone would have continued along in their various merry ways. But no more. Today, and since Opening Day in 2011, there's been a concussion protocol in place for such situations. So the trainer jogs over, and checks Maxwell out.

Granted, there was always a de facto protocol: *Hey buddy, can ya stand up? Can you run around without getting terribly dizzy? Can you see at least one of those baseballs well enough to catch it? Go get 'em, champ! You're in the lineup today!*

There is no sort of real accounting of how many baseball careers have been railroaded, or just plumb destroyed, by concussions and various other brain trauma. Let alone by the lack of attention to them.

On the twenty-eighth of August in 1978, Red Sox outfielder Dwight Evans got beaned by Seattle rookie Mike Parrott; Evans's batting helmet got smashed, and he had to leave the game.

Evans had been beaned before. That was in late August 1973, when Evans was a rookie. Less than forty-eight hours later, having flown to catch up with the Red Sox in Anaheim, he showed up in the locker room and his manager said, "Can you play?" Evans played. The next night, he was in the lineup against Nolan Ryan. After rejoining the club in Anaheim, Evans batted .196 the rest of the season.

Five years later, Evans got back into the lineup five days after Parrott beaned him, and was in the lineup almost every day for the next few weeks. And he was just awful, both in the field and at the plate. Evans recalls telling his manager that when he looked up, he saw five baseballs, and his manager saying, "Just catch the one in the middle."

Not coincidentally, September '78 was when the Red Sox blew their huge lead over the Yankees, ultimately losing the division title in a one-game playoff. Oh, and Evans's manager in '78? Don Zimmer, who himself had been badly beaned during his playing career.*

But that's just the way it used to be. And not just in 1978.

In 2006, Brewers third baseman Corey Koskie suffered a concussion that ended his career *and* left him in bad shape for a while afterward. "It was two and a half years of my own personal hell," Koskie later said.

In 2008, Mets outfielder Ryan Church suffered a concussion during spring training, and then another in May. The second concussion knocked Church out of the starting lineup, but forty-eight hours later he joined his team on a flight to Denver. Church would finally be sidelined for a few days, and later land on the disabled list twice with concussion-related symptoms. He never really recovered.

In 2010, Jason Bay—another Mets outfielder—ran into a wall while making a great catch at Dodger Stadium. He finished the game, but a headache was later diagnosed as a concussion, and Bay was sidelined for the last two months of the season; later he would describe his symptoms as "scary." He did return to the lineup in 2011, but struggled that season and his career cratered within two years. At thirty-four, just four years after drawing MVP support with a big season for the Red Sox, Bay's career was over.

Also in 2010, Twins first baseman Justin Morneau was having a tremendous first half of the season. But while running the bases on July 7, he suffered a concussion when struck by an infielder's knee. Morneau did not come back quickly, as Evans had; in fact he missed the rest of that season.

---

* Zimmer's propensity for getting beaned actually became a big part of his story . . . a *funny* part of his story, if not quite as funny these days.

But Morneau did come back in 2011. Suffering a variety of injuries—and yes, perhaps the lingering effects of that concussion—Morneau played in only sixty-nine games and (as he told Peter Gammons six years later) "had more operations than homers."

All those other injuries might well have happened without the concussion. One thing we know: in his twenties, before he was concussed, Morneau batted .286 with 181 home runs in 948 games. In his thirties, after he was concussed, Morneau batted .275 with 66 home runs in 597 games. He had half a great career, and then he had something quite different.*

There are worse stories.

Ryan Freel was a super-utilityman who played in parts of eight seasons in the majors, mostly with Cincinnati. He last played in 2010, having suffered, by his count, "nine or ten concussions." In 2012, he committed suicide. A year later, a postmortem determined that he'd suffered from Stage 2 chronic traumatic encephalopathy (CTE), making him the first ex–major leaguer to receive that posthumous diagnosis.

In football, there are worse stories still.

But in Baseball, strides have been made. Sure, it would be naive to think the people who run Baseball are *better* than the people who run football. What's more likely: Baseball had (and has) far less to lose from the acknowledgment of the concussion issue. For the simple reason that baseball was not designed as a contact sport; a baseball player might reasonably expect to play an entire career without being concussed more than once or twice. At least if he's not a catcher. And football? Well, you know. If you're not rattling the other guy's brain, you're doing it wrong.

---

* Morneau's late-career numbers benefited greatly from a couple of seasons with the Rockies; in 2014, his last full season, Morneau actually won the National League batting title.

That said, it is the catchers who bear the largest risk. In 2017, the 7-day concussion disabled list—created in 2011—will be used by eleven players, and seven will be catchers (including Francisco Cervelli twice). Overall, there will be nineteen concussions leading to DL stints, 7-day and otherwise, and thirteen of those will involve catchers. In fact, Bruce Maxwell was promoted from the minors back in May to replace catcher Josh Phegley . . . who himself spent about a week on the DL, recovering from a concussion. And just last month, Astros catcher Evan Gattis went on the 7-day concussion DL with a *mild* concussion . . . except plenty of people who care about such things have little patience with the word *mild* when it comes to concussions, and in fact Gattis was out of action not for a week, but for three weeks.

The great majority of the time, catchers are concussed when a foul ball hits them squarely in the mask. As a result, there are now great efforts to create (and market!) masks that prevent, or at lessen the chance of, concussions.

Bruce Maxwell wears a lightweight mask made by All-Star Sporting Goods. "Not getting concussions is part of our job," Maxwell tells me next spring. "Our biggest thing is about being safe back there, and using gear that's light, and at the same time protects us from the majority of the impacts that we do receive back there. So I've done my research, I've thought about it, and I'm really close with the guys at All-Star. They tell me how the testing went, they tell me the differences between their masks and other masks. I mean, I pay attention to stuff like that."

But these days there's another, heavier, truly innovative option. More and more catchers are sporting the Force3 Defender mask, manufactured by a company that's drawn financial investments from two major leaguers, Tyler Flowers and Yasmani Grandal. From the front, the Defender looks like the traditional sort of mask; which is to say, not like the hockey goalie–style masks that have been in vogue for some years now. From the side, though, if you look closely you can spot stainless-steel springs that separate the outer, padded wire cage and the inner cage that rests against the usual brimless helmet.

Flowers was the first in the majors to wear the helmet, last year. This season, Grandal switched to the Defender. They're not alone, but *officially* it's difficult to track down Defender users. Why? Typically when a catcher signs an endorsement deal, it's for *all* his gear: shin guards, chest protector, and mask. Which is probably why Brian McCann, who endorses Under Armour gear, told me he really likes his spring-loaded mask, but "I don't know anything other than that." (He might not know much about the technology, but he must know who makes it.)

"At the end of the day," Maxwell says, "it's just like football helmets. You could make the safest football helmet, and just the impact of two large humans colliding, you're still going to have concussions, still going to have head injuries. So I think it's more of a personal preference kind of thing."

Or as Gattis puts it, "Some hits, I just think you're gonna be concussed. Like me last year, was a Corey Dickerson backswing. It was serious stuff. I'm sure I'd had a concussion at some point in my life, but nothing like that."

Unless the technology's truly a game changer, we shouldn't be surprised if Catchers of the Future simply won't be expected to play more than 120-some games per season, or last for as many years as they used to. And much the same might be said about umpires. Remember Dale Scott, the first (and so far, only) publicly gay umpire in the majors? In his fifth game last spring, he took a foul ball off the mask and suffered his fourth concussion in five years, and second in nine months. "There's no doubt in my mind," he told me, "that early in my career, there were games I shouldn't have finished."

And so that fifth game in 2017—the 3,897th regular-season game in his long career—would be his last, although Scott didn't officially retire until after the season. "I figured I'd been playing on house money," he says, "so now I'm going to walk away."

For great-hitting catchers like Joe Mauer and Buster Posey, there's the option of occasionally playing other positions in the short term (as both have), and making the transition completely in the long term (as Mauer has, semisuccessfully).

There aren't many Mauers and Poseys. *Most* catchers are in the majors not because they can hit, but because they can catch and throw. That's actually a term. When a catcher can't hit much—which again, is most of them—scouts will call him a "catch-and-throw guy."

If Bruce Maxwell can't catch, Bruce Maxwell can't play.

Which means that if some solution isn't found, future catchers simply won't play as much. Will the union do something extra for those guys? Maybe with a pension that's got a more aggressive vesting schedule for catchers?

And that's to say nothing about kids. While concussions might lead to parents pushing their kids away from football and toward baseball, might the same impulse also lead to parents pushing their kids away from catching? Do you want *your* kid taking repeated blows to the head? And if youth leagues introduce a version of MLB's concussion protocol, who will be qualified to administer it? Will we reach a point where literally every youth sports competition is legally required to have a certified sports trainer on hand? If the solution is high-tech helmets, who's going to pay for them?

Most of these questions mean little to Baseball now, even if, as Dale Scott says, "Baseball is very forward thinking on concussions." Maybe even little in the long term, as the Dominican Republic and Venezuela and Cuba will no doubt continue producing top-flight catchers for as many years as you care to project. Still, how do you play a Little League game without a catcher? "You have to have a catcher," Casey Stengel remarked, "because if you don't you're likely to have a lot of passed balls."

On the field, Maxwell "passes" the protocol administered by the A's trainer, and reassumes his position.*

On a 2-2 pitch, Marisnick takes off again, swiping second easily. But while Hendriks doesn't throw particularly hard—not by Postmodern standards, as he'll be the first to admit—he does say, "When I know I have a little bit of life with my fastball, I can attack with that." Here, he attacks: another four-seam fastball, "only" 93 but enough to fool Maybin, who takes a big cut for the inning-ending strikeout. He turns to ask umpire Sam Holbrook if the pitch was in the strike zone (it was, but close enough to the edge that we can't know what Holbrook thought).

Score: Astros 7, Athletics 7
Win Probability: A's 61%

---

* But later this month, he'll be forced from a game after taking another foul ball squarely in the mask. Despite an early prognosis of *no concussion*, Maxwell will miss three games, returning to the A's lineup on the twenty-fifth. Two days earlier, while still convalescing, Maxwell had become the first major leaguer to kneel during the national anthem. None of his teammates join him, but a few will publicly express support. Afterward, A's outfielder Mark Canha says, "Every fiber in my being was telling me that he needed a brother today.. . . . I'm going to be there with Bruce every day." He'll also be the only one to kneel in 2017. And will join every other major leaguer in early 2018, standing for the Anthem before every game. So you can't tell the world you're gay, or smoke pot, or engage in a mild form of civic protest. Not in 2017, and probably not in 2018 either.

Home Eighth

My father once told me the harder you throw it, the less time you have to duck.

—DOUG JONES (B. 1957)

Now it's Joe Musgrove's turn to pitch, and his job is simple: preserve this 7–7 tie. Brent Strom's scouting report on Musgrove: "Premier strike-thrower, almost throws too many strikes. If you can throw good strikes, you can throw good balls." Might "too many strikes" help explain his struggles as a starter, earlier this season? It might. But his future remains bright, considering his track record and his powerful right arm.

Including Musgrove, here are the *average* fastball speeds this season for all the relievers we've seen in this game, so far:

97	Michael Feliz
91	Tony Sipp
96	Raul Alcántara
90	Mike Fiers
90	Luke Gregerson
91	Danny Coulombe
95	Liam Hendriks
94	Joe Musgrove

Those numbers understate Fiers's and Musgrove's *relief* fast-balls, as both spent most of the season as starters and (because they had to pace themselves) didn't throw quite as hard in that role. Since moving to the bullpen in late July, Musgrove's averaged more than 95 on his fastball.

And so here we see again, quite clearly, the pitching side of the power/power equation. "Now," longtime Rockies general manager Dan O'Dowd says, "kids of the last two generations have morphed: 'I'm going to get paid based on how hard I can throw.' And there is a science behind how to do that." When Dan Okrent was working on *Nine Innings* back in the early 1980s, you were considered exceptional, or at least above average, if you threw 90. No more. Today, if your fastball sits around 90, you need something else impressive, whether Coulombe's twin breaking balls or Gregerson's (once) baffling slider.

Oh, and by the way? We've not yet seen these teams' hardest-throwing pitchers. A's closer Blake Treinen and Astros closer Ken Giles are both among the seventeen major-league relievers who will throw at least fifty innings this season and average at least 97 miles an hour with their fastballs.

How many relievers did the same ten years ago?

None. No relievers did that. In 2007, the hardest-throwing relief pitcher was Marlins setup man Matt Lindstrom, at 98.7 miles an hour. Twenty-seven relief pitchers threw at least fifty innings and averaged at least 95 miles an hour.

This season, *sixty-nine* pitchers will do that. And most of them, a reasonably well-informed fan couldn't pick out of a lineup. Even if they were wearing their uniforms. And spotted you their initials. Yes, the world's greatest hitters have adjusted, but . . . well, you know. There's only so much they can do.

Matt Olson leads off against Musgrove. After two quick mid-90s strikes, and (as usual) conceding nothing, Olson smashes a 94-mile-an-hour fastball . . . right into the teeth of the Astros' infield shift; well into the outfield grass, Altuve gathers up the hard "grounder"—

it's actually a line drive that first touches earth a hundred feet from the plate, and at 105.5 miles an hour, it's got the fifth-hardest exit velocity of the entire game—and easily retires Olson at first base. As Ken Korach says, up in the booth, "That's baseball in two thousand seventeen: normally a base hit, well before all the shifting."

Musgrove's a large man, listed at six feet five and 268 pounds. He carries that 268 well. And while 268 is obviously big, it's not *exceptionally* big. Not in 2017. This season, there are probably a dozen or so pitchers with bigger listed weights. And six feet five? Hell, these days six feet five is nothing. There are sixty-four major-league pitchers listed at six feet five, and another fifty-six pitchers even bigger. Now, being six feet five doesn't mean you'll throw 95. It sure helps, though. *Give me a lever, and I'll move the loins of a scout.* Musgrove actually throws 98, at least when he's working out of the bullpen. Which makes his 12-to-6 curveball, just 82 miles an hour, look even better. Or worse, if you're a hitter.

Let's get this out of the way, though: you don't have to dunk a basketball to throw 95, and you also don't have to look like the Incredible Hulk to hit home runs.

Granted, it's not that big hitters don't have a power advantage. It's not that, at all.

From 2015 through the end of this season, 214 batted balls will be recorded with exit velocities of at least 115 miles an hour. Bizarrely, only two players will account for 90 of them: 42 percent from just Giancarlo Stanton and Aaron Judge (and most of Judge's are just in 2017, as he hardly played before). Three teams—the Phillies, the Indians, and the Reds—will combine for zero 115+ exit velocities in those three seasons.

Six teams show up on the list just once. Including the A's, with Khris Davis generating a 116 reading last year. Again: just once.

And the Astros? They've got five: three from Springer (six feet three), two from Correa (six feet four) . . . and none from (as an Astros staffer once called Altuve) *the midget who can hit.*

Like the Indians, the Astros have scored plenty of runs. Turns out that scary, otherworldly, look-what-one-of-these-big-soft-machines-really-can-do exit velocity is one hell of a nice-to-have, but it's hardly a must.

We don't have exit velocities for Hank Aaron, who hit 755 home runs, or for Willie Mays, who hit 660. We do have their listed heights: six feet and five feet ten. Aaron and Mays didn't often hit them far; they simply hit them, without a great deal of apparent effort, far enough.

And this is where I'm obligated to mention, at least in passing, that in 2017, when Judge and Stanton will combine for 111 home runs, they'll also combine for 371 strikeouts. And that in 1963, when Aaron and Mays combined for 82 home runs, they also combined for 177 strikeouts.

One of the most delightful things about baseball is its inherent tolerance for players with dramatically different bodies. This summer, we were blessed with a photo of the American League's two best Most Valuable Player candidates standing next to each other: six-feet-seven Aaron Judge and (let's be honest) five-feet-five Jose Altuve. For a few years back in the 1990s, the two best pitchers in the league were (almost) seven-footer Randy Johnson and (almost) six-footer Pedro Martinez. Both of them proving you don't have to be built like Roger Clemens—all six feet four and 220 pounds of perfection, give or take—to punch your ticket to Cooperstown.[*]

It helps, though. Granted, you always have to take the official heights with a grain of salt, because today's players routinely fudge their measurements when they think it'll help their chances of getting drafted or signed. Just as players in the old days—and I'm talking about U.S.-born players, through the 1940s and beyond—*routinely* shaved a year or two (or three!) from their ages. (As far as I know, the last U.S.-born player to carry out the charade for long

---

[*] No, Clemens is not in the Hall of Fame. He will be.

was Hal McRae, who debuted as a major leaguer in 1968 with the Reds, and finally in 1986, his last full season, admitted to turning forty rather than thirty-nine.)

Of course, the whole thing became a scandal not when all the stars of the olden days were doing it, but in the 1990s when we found out huge numbers of Dominican-born players were shaving years from their ages. For the same reason U.S.-born players used to do it: to get signed, and get more money when they signed.

These days, nearly every player in the majors is exactly how old he says he is. But the same isn't true of heights. Or for that matter, weights.

Many players' "listed" weights—that is, the weight that's published in media guides and record books and on Baseball-Reference.com—is a relic of their younger days, perhaps even from when they signed their first professional contract, as a teenager or right out of college. Even if the official weight is changed by the team, it's not always changed in the database for the rest of us. Because that would be complicated. The encyclopedias—nearly all of which are now just on the internet, of course—have chosen to associate just one weight with each player, which is defensible from a design standpoint, but often wildly misleading.

Officially, Roger Clemens is "listed" at 205 pounds. But that was Clemens in 1984, when he joined the Red Sox as a fresh-faced rookie. Twenty-three years later, when he bowed out of the majors with the Yankees, he was listed at 235. And one might guess that was generous by a few pounds. At least. Twenty-three years is a long time.

And then there's Bartolo Colón, listed at six feet even and 185 pounds when he debuted in 1997. Twenty years later, he's still pitching in the majors. At (officially) five feet eleven and 285 pounds, with (unofficially) the nickname Big Sexy.

As I said, in baseball there's still room for all sorts of fellows. But if you're going back and trying to use historical weights to study something, you're dealing with a huge amount of systemic

inaccuracy and uncertainty, simply because players' weights fluc-
tuate so wildly. Especially players with long careers.*

Heights, on the other hand, don't change much at all. Even over
the course of a twenty-year career. Which would make the data on
heights really easy to use . . . except so many listed heights are lies.
Especially when it comes to (relatively) short pitchers, and *especially*
when it comes to (relatively) short *right-handed* pitchers.

What does this mean in the real world? Every pitcher wants his
height to start with a six. If he's really five feet eleven in his socks,
he's going to be six feet in his shoes. And in the official listings.
If he's really five feet ten? Same thing. I'm six feet tall. Maybe
six feet one in my shoes. I've stood next to various major-league
pitchers listed as five feet eleven or six feet even, and I had two or
three inches on them. And if a pitcher, particularly a right-handed
pitcher, is really only five feet eight or five feet nine? Tack on a
couple of inches and *hope* somebody will still give you a shot, even
without the six in front.

With all that said, the tendencies and inducements to/for lying
about heights, and the natural fluctuations in weight, have generally been the same over the years. Which means we *can* study the
trends with some precision and have some confidence in our con-
clusions. And in fact the conclusion is inescapable: baseball players
are bigger than they've ever been, and getting bigger all the time.

In 1948, Cincinnati's Virgil Stallcup and the Cubs' Roy Smalley
became the first six-feet-three everyday shortstops—and by default
the tallest ever—in major-league history.

In 1957, young Tony Kubek joined the Yankees, and manager
Casey Stengel, always looking for an edge, used Kubek as a super-
utilityman. But in '58, the six-feet-three Kubek became the Yankees'
regular shortstop, a job he would hold, for the most part anyway,
until retiring after the '65 season. In 1960, six-feet-three Orioles

---

* Also, Barry Bonds.

rookie Ron Hansen hit twenty-two home runs, started 149 games at shortstop, and finished fifth in MVP balloting.[*]

Hansen was a legitimately great player, Hall of Fame–level talent. But he was wildly inconsistent, just couldn't stay healthy. His last stint as an everyday shortstop came in 1968, and ended when the Senators traded him to the White Sox. And in terms of "big" shortstops, that's where things stood until July 1, 1982. That was the day when Orioles manager Earl Weaver made Cal Ripken, all seventy-six inches of him, the first six-four everyday shortstop ever, after the organization had essentially been committed for years to the idea that Ripken was more suited to third base, simply too big to make the plays at shortstop. All he would do is hold the job for another fourteen seasons. *Really* hold the job.

In the wake of Junior Ripken, there would be other big shortstops. Not six-feet-four Ripken big, but six-feet-three Hansen big, as the next twenty years brought Derek Jeter, Bobby Crosby, Troy Tulowitzki, Ian Desmond, Didi Gregorius, and Jordy Mercer to the majors, and at least occasional stardom for most of them. Beginning with Jeter in 1995, there were more six-feet-three shortstops over the next twenty years than there'd been in the previous—well, ever. In the previous forever.

In 2015, things *really* got interesting. In the American League, six-feet-four (215-pounds) Carlos Correa showed up, and showed well enough to win the Rookie of the Year Award. In the National League, six-four (220-pound) Corey Seager showed up in September with the Dodgers; in 2016, Seager would also win a Rookie of the Year Award. Basically, in roughly a century there was one Cal Ripken. Then there were two, in one year. Both of them fantastic hitters who could also make all the plays at shortstop.

---

[*] The only four ahead of Hansen: superstars Roger Maris, Mickey Mantle, Brooks Robinson, and Minnie Miñoso. On the other hand, the four behind Hansen were non-superstars Al Smith, Roy Sievers, Earl Battey, and Moose Skowron.

That's a tiny number of data points. So let's consider pitchers. In 1967, there were twenty-one major-league pitchers who stood at least six feet four and threw at least a hundred innings; in 2017, there will be fifty-five of these beasts.

Yes, there are a lot more teams now: thirty, compared to just twenty in '67. So here's another way of looking at the growth of big-league pitchers. In '67, 17 percent of all the pitchers in the majors were six feet four or bigger. This year, *30 percent* are that big. There will be 222 pitchers in the majors this season—roughly speaking, seven or eight per team—who are as tall as Cal Ripken. Who was (and is) a big man.

Also in '67, 15 percent of all the pitchers were listed shorter than six feet. This year it's around 8 percent.

If you want to look at all those numbers and conclude that baseball players, or pitchers anyway, have gotten ONE HUNDRED PERCENT BIGGER over the last fifty years . . . well, of course you would be wrong. Technically speaking. But they're definitely bigger, and dramatically so. When you've got six-feet-four shortstops running around and hitting home runs and making great plays and nobody thinks that's remotely strange, you know we're in a new world.

Ryon Healy, batting first for the A's, is just as tall as Musgrove, whose first offering here in the eighth is one of those tough curveballs, which carves a path right through the strike zone; all Healy can do is admire it, and hope for something more hittable next time. Instead he gets *another* curveball, this one even lower, and takes a big looping swing that misses.

So Musgrove's got Healy right where he wants him.

You know what happens next. Musgrove somehow throws a fastball in the strike zone. It's not a *bad* pitch—it's just above the knees, on the outer edge of the zone, and for God's sake it's 98 miles an hour—and Healy doesn't do a *lot* with it. But he still pokes the baseball into the right-field corner, and slides safely into second base.

Healy is not among the faster players on the roster; representing the go-ahead run, he's quickly replaced by pinch-runner Franklin Barreto, a twenty-one-year-old rookie who entered this season as one of the A's top prospects, having arrived in the big Josh Donald-son trade a while back.

Barreto debuted in the majors in late June and was in the lineup for a couple of weeks. But he didn't hit much, spent the rest of the summer with Triple-A Sacramento, and he's on the roster now solely because the active rosters were expanded a week ago.

To this point, Baseball has *almost* resisted all entreaties to expand the rosters. Until September anyway, when you can do basically anything the hell you want. In fact, in one sense the rosters are *smaller* than they used to be. Until the 1960s, teams could carry more than twenty-five players until a certain date in May. Now, though, from Opening Day through August—and then again in the postseason—teams are *almost* limited to just twenty-five players on the active roster.

We'll get to the almosts (and September) in a minute, but it's worth stealing this extra minute to mention just how extraordinary baseball is.

With the exceptions of a few changes because of wars (with foreign powers, or the union), the MLB team's active roster has been set at twenty-five players *since the First World War*. A whole century.

Meanwhile, over the same span the active roster for NFL teams has gone from sixteen to thirty to forty to (now) forty-six . . . with cries for more. Constant cries for more.

For many years, the NBA's active roster limit was twelve. But today each team must carry *at least thirteen* players, one of whom can be listed as inactive, and they *may* carry fifteen players. In fact, if they don't *average* fourteen players during the season, per team, the league must pay a "surcharge" to the union.

Now, you might reasonably wonder why a basketball coach would need thirteen or fourteen or fifteen players, when he can use only five at a time. And (let's be honest) only eight or nine guys per team are good enough to play regularly for a good team. Which is why so many players never get off the bench in a close game.

Baseball, though. Twenty-five on the active roster for as long as anyone can remember.

Well, almost. Until 1968, teams were permitted to carry more than twenty-five players well into May, theoretically because spring training wasn't long enough to sort through all the roster hopefuls. And to this day, teams may carry as many as forty players on the active roster beginning on September 1. In practice, it's typically in the low thirties, with teams adding younger players to get a better look, or occasionally adding real value in the hunt for a playoff spot.

Another almost. Beginning in 2012, teams were allowed to add a twenty-sixth player—almost invariably yet another bullpenner—for the highly uncommon doubleheader.*

More substantively, the roster rules have become so flexible, and the use of the disabled list so routinely abused, that most teams essentially use twenty-six- or twenty-seven-man rosters until September. If management thinks the manager is stuck with (*only*) five or six fully charged relief pitchers, there are various ways to swap out a tired arm for a fresh one in Triple-A or even Double-A.

Which is a problem. This surfeit of replacement-level, easily accessible relief pitchers contributes to at least two issues that should worry Commissioner Rob Manfred: pace of play, and the precipitous decline in batted balls in play.†

---

* Today, doubleheaders are so uncommon because both the owners and players hate them. It's one of the few things everybody agrees on. And yes, there are other almosts. During the Great Depression, and during World War II, roster limits were lowered. And in a cost-cutting move, the active rosters were "voluntarily" set at twenty-four players from 1986 through '89. With minimum salaries set at roughly sixty thousand dollars during those years, the roster contraction seems to have been less practical than punitive.

† Plus, when you can yo-yo players up and down with hardly any limits, you're almost guaranteed to treat them like numbers rather than people. Before finally arriving for good a month ago, Matt Olson was demoted to Triple-A five times this season. Danny Coulombe told me that when he was with the Dodgers in 2015, he was promoted and demoted six times, spending the grand total of nine days in the majors. "You don't really feel like you're really a part of the team. It's a tough situation, but you'd still rather be in the big leagues than be the guy stuck in Triple-A," he said.

Fewer batted balls in play, because all those pitching changes are nearly always to the defense's advantage, with the new reliever likely to (a) throw around 95, and (b) have the platoon advantage, both items making a strikeout more likely. If there was just one fewer pitching change per game, there would be fewer strikeouts and more balls in play. Oh, and the games would be slightly more entertaining.

That's the theory, anyway. Commissioner Manfred has claimed that fans *like* home runs and strikeouts. Of course, nobody's doing any real surveys except maybe MLB, and they're not going to show us the crosstabs. So it's almost impossible to know what fans really want, or what they might prefer if given a chance. Well, except for their favorite teams winning. We're pretty sure they want that.

There's any number of ways to limit pitching changes, even *with* a larger roster. You could mandate that every pitcher face at least two hitters *or* finish an inning. You could limit every team to twelve pitchers on the active roster *and* tighten (or at least enforce) the rules about minor-league call-ups and the disabled list. These are obvious, commonsense fixes that might be done, after plenty of study, in one reasonably quick meeting . . . except the union has a great deal to say about rosters, and about pitchers.

The union simply must be on board with any changes to roster size and limitations. And while the union would be *thrilled* with a larger roster—and if twenty-six isn't enough, how's about twenty-seven!—anything cutting pitcher usage might be a nonstarter. For one thing, more than half the union *are* pitchers; they don't want fewer of themselves. And two, the union will almost certainly frame any proposed limits as a workplace-safety issue. If relievers are compelled to throw slightly more pitches, they'll argue, they're more likely to get hurt.

Which might be true. However slightly.

You shouldn't run a league that way, though.

In fact, roster expansion in every sport has very little to do with making the game better for fans, and almost everything to do with mollifying unions. Well, and making coaches' jobs easier. In every negotiation, the players want more money and the owners don't wanna give it to them. From there, everything gained by the players is in lieu of more money. When the players negotiated for paternity leave? In lieu of more money. When the players negotiated for hotel suites on road trips, and two seats on the bus in spring training? More off days during the season? In lieu of more money.

Maybe this is just how things must be. In every negotiation with a successful, amicable resolution, it's probably because—and remember, it's been nearly twenty years since the last strike or lockout, so they've been doing something right—both sides get something they want: the owners, not giving the players more than around half the money; the players, getting around half the money *and* nearly all the ticky-tacky things like big hotel rooms and paid family leave and an extra day off every month or two.

Did I mention the money? This year, the minimum major-league salary is $535,000 per season, and that's roughly what most players make in each of their first three full seasons. After which, if they're good, their salaries rise dramatically. This season the average major-league salary is $4.5 million; the *median* salary, $1.5 million.

But while the gap between richest and "poorest" is massive—this season, Clayton Kershaw (among MLB's most talented pitchers) earns roughly $32.5 million more than rookie sensation Aaron Judge (among MLB's most talented hitters)—it wasn't so long ago that a young major leaguer was solidly middle class in America, and might well cast about for an off-season job. Digging graves, substitute teaching, haberdashery, selling Pontiacs, that sort of thing. Today, if you spend all or most of a season in the majors, you're making damn good money, lifestylewise. And in the off-season, you're not working; you're working *out*.

For a while, anyway. It's worth mentioning that with all the turnover in Baseball today, and particularly among pitchers, being a "major leaguer" is hardly a guarantee of wealth. Not when good Triple-A players are getting paid something like three thousand dollars per month; roughly speaking, about the same as a young personal trainer at your local gym. One *might* even argue that the difference between the major-league minimum salary and the typical Triple-A salary is . . . well, perhaps not scandalous. But wildly inequitable, at best. Considering the negligible difference in talent. If there's a difference at all. Considering how many players, especially pitchers, are on a shuttle between Triple-A and the majors, one can't really argue there's any substantive difference.

So how does this inequity persist? Well, the minor leaguers don't have a union, so there's really no way for them to conduct an organized push for higher salaries or better working conditions. You might *think* the Major League Baseball Players Association would stick up for their minor-league brethren. Either by expanding the ranks to include minor leaguers, or at least supporting the formation of another union.

You might think that, but you would be wrong. There's never been a *hint* of the major leaguers doing anything to support the minor leaguers. Publicly, anyway, in the last half century the players' union has not lifted even a single pinky to improve the lives or the working conditions of the young players in the minors with *exactly* the same dreams and problems the big boys once had.

Go figure.

Okay, so the major-league players obviously don't worry much about the minor leaguers. What about management? If you've got a developing Jose Altuve or Jharel Cotton in your farm system, don't you want him eating nutritious food and resting in comfortable lodgings, all the year 'round? Do you really want him trying to sleep four to a room, and subsisting on the cheapest burgers he can find?

I posed this question to Jeff Luhnow a few years ago, just before we took the stage at a conference. His response: "We like 'em hungry." Granted, Luhnow might have simply been overly glib, metaphorical even, in the moment. He might also have been channeling Joe DiMaggio, who once said, "A ballplayer's got to be kept hungry to become a big leaguer."

For which there is, perhaps, *something* to be said? But there are some wealthy minor leaguers. The second half of the DiMaggio quote: "That's why no boy from a rich family ever made it to the big leagues." Which was preposterous on its face when DiMaggio said it, and even more preposterous now. Just off the top of my head, Mike Piazza's father was tremendously wealthy—once nearly lured the San Francisco Giants to Florida, which would have been a great thing for the A's, but of course that's a much different, much longer story—not to mention all the players drafted in the first round of the June amateur draft, most of whom become instant millionaires upon signing their first professional contract. Think Nuke LaLoosh.

But the wealthy minor leaguers driving Italian sports cars and monster trucks are distinctly in the minority. And while the older minor leaguers at the higher levels do make more money than the younger players, they're also more likely to have kids to think about. And it's not uncommon for a player's wife to essentially support the family. Of course, the potential payoff is huge. It's also uncommon, as only 17 percent of the players who are drafted will ever reach the majors. Let alone enjoy a career that ensures long-term financial security.

But why not consider the care and feeding of minor leaguers a market inefficiency, that might be exploited with a relatively tiny investment? Hungry, really? "I'm very much an environmentalist," erstwhile Astros general manager Tim Purpura (now the president of the Double-A Texas League) says, "an advocate of doing things from a major-league average point of view. I think the hunger to get better, to reach the next level, *comes from inside the players.*"

Baseball Prospectus's Russell Carleton writes well on the subject of resource allocation, and he's made a tremendous case for allocating *more* resources to the minor leagues. Five years ago, he wrote that while fast food "will provide that nice 'full' feeling . . . being full is not the same as being well-fed. Eventually, the body will need nutrients to maintain some basic functions. But what's more, poor nutrition impacts learning, and the whole point of a minor-league system is to be a training ground for young players. In some sense, these men are in a type of school and majoring in baseball."

Yes, that was five years ago. But with a few exceptions—most notably, the Dodgers now spend real money to give their minor leaguers healthy meal options—most teams are still far, far less worried about nutrition than any rational analysis would recommend. Why? Because when it comes to food and salaries, the rational financial investments come with six zeroes, and to this point few baseball executives have done much to convince their bosses that all those zeroes are as worthy as, say, the fifth or sixth arm in the bullpen.

Hey, nobody said it makes sense.*

The takeaway here? There is just a tiny difference, often no difference at all, in talent between the seventh man in the bullpen and a good Triple-A pitcher, or between a team's fifth-best outfielder and the farm system's best outfielder. But the difference between their salaries over a full season is startling.

Of course, while the difference is dramatically larger than it's ever been, it might also be less *meaningful* than it's ever been. In a league where the A's will ultimately use fifty-four players this season and the Astros forty-six, it's obvious that if you show much of anything at all in the high minors, you'll get at least a taste of that sweet, sweet major-league money. Oh, and you get to be a *major leaguer* for the rest of your life. For which there really is no substitute.

In 1982, exactly 932 baseball players were officially major leaguers; that is, they were credited for appearing in at least one major-league game. In 2017, the figure will be 1,358. Thirty-six per team in 1982 versus forty-five per team this year, or 26 percent more. Which is especially dramatic when you recall that the active roster size has not changed in the intervening thirty-five years.

Maxwell's up next, with a measly single probably enough to give the A's the lead. Like Healy, Maxwell takes a first-pitch curveball

---

* Astros executive Sig Mejdal learned a great deal from his experiences as a minor-league coach this summer, but he would speak to me specifically about just one: the need for better food in the minors.

for strike one, then a low fastball for ball one. Then yet another curveball, which Maxwell chops to Gurriel at first base. Waving off Musgrove, Gurriel trots to the base well before Maxwell arrives, with Barreto scooting to third.

Between Gurriel stepping on first base and Musgrove firing his first pitch toward Matt Chapman, there's exactly seventy-nine seconds of . . . well, of nothing. Roughly thirty seconds of that is perfectly normal, but the other forty-nine seconds was a visit to the mound from catcher Juan Centeno—who took over behind the plate in this inning, after Marisnick pinch-ran for McCann earlier—and pitching coach Brent Strom.

Granted, forty-nine seconds isn't much, and Strom and Centeno retreated before umpire Holbrook felt compelled to come out and hurry things along.

Historically, though, coaches would visit the mound for a couple of reasons: to remove the pitcher; to settle down the pitcher, physically and/or mentally; or to discuss a tricky situation, if a bunt or some baserunning chicanery seemed likely.

More and more, though, coaches visit the mound simply to talk about how they're going to work the next hitter. Catchers, even more so. They'll tell you it's because sign stealing has become rampant, and they're probably not lying. But it's also just another symptom of the players' compulsion to control the action, and without some real limit on mound visits, this problem's only going to get worse.

Finally the action resumes, with Musgrove throwing Chapman a curveball that misses just inside. Then another curve, this one for a called strike. After missing high with a fastball, Musgrove looses yet another curveball. Reaching for it, Chapman tops an easy grounder to the mound, and Musgrove escapes this modest jam.

Score: Astros 7, Athletics 7
Win Probability: Even

Visitors Ninth

I never keep a scorecard or the batting averages. I hate statistics.
What I got to know, I keep in my head.

—DIZZY DEAN (1910–1974)

For all the hard throwers we've seen so far, new A's reliever Blake
Treinen—like Danny Coulombe and Joe Musgrove before him,
the best he can do is keep this game tied at seven apiece—is the
hardest thrower; his first pitch is 98 miles an hour . . . and George
Springer turns it right around for a line-drive single into right field.
Proving once more the old adage: a big leaguer can hit a bullet, if
it's straight.

Treinen proves another adage, if you'll just give me the license to
create an adage at this moment: shake a tree, and a hard-throwing
reliever will fall out (and with a good secondary pitch he'll give you
a few good years wherever you want to use him).

Okay, so it's not much of an adage. But Treinen is our hardest-
throwing example (so far) of the *fungibility* of relief pitchers. Just
like Luke Gregerson, Treinen wasn't a closer . . . and then he was.

Gregerson was drafted by the St. Louis Cardinals nine years ago,
with the 856th pick in the amateur draft, from tiny St. Xavier University near Chicago. The last pick in the twenty-eighth round of
the draft.

The twenty-eighth round does not produce many major leaguers;

in fact, only three from the twenty-eighth round in 2008 have reached the majors: Gregerson, and two guys who are no longer playing professional baseball. So he beat huge odds, just getting here.

Which he did in fairly short order—for a twenty-eighth-rounder, or anyone else, really—thanks to a terrific slider that simply outmatched minor-league hitters.

For most of six seasons, Gregerson thrived as a "setup man": (supposedly) not good enough to preserve a small lead in the ninth inning, but good enough to preserve a small lead in the seventh or eighth, thus setting up a save situation for the Proven Closer™.

Hey, I'm not saying it made (or makes) sense. But it was (and is) popularly believed that some real, meaningful number of fine relief pitchers *just don't have what it takes* to get those last three outs of the game. And so Gregerson, in his first six seasons, posted a solid 2.75 earned run average, struck out nearly three and a half times as many batters as he walked, yet earned only nineteen saves.

Gregerson became eligible for free agency following the 2014 season, his sixth in the majors, and signed a three-year, $18.5 million contract with the Astros that would have been more lucrative if he'd been getting saves instead of holds with his previous team. Of course, then the Astros wouldn't have signed him. They hadn't really deployed a regular closer in '14, but Gregerson got the job in '15. Belying the suspicion that setup men can't simply step into the ninth inning and thrive, Gregerson earned thirty-one saves, with his other statistics right in line with (or better than) what he'd done before.

Nevertheless, in 2016 the Astros found themselves with a dreaded *closer controversy* in spring training (think *quarterback controversy*, except fundamentally less important times infinity). Because in the off-season, the Astros had traded for the Phillies' young closer, Ken Giles, who'd posted a 1.56 ERA and struck out nearly a dozen batters per nine innings in his first two seasons. Gregerson's fastball topped out in the low 90s, while Giles routinely hit the high 90s, much more in keeping with the image of the intimidating lights-out, blow-your-doors-off relief ace.

Gregerson, despite knowing that whatever his job description, he would earn $12.5 million over the next two seasons, wasn't shy about his preference, telling the *Houston Chronicle*, "How do you think I did last year? I don't see any reason things should change."

That was a selective quote! In the same interview, Gregerson also said some good teammate things. In the event, Giles struggled in spring training, at the end of which A. J. Hinch announced that Gregerson would keep his "closer" title (and Hinch referenced Gregerson's "slow heartbeat"; really, he did).

At the time, one writer actually described the Astros' (theoretical) flexible use of Giles—analytically speaking, *easily* their best relief pitcher—as *progressive*. Which it would have been. If that's what Hinch was actually doing. But he wasn't, really. Like essentially every other manager, even those working for *progressive* teams like the Astros, Hinch wants to use the same pitcher in ninth-inning save situations, nearly every time. On paper? Your best strategy is the infamous "closer by committee." If you're ahead 2–1 in the eighth inning and the other team's best hitters are coming up, isn't *that* when you should use your best available pitcher? Of course. But there is literally not a single manager in the major leagues who plays it that way. There wasn't one in 2016, and there isn't in 2017. Not one out of thirty. When a manager doesn't use the same guy every time, it's because he hasn't found a closer he trusts. Yet.

As military men are fond of saying, no plan survives contact with the enemy.

That is not always true. Depends on the enemy, and fortune. And generalship. Sometimes the guy you've anointed "closer" on Opening Day will still be "closer" in Game 162. But here's a true thing: of the twenty pitchers who racked up at least twenty-five saves in 2016—that is, the pitchers who served as closers for more than half the season, usually quite a lot more than half—only eight will repeat in 2017.

Eight.

Another true thing: In 2016, the top six save guys in the majors combined for 276 saves. In 2017, those six Proven Closers™, those aces, those *studs*, will combine for just 107 saves . . . and 68 of those from only two studs: Jansen (41) and A. J. Ramos (20 saves with the Marlins, then seven more after joining the Mets).

So you might already have guessed what happened with Luke Gregerson, Ken Giles, and the Houston Astros. Early in the season, Gregerson was shaky. Or *seemed* shaky. Considering the inherently small sample sizes that are part and parcel of relief pitching—it's literally true that one particularly terrible (or unlucky) outing can ruin a relief pitcher's ERA for months—it's incredibly difficult to separate, over the course of just a month or two, let alone a few weeks, meaningful performance from random variation and statistical noise. What we do know is that after two shaky months (and five blown saves) last season, Gregerson was out, and before long Giles was in. And Giles has been in—which is to say, he's been the Astros' decidedly nonprogressive Proven Closer™—ever since. So at this moment, he's limbering up in the bullpen.

But setup man is a pretty good job too. Perhaps even a little harder too; due to the vagaries of lineup math, pitchers in the eighth inning actually face somewhat better hitters than pitchers in the ninth, according to a recent study.

Like Gregerson, Blake Treinen has done both jobs. Unlike Gregerson, Treinen's a closer *now*.

It's been a long winding road for Treinen, a strapping fella who looks like he throws at least 95, and does. After his junior season at South Dakota State, the Marlins grabbed Treinen in the twenty-third round of the amateur draft, despite his 6.09 ERA that spring . . . only to withdraw their initial contract offer upon seeing an MRI that showed shoulder inflammation. A year later, the A's were so impressed with Treinen's arm, they used their seventh-round pick to draft him: lofty status for a twenty-three-year-old senior.

That was in 2011. After Treinen's second season in the A's farm system, he went to the Washington Nationals in a three-team trade that also involved major leaguers John Jaso and Mike Morse. Reaching the majors at twenty-five, Treinen pitched pretty well except for too many walks, which was balanced with few home runs allowed. Thanks largely to Treinen's (almost) unique sinking fastball: not the traditional two-seamer, but rather a sort of *one*-seamer.

Most pitchers throw either a sinking two-seam fastball, gripped *along* two seams of the baseball, or a "rising" four-seam fastball, gripped *across* the seams. Or both. But Treinen begins with the traditional two-seam grip, then turns the ball ever so slightly, leaving him with his index and middle finger nearly straddling just one seam. It's not a unique pitch, but Treinen's one of the few major leaguers who throws it, and he throws his the hardest. At its best, which is actually most of the time, the pitch has what Treinen calls a "two-plane movement"—both down *and* away from a right-handed hitter—and at 97 or 98 miles an hour, it's nearly unhittable.

In the first half of this season, his ERA was elevated (5.73), but the underlying numbers—you know, the numbers that matter to Postmodern baseball teams—suggested that Treinen's skills hadn't changed; he was just pitching in some tough luck.

Just after the All-Star Game, the A's shipped their two best relief pitchers, Sean Doolittle and Ryan Madson, to the Washington Nationals for Treinen and a couple of reasonably hot prospects. A month ago, Treinen was installed as a closer for the first time in his career.

With Springer on first base as the potential go-ahead run, Treinen's in the unenviable position of dealing with Altuve—whose two hits tonight have lifted his batting average to .354, light-years ahead of everyone else in the American League—and then Correa and probably more. And believe it or not, Treinen's *not* thinking about strikeouts in this situation. Even throwing 98. "They're pretty aggressive hitters," he later says. "They don't miss fastballs. So the idea is not necessarily to strike them out, but get 'em to have weak contact, and then you take your chances. You can trick people, at the lower levels—college, high school, maybe in the minors at times—but in the big leagues, very seldom do you get tricked. It's all about execution. Everybody knows what's coming. Just, are you going to execute better than the next guy."

After missing outside with one of his one-seamers—might actually have clipped the strike zone, actually—Treinen comes back with another, but this one crowds Altuve, who lifts a pop fly that first baseman Olson collects in foul territory, just a few steps from Springer, rooted on the bag. Better execution.

Correa's next, and Treinen ultimately gets a strikeout he doesn't particularly want: "It was a fastball inside that I think more times than not, he fights off or puts in play. That was my goal. I wanted him to put it in play. I was actually probably kind of frustrated that I struck him out, because I wanted to get a ground-ball double play and get out of the inning."

Still, two outs with a man on first. That's a reasonably safe situation.

Reddick's next. Treinen's got a good memory, can *almost* remember all the details from this outing, six months later. But sometimes you don't *want* to remember. "Usually you focus more on the negatives," Treinen says. "That's how our minds work, so you have to try to force yourself to focus on the positives. Which is a short sample size, because I've faced Houston only a couple of times."

When he was pitching for the Nationals, Treinen never faced the Astros. And in seven weeks since joining the A's, he's actually pitched against Houston just once, a nearly flawless two-inning stint three weeks ago, in which he struck out Reddick on three pitches, the last of them a slider in the dirt. Which seems like something worth remembering.

Whatever his memories in this moment, Treinen almost immediately gives up the tiebreaking run. Treinen will later remember Reddick's double as a ground ball that just snuck through the infield—*focus on the positives*—but it's actually a line drive that Olson can't snag, landing in short right field before skipping all the way to the wall in the right-field corner. Joyce gets to the corner smartly, gathers the ball and throws a strike to cutoff man Lowrie, who then spins and throws, without great accuracy, a one-hopper to Maxwell. He spins around for the tag, but Springer's already sliding safely past him.

Unbelievable, Ray Fosse intones. *Unbelievable.*

Or not. Treinen's good but hardly great, and he's facing the best hitters in a tremendous lineup. Seeing a run in this situation actually seems like one of the more believable things we've seen all evening.*

The play at the plate isn't particularly close, and Maxwell hadn't been in any position to keep Springer from scoring. Not with the throw coming from right field. But if the throw had been coming from left field, just a few years ago, Maxwell (and his already-concussed brain) might well have felt compelled to straddle the baseline in front of the plate, essentially daring Springer to steamroll him. And Springer, all 215 pounds of him, might well have done just that.

Which used to be a fairly common sight. One big (fast) man crashing into another big (armored) man. With perhaps fewer resulting injuries than you might imagine, but still more than Baseball should have tolerated. But enough wasn't enough until six years ago.

In 2010, San Francisco Giants catcher Buster Posey was the National League's Rookie of the Year. Handsome and likeable and supremely talented both as a catcher and hitter, Posey looked like

---

* Next year, Treinen *will* be great, making the All-Star team in July with a 0.94 ERA, thanks largely to giving up just one home run in forty-eight innings.

as good a bet as any to become one of Major League Baseball's favorite poster boys.

On the twenty-fifth of May, the next spring, Posey's Giants were
tied 6–6 with the Marlins in the twelfth inning when Emilio Bon-
ifacio drove a fly ball to medium-depth right-center field. At third
base, Scott Cousins tagged up and steamed toward the plate. Posey
set up to receive a throw from the right fielder, leaving approximately half the plate for Cousins to slide.

Cousins didn't slide. Instead, he veered slightly to his left and
just blasted through Posey, with the ball popping loose. *Blew him
up*, as they say. So Cousins scored, with the unfortunate side effect
of Posey suffering severe leg injuries that cost him (and the Giants, and their fans) the rest of the season. Now, technically what
Cousins did might have been against the rules. But if so, the rules
hadn't been enforced in a long, long time. Essentially, runners had
been able to do just about anything they liked *and* catchers were
permitted to completely shut off access to the plate, even before
they'd received a throw.

Baseball wasn't *designed* to be played like football or rugby; yet
somehow that is how it came to be played, at least around the plate
(and too often at second base). And it took a star player suffering
a season-ending, perhaps career-threatening injury for Baseball to
finally discourage the violence.

Not that anything happened quickly. But in 2014, three seasons
removed from Posey's injury, a new rule was added. At the time,
Rule 7.13 essentially mandated that a runner couldn't deviate from
his path to the plate in order to hit the catcher (as Cousins did), *and*
that catchers couldn't completely block the path to the plate unless
they already had the ball (as catchers had been doing for eons).

Officially, the new rule was "experimental" and of course there
were glitches as everyone got used to playing differently. Today it's
Rule 6.01(i) and it's complicated . . . but for the most part, it works.
There are many fewer collisions, and many more *baseball plays*; you

know, deft tags and nimble slides and players actually making seat-of-their-pants decisions (granted, Cubs manager Joe Maddon still argues that jarring collisions are "baseball plays," but he's an old football player who, deep in the depths of his soul, seems to believe the *best* game would combine the two sports).

Oh, and then two years later we got Rule 6.01(j): the Chase Utley rule.

Unofficially, that is. But the rule's nicknamed for Utley because of a violent takeout slide the Dodger leveled against a shortstop in the 2015 postseason. Utley's slide was clearly against the letter of the existing rules, but the rules were rarely enforced, and this incident would have gone largely unnoticed . . . except Utley's late slide resulted in Mets shortstop Rubén Tejada suffering a broken leg.

People tend to notice broken legs. Especially in October. So there were calls for change, and this time—perhaps in part because of the precedent set by the Posey rule—the change came quickly, in the form of a requirement that a baserunner must make a *bona fide slide*; that is, a slide that's intended, or at least meets reasonable criteria of intention, to result in the runner at second base being safe. As opposed to the obvious intention of simply hindering an infielder in the process of turning a double play.

Of course, the goal of both the Buster Posey and Chase Utley rules are fewer broken legs, fewer concussions, etc. And it's difficult to argue that they haven't worked in just that way. Which is obviously a positive development if you *do* prefer to see the best baseball players playing baseball, and *don't* enjoy seeing players get hurt. (Joe Maddon's a relatively progressive guy in a decidedly nonprogressive culture, but he's hardly perfect.)

Reddick hit a slider that caught way too much of the strike zone. Treinen doesn't take the same chance against Gurriel. First pitch: 98-mile-an-hour sinker that Gurriel swings over. Second pitch: 98-mile-an-hour sinker that Gurriel tops to third base, where Chapman makes the routine play to end the inning.

Astros closer Ken Giles has been getting loose in the bullpen, and he'll undoubtedly be pursuing his thirtieth save this season. Giles throws even harder than Treinen.

Hundred Miles, they call him.

Score: Astros 8, Athletics 7
Win Probability: Astros 80%

Home Ninth

There is nothing so uncertain as a dead sure thing.

—GEORGE M. COHAN (1878–1942)

Ken Giles, one of MLB's premier relief pitchers, has taken the mound for the most difficult job that's routinely assigned: protect a one-run lead in the ninth inning, the enemy manager doing everything he can to wipe out that lead.

Humans are naturally drawn to post facto analysis. Sports fans too. Maybe sports fans, especially. When something happens, we naturally assume it was inevitable. Or at least that it was most likely.

But nothing is inevitable, and we're not much good at knowing what's most likely. I have read, any number of times, that once the United States entered World War II, the conclusion was *inevitable*. Now, it might be true that the U.S. wasn't going to *lose* the war, no matter what happened. Its manufacturing power and geographic isolation made some sort of Axis invasion essentially impossible. But it's not actually so difficult for a decent historian with a fair imagination to come up with scenarios whereby the U.S. doesn't overpower Japan in the summer of 1945; where Germany doesn't capitulate a few months earlier. A few V-2 rockets, for example, tipped with atomic explosives could have led to a vastly different outcome. In *most* possible realities, Japan is crushed (mostly) by the U.S., Germany (mostly) by the Soviet Union. But not in every reality. There are a *lot* of realities.*

Baseball is even dicier. Look at the 2016 Cubs. *Before* the season, they were among the favorites to win the World Series. Yes, despite the Curse of the Billy Goat. After the season, of *course* they won the World Series. But even leaving aside that the Cubs needed a Game 7—ten innings of Game 7, no less—to lock down their first World Championship since 1908, there's this: the Cubs essentially lucked into a couple of their best players. Actually, it would be more than a couple of them, if we wanted to dig deep enough. But let's just look at first baseman Anthony Rizzo and starting pitcher Kyle Hendricks.

Rizzo was an All-Star last year, and probably the Cubs' second-best player; his teammate Kris Bryant won the MVP Award, and Rizzo finished fourth in the voting. But Rizzo was available when the Cubs traded for him after the 2012 season because (a) he'd played poorly for his team (the Padres) in forty-nine games that season, (b) the people running his team obviously didn't realize how talented he was, and (c) the people running his team had recently traded for another, less-talented first baseman.†

Or maybe the Padres knew exactly what they were doing. After all, they did get pitcher Andrew Cashner in the deal, and Cashner wasn't Just Another Guy. He was a young, not-so-long-ago high draft pick who'd reached the majors at twenty-three after breezing through the minors.

Well, not breezing. As a first-year pro in the low minors, Cashner posted a 5.85 ERA. The next year he struggled some in Double-A. But his pedigree and triple-digit fastball were still exciting, and plenty of teams would love to have had him. The point isn't that the Cubs fleeced the Padres (whose general manager had worked for

---

* Including at least a few with Jon Singleton in tonight's starting lineup.

† Actually, that first baseman was Yonder Alonso, who is directly responsible for the presence in tonight's game of Boog Powell.

Theo Epstein in Boston). The point is that whatever Cashner's talents, Rizzo was available only because of a sort of statistical fluke: his poor performance in those forty-nine games with San Diego.

As ex-Padres and then Cubs executive Jed Hoyer would later say, "The Cubs are really fortunate. If when he came up he'd played really well, there's no chance the Padres would have traded him. He was their first baseman of the future and there was no one to compete with him."

Now, you might be excused for thinking—because yes, Theo Epstein really was (and is) a tremendous baseball executive who's going to Cooperstown someday—that if Rizzo had not been available, well then Epstein would simply have traded Cashner (or someone else) for another "impact player" (Epstein's term for his goal when acquiring Rizzo).

Perhaps.

But guess what. *It's not that easy.*

Case in point: Kyle Hendricks.

Epstein traded for Hendricks at the non-waiver deadline in 2012. The Rangers were looking for a veteran pitcher for their stretch run—ultimately successful, notwithstanding a quick postseason exit—and Ryan Dempster fit the bill perfectly, going 7-3 after coming over from the Cubs.

This is exactly the sort of deal that teams in utterly different positions on the "success cycle" hope to make every July (or August, sometimes). The Rangers got a pitcher who did help push them over the line, and the Cubs got a couple of promising young players, cheap and cost controlled for at least the next six-plus seasons.*

---

* Along with Hendricks, the Cubs also scooped up Christian Villanueva, a twenty-one-year-old third baseman in Class A who had ranked among the Rangers' better prospects before the season. His development seemed to stall in the Cubs' farm system, and last winter they cut him loose. He signed with . . . the Padres, and got his career back on track with a nice Triple-A season. So what does Villanueva's trajectory say about the Cubs? Who knows.

Just another example of Theo Epstein's Hall of Fame intellect, right?

Well, sure. He and his people sifted through a list of minor-league Rangers, and somehow alit on the pitcher who would lead the National League in ERA just four years later *and* post a 1.42 ERA in five postseason starts that fall. You know, when the Cubs won the World Series.

So, yes. Tremendous work, Theo. Bravissimo, etc.

But then you run across this passage in Ned Colletti's book. In the summer of 2012, Colletti was Epstein's counterpart with the Dodgers and, like the Rangers, the Dodgers were in the market for an experienced starting pitcher. By 2016, Colletti was doing TV work and writing his memoir, which includes:

> *I caught up with Theo around the batting cage before Game 3 of the World Series and told him he ought to thank me for not giving him Allen Webster, the pitcher he wanted as part of the deal I tried to make for Dempster. He never would have had Dempster to send to Texas for Hendricks if we had made the deal.*
>
> *"That's funny and true," he said. "And to think, the guy we were set on—the player you wouldn't trade—had an ERA of seven in Korea this past season. We 'settled' on Hendricks, who was throwing eighty-eight when we acquired him."*

Do the Cubs win the World Series in 2016 if Rizzo had played better with the Padres in 2012 and Colletti had been willing to include Webster in a deal for Dempster?

Just looking at the specifics, it seems highly unlikely! You know, considering that both performed exceptionally well during the regular season *and* in the League Championship Series against the Dodgers *and* in the World Series against the Indians. Would the Cubs even have been in *position* to win the World Series without those guys?

Perhaps. If Epstein hadn't found a hard-hitting first baseman and a Hendricks-caliber starting pitcher well before 2016, he might well have found them by October. The Cubs won their division in 2016 by 17^1/$_2$ games, so they would have finished in first place even with anonymous replacement-level players in those slots.

In Tom Verducci's book about the Cubs' championship run, he writes, "The construction of a championship team is granular. The final picture is a Seurat painting. As with many tiny dots of color, there are millions of reasons and thousands of cascading events that help explain how in five years the Cubs morphed from a 101-loss team into a world championship team."

The Seurat metaphor is interesting and useful . . . but only to a point. While *every* move in a well-run organization is purposeful—just as each of Seurat's contrasting oil dots was purposeful—a baseball team's moves are highly subject to luck, random variation, all the rest. And that's even before you start playing the actual games. There are still real inefficiencies to be found, and it's possible that Billy Beane will find the next one.

My shit doesn't work in the playoffs. Another of Billy Beane's famous lines in *Moneyball* (the book). Okay. Two things about that. One, it doesn't always work in the regular season either. The Athletics' seven losing seasons since 2006 prove that. And two, Beane said that *before* a number of heartbreaking postseason losses. To date, Beane's A's have reached the postseason eight times, but won just one postseason series while losing eight, including a horrific loss to Kansas City in 2014's Wild Card playoff. Beane's A's have gone 0 and 7 in winner-take-all games.[*]

It might not be an exaggeration to suggest that if two or three of those games had gone the other way, the A's would have won a World Series or two. The Twins once won two Series in five years;

---

[*] With one out in the bottom of the eighth inning in that Wild Card Game against the Royals, the A's Win Expectancy was 95%. With one out in the bottom of the twelfth inning, the A's Win Expectancy was nearly 90%. They lost anyway.

the Marlins, two in seven years. With a championship or two on his résumé, Beane would already have punched his ticket for the Hall of Fame.

Without, though? He's not really a viable candidate. While very few players have been elected to the Hall on the strength of a game or two—it's literally against the rules, and voters have arguably broken the rules only for Jack Morris and perhaps Bill Mazeroski—managers and executives are elected almost completely because of championships plus lengthy tenures. Leo Durocher's in the Hall of Fame largely because he managed a World Series-winning team in 1954; Gene Mauch's *not* in the Hall of Fame largely because he didn't manage a championship team in 1964.

Beane certainly has the requisite tenure. Or will. What he doesn't have is even a single championship. Not close. In his team's only American League Championship Series—the last step before the World Series—the A's were swept by the Tigers.

Essentially, there are three ways to objectively assess a general manager. Or more broadly, a management team that includes ownership.

Just looking at wins and losses is easy, but doesn't take financial resources into consideration. "Moneyball" might have given the A's an edge early in this century, but wouldn't Beane have ultimately won even more games if he'd been playing "Moneyball with money"? As Theo Epstein and the Red Sox were said to have done, while winning two championships?

Just looking at championships—now three for Epstein, still none for Beane—is easy, but it doesn't nearly account for the luck you need to win three postseason series (plus a Wild Card Game, if you didn't win your division, and God forbid you're stuck in a division with the Cubs, Astros, or Dodgers).

This will be another championship-free season for Beane's team; just two more losses over these next few weeks, and they're guaranteed their third straight losing campaign.

A better team, or perhaps even a lousy team with a deeper bench, might begin the bottom of this ninth inning with a pinch-hitter.

After all, Boog Powell's hit just one home run in the major leagues; there's a reason he's the last name on the lineup card. After all, Ken Giles is now standing on the mound. He's one of the very hardest-throwing pitchers on the planet. And as Powell will allow, some months later, "I have a tendency to be late on faster pitching."

But A's manager Bob Melvin probably doesn't have a better hitter on the bench, plus he's already thinking about next season. So why not see what this kid can do?

"I was just trying to be early on his pitches," Powell tells me. "I remember he blew me away with two fastballs that were just—he blew 'em by me."

Powell took that first fastball, right down the middle, but he got a piece of the second one. Maybe that's why Centeno, behind the plate, flashes the sign for a slider. After getting all geared up for Giles and his 100 miles, how could a fresh kid like Powell possibly adjust to one of Giles's nuclear sliders?

Anyway, the pitch won't be where Powell can hit it. As Giles is going into his motion, Centeno actually taps the ground with his open mitt; this pitch is going to start low and end lower.

Except it doesn't. It's a hanger. A mistake. Somehow, Powell adjusts. "Honestly, I was just trying to put the ball in play," he says, "and let the rest take care of itself. And, it did. I couldn't tell you how. He put it right where I wanted it, and next thing you know it's out of the park."

While the baseball was soaring over the right-field wall, Powell was actually sprinting around the bases. Even slowing down just a bit to slap hands with his third-base coach, he makes the trip in just seventeen seconds, five seconds faster than the average "tater trot," and quite possibly among the dozen or so fastest in the major leagues, all season.

Giles made a mistake. He doesn't make many of them. Over the last three calendar months—almost exactly half of a whole season—Giles has converted fourteen of his fifteen save opportunities; in thirty innings over that span, he's given up just fifteen hits and three runs while racking up forty-six strikeouts. Over the last three months, Ken Giles has pitched nearly as well as anyone *can* pitch.

What's more, there's very little (if any) correlation between how a pitcher fared against *that* hitter, and how he'll fare against *this* hitter. Once in a blue moon, Ken Giles is going to hang a slider, or throw a straight fastball to just the wrong place. But doing it once doesn't meaningfully increase the likelihood that he'll do it again.

None of which changes Marcus Semien's job as he steps into the batter's box, now representing the winning run: get on.

"When you throw a hundred," Semien says later, "it's hard to be on both. You have to be on the fastball, but he was throwing his slider down in the zone and getting more strikeouts. His fastball's a four-seamer. So it's still a straight ball. You just have to be a little bit earlier, on time. So, early in the count you don't want to chase a slider. You want to get a fastball."

He got a fastball: 99, straight. And he was plenty early enough, with a line drive to left field that *might* have been caught if Reddick were playing in his normal position. But he was in the standard "no-doubles" defense, deeper than usual, so didn't have a chance to make the play. Oh, and this was *not a bad pitch*. It was 99 miles an hour *and* on the inside corner: middle-in, sure, but *really* in. Marcus Semien is a world-class athlete, and there's not been another moment in this game, maybe not another moment all summer, in which his athletic brilliance is more obvious.

Giles isn't visibly rattled. But even the world's best pitchers, it seems, aren't immune to failure. Giles throws Matt Joyce four straight fastballs, all 98 or 99, all outside the strike zone. One of those pitches isn't close to the zone but three are; somehow Joyce merely watches all four, and trots down to first base. Semien's already on second, having taken off as Giles was still delivering the fourth heater.

Next up: Jed Lowrie, still with nobody out.

When I asked Lowrie how you think about facing someone who throws as hard as Giles, he said, "Get a good pitch to hit."

Full stop. We stare at each other.

I blink first.

Okay (I say), so it's really that easy? Just get your pitch, and a hundred's no big deal?

"It is a big deal," Lowrie said. "I mean, a hundred miles an hour is fast. But this is the big leagues. So you gotta be ready for stuff like that. Sounds stupid, what I said earlier, sounds simple, just getting a good pitch, but that's what it's all about. Because if you're chasing a hundred out of the zone, or you're cheating on it, you're gonna look bad on the slider. So first and foremost, you gotta get a good pitch."

But Lowrie's not cheating on Giles's first pitch, a down-and-in slider; he's squared around to bunt, although it's not obvious whether he actually wants to bunt—moving Semien to third base with the winning run and avoiding a potential double play—or has every intention of taking the first pitch, and squared around to maybe rattle Giles a bit more. Funny thing is, the pitch might actually catch just the tiniest sliver of the strike zone. But it looks like a ball on television, and it looks like a ball to the only man with the power to call it a strike.

Up in the booth, the old catcher Ray Fosse says, "That was another breaking ball. He may take a strike, *force* him to throw a strike, because right now that's five out of the strike zone."

Lowrie's not looking to take a strike. Lowrie's looking for a good pitch. You know. To hit.

The next one is almost a hundred. It's also heading almost directly to the very center of the strike zone. Lowrie got the good pitch. He's *ready* for the good pitch.

Lowrie's swinging away, Glen Kuiper says, next to Fosse. *Lines one, left-center field, Maybin coming in, he can't get it! And the A's are gonna win the game as Marcus Semien slides home, unbelievable!*

In the old days, you might see a small celebration on the field, after a big win. Say, in the World Series. Now, there's a public celebration after *every* win, usually two lines of players high-fiving. Which seems odd, considering they could just as easily high-five or shake hands or even hug a little, back in their locker room. But that's just how it's done today.

A walk-off win, though, like tonight's? With the expanded roster, it looks like (as Fosse says) the whole ballpark's running onto the field. Lowrie's mobbed by his teammates, everybody jumping up and down and high-fiving, and a few minutes later, while doing an interview with the TV crew, Lowrie will be attacked with two shaving-cream pies *and* be drenched with two water coolers: one filled with ice water, the other with Gatorade. Lowrie's a gamer and gives it a shot, but this interview's over. He just had time to explain that no, he had no intention of bunting against Giles. He was looking for that good pitch.

There probably won't be a curtain call tonight for Lowrie. The announced attendance was just north of twelve thousand . . . but announced attendances are largely a fiction, as the figures describe tickets sold, not fannies in the seats, and it's not likely that much more than ten thousand people were actually in the stands tonight. And some real percentage of those must have left before the ninth inning. So while the fans remaining did their best, the real celebration happened on the field, enjoyed by a few dozen elated men in white uniforms, trimmed in green and yellow. They'll finish this season in last place for the third year in a row. But in this moment, nothing matters except this moment.

In the bottom of the ninth inning, Ken Giles threw the five fastest pitches in the entire game: four 99s and one 100. None of Oakland's three batted balls, all three of them hits, were among the twenty hardest-hit balls in the entire game.

Houston entered this series as one of the American League's very best teams; Oakland, one of the American League's very worst. In this game, though? The worse team was the better team. The worse team will beat the better team twice tomorrow, and then again the day after tomorrow to complete a rare four-game sweep.

Short hops, man. Short hops.

Score: Athletics 9, Astros 8
Win Probability: 100%

Epilogue:
October Ball

I'm about as old school as it gets. I don't like to overload myself with a lot of information. I just like to kinda go off a feel.

—GEORGE SPRINGER (B. 1989)

Ken Giles's blowup against the A's was just a blip, right? Look out, October?

Sure, we know closers don't last forever; there's only one Mariano Rivera, and he hasn't actually been Mariano Rivera for a few years now. But four games after blowing up against the A's, Giles was right back in there for a save, which he converted. After the eighth of September, in fact, Giles pitched in eight games and didn't give up a run.

Including Boog Powell's equalizer on that eighth of September, Giles ultimately gave up only four home runs in sixty-three innings during the regular season . . . and then in the postseason, he gave up three homers in seven and two-thirds innings. He recorded two saves, but gave up homers in both of those games.

In Game 2 of the World Series—the Astros having already vanquished the Red Sox and Yankees in the American League playoffs—Giles pitched a perfect ninth inning to preserve a 3–3 tie against the Los Angeles Dodgers. In the top of the tenth, Altuve and Correa hit back-to-back home runs to make the score 5–3 . . . and then Giles gave up two runs in the bottom of the tenth, thanks in part to a leadoff homer and later a wild pitch. Setup man Chris Devenski finally came on to prevent further damage, and on they went to the eleventh. In which the Astros took another two-run lead, on yet *another* home run, this one coming from George Springer, off Brandon McCarthy. In the bottom of the eleventh, the Dodgers touched Devenski for a lineout, another lineout, and then a solo home run. But Devenski, who routinely throws 96, struck out Yasiel Puig on an 84-mile-per-hour changeup to seal the victory.

The two clubs split the first four games of the Series, leading to a Game 5 that ranks among the wildest seesaw affairs ever: Astros 13, Dodgers 12 in ten innings, the contest finally ending on Alex Bregman's walk-off single against (usually) lights-out closer Kenley Jansen. The Dodgers beat Verlander in a tight Game 6, setting up Baseball's greatest event: Game 7.

Throughout the Series, it was almost as if the Astros and Dodgers said, "You liked what you saw during the regular season? Here! We'll give you even more of that!" The Astros would eventually hit fifteen round-trippers; with the Dodgers hitting ten of their own, the combined total of twenty-five shattered the World Series record for both teams. Springer tied the all-time record with five homers in the Series, and he set a new record with twenty-nine total bases. Dodgers shortstop Cody Bellinger, coming off a brilliant rookie season, set a record of his own with seventeen strikeouts.

And in Game 7, neither starter lasted even three whole innings. The Astros knocked out Yu Darvish in the second inning, going ahead 5–0. But Houston's Lance McCullers was lifted in the third, despite having thrown only forty-nine pitches while pitching scoreless, walkless ball. So the last six-plus innings of the game was a long parade of relief pitchers, all of whom were nearly flawless. Most notably, Charlie Morton—who had started against the Yankees in Game 7 of the American League Championship Series, and tossed five shutout innings—closed out the Dodgers in *this* Game 7 with four innings in which he gave up just two hits and one run.

Just three years after George Springer and the Astros were on the cover of *Sports Illustrated* in the middle of a last-place season, they were right where that cover said they would be: sitting atop the Baseball world, as Postmodern a team as you will find.

In 2017, at least. Because we hadn't seen nothing, yet.

Extras: Future Ball

The best time to plant a tree was twenty years ago. The second-best time is now.

—CHINESE PROVERB

In the Astros' first game in 2018, World Series MVP George Springer led off with a home run, Justin Verlander pitched brilliantly, and A. J. Hinch debuted his new (but hardly unprecedented) four-man outfield against Rangers slugger Joey Gallo. As my friend Craig Calcaterra wrote, "It's like 2017 never ended."

Actually, it's more like 2017 was just a warmup.

In March and April of 2017, major-league pitchers struck out almost 22 percent of the batters they faced, which was an all-time record. In March and April of 2018, the figure was nearly 23 percent. We simply haven't reached a strikeouts limit, and can't even identify a *realistic* limit. If 23 percent is fine, why not 24 percent, or 25? When Okrent's *Nine Innings* was published in 1985, 14 percent of all plate appearances ended with strikeouts. The difference between these figures represents a radical change in the nature of the sport, and yet nobody *in* the sport seems willing to acknowledge what's so obvious to anyone with just a touch of historical perspective.

Hinch's four-man outfield wasn't the only radical move in the spring of 2018. In the Philadelphia Phillies' first two games, rookie manager Gabe Kapler used fifteen pitchers, setting a new record. Later in the spring, the Tampa Bay Rays become the first team in history to regularly use an "opener": a starting pitcher who would be permitted to go just *once* through the other team's batting order. All of which might well be conducive to winning; none of which make the games more entertaining for the common fan.

In the 1960s, in a national baseball magazine, a New York writer penned an essay headlined "What's Wrong with Baseball?" This was more than fifty years ago, and yet this should today sound familiar: "The long, drawn-out three-hour game is probably the most obnoxious feature of baseball—and its biggest drawback, right now."

And so it's always gone. While it's easy to bemoan the state of today's game, and tempting to think the gravy train can't steam on forever, history suggests that Major League Baseball will outlast me, and quite possibly you.

As long as the billions of dollars keep rolling in, it's difficult to imagine even a semi-likely scenario in which Baseball would seriously consider the systemic changes necessary to bring back more singles and doubles and triples and steals and first-to-thirds and acrobatic double plays. All we know is that Baseball will do something, in response to something, and that whatever Baseball does, there will be unintended consequences. Because Baseball is inherently a human enterprise, and humans don't know any other way.

One something: In 2018, Major League Baseball wanted pitch clocks, a presence in the minor leagues since 2015. It didn't happen, because of strenuous objections from the Major League Baseball Players Association. MLB could have gone ahead anyway, but in the interest of comity (or public relations), agreed to hold off for at least another year.

However, there *were* new, semi-significant time-saving initiatives in 2018.

In the minor leagues, at all levels, eternal tradition has been upended by a new rule stipulating that all extra innings will begin with a runner on second base. In the minors, marathon games are dead. This rule was officially included under the heading of "pace of play regulations," but killing long games has nothing to do with *pace*. Length of games, yes. Pace, no. Killing marathon games is purely about protecting pitchers, and making those poor beleaguered managers' jobs a little easier.

Meanwhile, in the minor leagues *and* the major leagues, for the first time since 1973, there are new rules limiting visits to the pitcher's mound. In 2018, in the majors and the high minors, you get six mound visits per game, not counting trips to remove a pitcher. Including visits from *not* just managers and coaches; teammates, too.

There's no evidence that the new mound-visit rules are *because* of the Houston Astros . . . but then again, if you were looking for a good reason to make new rules, you just had to watch the Houston Astros last fall. Especially in Game 7 of the World Series, when Brian McCann visited the mound *a dozen times in the first six innings*, murdering five minutes on national television. And it wasn't because of the pitcher, because there were a bunch of them: Lance McCullers Jr., Brad Peacock, Chris Devenski, Charlie Morton. If someone was pitching, McCann was visiting.

Theoretically, McCann was worried about the Dodgers stealing his signs. This was yet another obvious example of the players' best interests battling against the greater enterprise: exciting, action-packed baseball. If you're Brian McCann, you don't give a tinker's damn about the enterprise. If you're Brian McCann, all you want is to win the biggest game of your career.

Justin Verlander might have been speaking for most of his union brothers when he said of the new mound-visit restrictions, "I think this is a Band-Aid on what I wasn't considering a bigger issue. I think the game is fine the way it is."

Perhaps. But the game, at least in some respects, has become less fine every year.

When you're a tree, it's difficult to see the forest. Even if you're a tree as large as Justin Verlander. What players have a difficult time understanding is this: Even if you think *the game is fine the way it is,* inaction does *not* mean things will remain fine. With so many dynamics in play, change is inevitable. The question is, does Baseball want to guide the changes, or just let them happen?

In Oliver Sacks's last book, he wrote, "Nothing is more crucial to the survival and independence of organisms—be they elephants or protozoa—than the maintenance of a constant internal environment." This constancy is called *homeostasis*.

Further, Sacks writes, "It is especially when things are going wrong internally—when homeostasis is not being maintained, when the autonomic balance starts listing heavily to one side or the other—that this core consciousness, the feeling of *how one is*, takes on an intrusive, unpleasant quality, and now one will say, 'I feel ill—something is amiss.' At such times, one no longer *looks* well either."

Justin Verlander might not feel ill, but something is amiss; Baseball no longer *looks* well. When a team can go through an entire season and hit only five triples—as the Blue Jays did in 2017, setting a record low—it doesn't look well. John Thorn, MLB's official historian, who loves baseball as much as anyone I've ever known, says of Two True Outcomes baseball, "We love surprises, since we were children. But this is a game I don't like." Because the surprises—they're disappearing.

A month or so after the World Series, Steven Goldleaf wrote a long essay for Bill James's website, titled "How Sabermetrics Has Ruined Baseball."

That headline's just a grabber, but Goldleaf's central point is a good one: "Sabermetrics could ruin baseball, in that its goal is to create a type of game that optimizes winning, while fans want to see a type of game that is entertaining to watch."

It wasn't always this way. Baseball used to *do* something.

Way back when, hitters figured out how to foul off pitches at will; Baseball made some of those fouls count as strikes. Way back when, some wise guy realized he could forestall an easy double play, as a runner, by simply fielding the ball himself; Baseball nipped that one quickly. In the 1970s, Orioles manager Earl Weaver started writing a pitcher's name into the DH slot into his lineup, and then picked a real DH when the slot came up in the game, depending on the situation. Baseball fixed that one, too.

For many decades, for nearly all of the game's history, there was a sense that *if we don't give the fans what they want*, they won't come to the ballpark and *we will lose money*.

That's not Baseball today.

Historically, when Baseball as a moneymaker seemed in trouble, the owners acted. That's why the playing rules were dynamic for so many years, and that's why so many franchises were added or relocated from the late 1950s through the late '90s. But since 1998, only one franchise has moved, none have been added, and the only significant changes to the playing rules—unless you count the automatic intentional walk, which I wouldn't—have been made to lower injury risks, and *not* to make the game itself more entertaining. Sure, there are powerful forces arrayed against real change; against a return to the variety of baseball life that's not just the game's spice, but its *essence*.

Look, we hardly need a scattering of gimcrack measures, just for gimcrackery's sake.

But why not whack a few pesky moles, just to see? Endless mound visits from the catcher? Consider yourself whacked. Nobody's going to miss you, even the littlest of bits. Pitch clocks, with enforcement? Why the hell not? ESPN's Jon Sciambi says, "I do not believe a single player would underperform his true talent level because he's asked to play faster." John Baker, who played in the majors for years and now works for the Cubs on the mental side of things, says of a pitch clock, "It will never affect the quality of the game played on the field."

Relatively speaking, speeding up the game *some* is actually the easy thing. Reaching Commissioner Manfred's goal of a 2:50 average game just means cutting the time between pitches by a few seconds, along with perhaps cutting the number of pitches altogether;

just one or two per half-inning might do it. Sciambi's right: "We need just a little bit more *now now now now*, quicker quicker, *come on*. I think you have to do something, or you can have a problem in fifteen years." And they might actually do something. Soon, even.

What's not so easy is stopping or significantly slowing the rise of those Two True Outcomes: strikeouts and home runs. But if Baseball could somehow agree that the future exists *and* it's better with more non-Outcome action, what might that look like?

Obviously, if the (presumably) juiced baseballs get de-juiced, there won't be as many home runs. Which would mean fewer runs. Which was worrying Baseball before the (presumed, however unintentional) juicing. It's simply not enough to turn some of the home runs into doubles and triples and (if the hitters give in some) singles.

Yes, if home runs are harder to come by, *some* hitters will change their approaches, and some teams will place a higher value on non-power hitters. Again, though: It would not be enough. You hit the reset button and you're back in 2014 and people are complaining about not enough scoring and too many 2-1 games . . . while the pitchers just keep getting bigger and throwing harder and mastering the dark, related arts of foreign substances and spin rates.

Ultimately, something must be done about the pitchers. Which sounds radical and perhaps punitive only if (a) you're a pitcher, or (b) your grasp of history doesn't extend much before 1987. Or 2004.

Back in 1920, they outlawed the spitball. In 1969, they lowered the pitcher's mound. Any number of times, the strike zone has been changed, officially or otherwise, to boost scoring or depress scoring. Throughout *most of professional baseball's history*, rules were made and baseballs were constructed with essentially one aim: *make the game on the field more entertaining.*

Even today, it's not that the owners and players *can't* work together. They can. For many years, the players fought any sort of drug policy that would include mandatory testing. This argument was publicly predicated on the principle of privacy, but just being honest about this, it never had much to do with principles. It was mostly about convenience; if you are not using drugs, getting tested is inconvenient. If you are using drugs—as hundreds of players probably were, at the height of the Steroids Era, at least occasionally—it's *really* inconvenient.

Ultimately, pressure from the U.S. Congress *and* the media *and* the players who didn't want to use drugs . . . ultimately the players and owners came together to protect, if not the game itself, at least its public reputation. And yes, there were *undoubtedly* players, clean and dirty, who were looking for a way out. And if that meant peeing into a damn cup a few times every year, so be it.

But what might bring the owners and the players together in 2018? Or 2019 or '20 or '21? It might have to be something that threatens the players' health, the owners' profits, or the players' livelihoods.

There simply is not, as I write these words, any such threat on the near horizon. The Dodgers are only a few years into a 25-year, $8.35 billion contract for their local television rights. Which is an immense amount of money. Even the lowly Tampa Bay Rays, arguably the most beleaguered franchise in the majors, this winter entered into a fifteen-year deal that guarantees them $82 million per season (beginning at $50 million in 2018 and moving progressively higher). The Rays!

Owners and players alike have relatively little interest in the long-term health of the enterprise. Most of the players will be retired; most of the owners will have sold their teams. In the short term, there is simply little common cause between the people who run Baseball, and the people who watch baseball. Or between the people who run Baseball and the people who *play* baseball, outside of the major leagues. Witness Baseball's failure to subsidize youth baseball in a meaningful way, or create a schedule that's more friendly to fans than to players, or ensure that minor leaguers earn just a reasonable living wage. It's *almost* as if Baseball were content with their aging demographic base and all those televisions tuned to the games in memory-care facilities.

But if Baseball actually *wanted* new fans? I think you get them by making the game itself, the game most people are *seeing*, more interesting. And what would make it more interesting? Aside from simply stealing back a few seconds from the lollygagging players, here and there?

Let's talk about the strike zone.

The zone was last altered in 1996, when the bottom line was dropped from the top of the batter's knees to the bottom. This was theoretically going to make the pitcher's job easier, since of course it's *always* been said that "keeping the ball down" would lead to more ground balls and (of course) fewer home runs.

In 1997, Mark McGwire hit 58 home runs. In 1998, McGwire and Sammy Sosa combined for 136 home runs. In 2001, Barry Bonds hit 73 home runs. In just 476 at-bats. Now, the new strike zone wasn't the only reason for all the home-run records getting obliterated. But you hit home runs with uppercuts, and it's easier to uppercut a low pitch than a high one. There's also evidence of a *de facto* change in the strike zone a decade ago, when PITCHf/x technology led to an MLB initiative called Zone Evaluation, "which tracked missed calls after each game and judged umpires by their accuracy." Unsurprisingly, this led to better, more consistent umpiring of balls and strikes . . . and fewer "missed" strikes low in the zone.

What would happen if you lowered the pitcher's mound by an inch or three? What would happen if the strike zone was raised from the bottom of the knee to the top? Say, three or four inches? Fewer strikeouts, probably. But still a ton of them, and nearly as many home runs. Maybe you would want just a *slightly* smaller strike zone: shave those three or four inches from the bottom, but *add* two inches at the top. Maybe that's how you get fewer strikeouts *and* fewer home runs . . . and obviously more batted balls in play, because now the hitters aren't so incentivized to focus on uppercutting.

Not *so* incentivized. Somehow Babe Ruth and Ted Williams managed to uppercut plenty of home runs, even with a strike zone up to their armpits. But if you're going to take something away from the pitchers, you must take something from the hitters, too.

If, through experimentation, one could find a better sort of balance between pitching and hitting—a balance that would, by the way, also lead to *more* fielding and *more* baserunning . . . if you were free to tinker with the game, why on earth would you *not* do that? Why *not* fool around with a slightly smaller home plate? Why *not* mandate slightly smaller gloves for the fielders?

Yes, such things today seem almost impossible, for the simple reason that today Baseball prioritizes the desires of millionaire union members over the desires of the spectators and just about everyone else who's *not* in the union. As unions usually do, this one's acting purely in self-interest, with nary a care for anyone outside the union. Which isn't going to change.

But wait! Television might save us!

Ultimately it's the guys with the biggest dollars who will decide how all this plays out. If the television guys become convinced that their ratings might be a few percent better with quicker games; better, with more flashy running and fancy fielding . . . well, that's when you might begin to see some sort of consensus among all the interested parties. If it's billions.

Because, the dollars? They do matter. Baseball people still care about dollars.

The winter following the 2017 season was marked by an unprecedented chill in free-agent signings, with most of the top free agents still . . . well, *free* when spring training camps opened in February.

This was not completely unprecedented. In the winters following the 1985, '86, and '87 seasons, the owners colluded to essentially kill the market for free agents. Which was illegal. Ultimately the owners settled with the union for $280 million, which was then distributed (in a long, complicated process) to the affected players.

Back in the 1980s, there probably were teams *actually losing money.* Collusion was a sort of sad plea: SAVE US FROM OUR-SELVES. These days, nobody needs much saving. In 2017, revenues were up again. In 2018, everybody's getting a one-time, $50 million check for selling a big piece of Major League Baseball Advanced Media to the Disney Corporation. So last winter, the defining sentiment seemed to be, "Hey, I have the money. I just don't want to look like an idiot in six years when this guy isn't good enough to play but I'm still paying him $20 million."

Not wanting to look like an idiot can be a strong motivator, especially these days when so many people in so many media are looking for reasons to hammer you. And if the reason's actually fair? Well, all the better. The Angels will wind up paying Albert Pujols $165 million over the last six years of his contract, in return for approximately zero, you know, wins.

Without being gratuitous, you might also mention Ryan Howard and Jacoby Ellsbury and Adrián González and Josh Hamilton and Carl Crawford and a few more.

For essentially the first time since the invention of free agency back in the 1970s, hard cold data has trumped irrational exuberance. It simply doesn't make sense to commit many millions to veteran players on the downsides of their careers, when it costs not only those dollars, but also can result in the loss of amateur draft picks *and* permissible spending on young players from outside the U.S. (four of the Washington Nationals' top prospects were signed out of the Dominican Republic for less than $400,000—combined).

For fans, this means almost nothing. For the players, it means almost nothing. At least on a practical level, as erstwhile pitching ace Jake Arrieta's lifestyle hardly hinges on whether he earns $200 million over the next seven years (what he reportedly wanted, as a free agent last winter), or $75 million over the next three (what he finally got, very late in the signing season).

Where the new realities *might* make a difference is for the younger players. Because at this point, about the only way to seriously threaten the currently longstanding labor peace would be for the revenues/payroll ratio to get seriously out of whack—historically speaking and/or relative to the other big-time pro sports—for long.

But in recent years the players' compensation, *figured as a percentage of team revenues*, has held remarkably steady. When you consider not just salaries, but also signing bonuses and benefits and postseason bonuses, the players' share comes to almost exactly 50 percent in 2017 . . . which has essentially been true throughout this decade, just as it's been roughly true in the other big team sports. And if we expand our definition of "players" to include minor leaguers, we tack on another 6 or 7 percent.

Sportswriters, though, have a vested interest in controversy, which helps explain why—just two years after the current Collective Bargaining Agreement went into effect, and nearly four years before it expires—so many baseball writers in the 2017–2018 off-season came to predict all manners of doom and gloom, thanks to the owners' semi-unilateral efforts to speed up the game, and the soft market for free agents.

For as long as I can remember, the sporting press has shown a general tendency to forget about the fans. In the 1970s and '80s, when the players found their footing as a collective force, and went on strike a couple of times while reaping huge increases in their compensation, the writers were almost universally on the owners' side. In the late '70s, there must have been hundreds of newspaper columns predicting that free agency would literally destroy baseball. A million dollars for one player! The horror!

Baseball survived.

Somehow, Baseball survived. Despite the owners' blatant, illegal collusion in the late '80s, and the players' devastating strike in 1994 (and the drug-related p.r. hits in the middle '80s and then again twenty years later). And where the writers were largely behind the owners for those first twenty or thirty years of free agency, now they seem squarely behind the players.

Media types tend to forget something, though: the baseball business is not a two-sided coin, with the players on one side and the owners on the other. They forget about the millions of baseball fans who pay for all these nice things. The business does not exist without the fans, just as Kellogg's doesn't exist without hungry kids and Southwest Airlines doesn't exist without thrifty travelers. There would still be baseball without these millions of fans, but there would not be Baseball. And it's worth mentioning that in the first half of the 2018 season, attendance is down significantly: something like 6 or 7 percent. Perhaps because more teams than ever are following the Cubs/Astros paradigm, and losing a hundred games because they can't win ninety.

So my advice to the opinion-makers: First, remember that the owners are billionaires and the players—the players running the union, anyway—are millionaires, and then think about the fans, most of whom are *not* millionaires, and consider their inescapable, inevitable choice: take whatever Baseball's billionaires and millionaires and media conglomerates give them, or find another pastime.

Same as it ever was, and will be. But that doesn't mean the writers and the TV presenters and the radio people can't stop siding with the oligarchs and their exceptionally well-heeled employees, and focus instead on creating a better, smarter, more exciting version of Baseball for as many spectators as they can find.

If Baseball *and* baseball have a meaningful future, that should be it.

Rob Neyer
July 2018
Portland, Oregon

Acknowledgments

It's been a few years since my last book. I can't say I've missed the work, exactly. Even though (yes, it's true) the work is (generally) pleasurable. I can't say I've missed the "extra" checks, precisely. Even though the checks are (always) pleasurable.

What I've missed the most is the chance to express, with some measure of posterity, my gratitude to the many people who have supported me while on this quixotic quest to create something worth a few hours of your precious time.

First on the list, this time? My editor, Eric Nelson. This book was entirely Eric's idea, and I was lucky enough to be his second choice when his first choice couldn't do it. Eric was instrumental in choosing the game we covered herein, and he also wielded a deft editorial hand, allowing me to write just the book I wanted to write. If you found anything herein that seemed askew, it was probably despite Eric's best advice.

Along with Eric, the other good folks at HarperCollins who shepherded this book from concept to bookstore include Eric Meyers, Doug Jones, and John Jusino.

My agent these days is Peter Steinberg, of Foundry Literary + Media. We worked on a couple of projects that never quite came together, and finally justifying Peter's good faith and hard work has been tremendously heartening.

I wouldn't have considered this book even a remotely worthy successor to *Nine Innings* if I hadn't spent some time with a number of the players I was writing about. And I wouldn't have been able to do that without the gracious assistance of Oakland's Fernando Alcalá, Houston's Chris Peixoto, and Seattle's Tim Hevly and Kelly Munro.

My thanks to Sig Mejdal, Brent Strom, and Jeff Luhnow for answering my specific questions about their guys; thanks also to Billy Beane for all the colorful phone calls, all those years ago.

Mark Armour, Matthew Kory, Dave Jordan, Stephen Mast, David Todd, Craig Calcaterra, Jonah Keri, Pete Fornatale, and Jim Baker all read portions of this book early on, and all offered valuable suggestions.

Patrick Dubuque was this book's first point of contact with the outside world—that is, the world outside of my head—and he pointed out an embarrassingly large quantity of clumsy prose (and worse). I shudder to consider the absence of Patrick's judgment and wisdom. Jason Brannon's been my fact-checker for nearly twenty years, and once again he found an embarrassingly copious number of errors. How so many got in there, I don't have the slightest idea. But Jason's why most of those little bastards have now gotten out.

Just as Patrick and Jason made this book better than it was, photographer Nina Johnson made me look better than I am, for the dust-jacket photo. If you're in Portland and need some professional work done, Nina's the one.

Having greatly enjoyed *Nine Innings* when it was first published, and then been fortunate enough to spend some time with Dan Okrent over the years, I was trepidatious about writing a similar book. I felt less trepidatious upon receiving Dan's gracious blessing, and I hope he sees at least a few hints of his own work here.

Obviously, this wouldn't be anything without all the people who spoke with me for this book. Aside from the various A's and Astros, whom I interviewed in their clubhouses in Arizona and Seattle, I also benefitted from the insights and experiences of the following: Jeff Heckelman, Mitchel Lichtman, C. J. Nitkowski, Doug Glanville, John McLaren, Mike McMurray, Jon Sciambi, John Baker,

Joe Bohringer, Dan Haren, Fred Claire, Joe Lemire, Dan O'Dowd, Zachary Levine, Evan Drellich, Jim Coffman, Tim Purpura, Brandon McCarthy, John Thorn, Christina Kahrl, Sean Forman, Cory Schwartz, Keith Woolner, Sam Mondry-Cohen, Daren Willman, Sam Grossman, Manny Acta, Dale Scott, Bill Bavasi, Tom Farrey, and Bill DeWitt Jr.

Most of those gentlemen are quoted in the book, but those who aren't still informed the material here. Writing a book is actually work, often difficult work; but talking to people who love baseball is an abject pleasure. Oh, and for anyone who might be unaccountably missing from the list, you have my profound apology.

Bill James has been a large part of my life, one way or another, since 1984, and I continue to thank the heavens for that moment when I first laid eyes upon his work.

In addition to Bill and Dan, I'm grateful also to Jeff Pearlman, Jane Leavy, Dirk Hayhurst, Daryl Morey, Will Leitch, and Ben Mankiewicz for their kind words about this book.

One of my great enduring pleasures is talking about baseball on the radio, and so I'm grateful for the continuing opportunities afforded by Gary Hill, Kevin Cremin, Aaron Goldsmith, Bob Valvano, Sean Levine, Dwight Jaynes, Nestor Aparicio, Damon Bruce, John Canzano, and the whole JT The Brick crew.

In the general catch-all category of Helping Me Get Through a Tough Time, I gratefully include Jim Baker, Kathleen Kinder, Rob Nelson, Mark Armour, Carson Cistulli, Gabe Kapler, David Todd, Steve Hofstetter, Bob Klapisch, Joe Sheehan, Ben Lindbergh, Sam Miller, Craig Calcaterra, Meg Rowley, Cee Angi, Jeff Snider, Tim Brown, Kevin Burkhardt, Owen King, Dan Epstein, Josh Wilker, Jason Turbow, Michael Lewis, Tabitha Soren, Pete Fornatale, and Joshua Prager.

Among the great blessings of my life are my birding and climbing friends, two completely different groups of people, without whom I would be lost.

Special thanks to Jeff Bower and Vivian Little for letting me crash in their flat, and to Jonah Keri for being exactly the right person at exactly the right moment. Even specialier thanks to my parents for creating me, and to my wife's mother for creating my wife (and for her preternaturally cheerful island hospitality). Oh, and to my brother for being my brother.

One doesn't know how to properly thank one's wife and daughter; fortunately, there's a dedication page for them.

Finally, my apologies to anyone I might have missed. If I remember later, or you remind me, I'll do my best to make amends. Peace and love, all . . .

Index

Note: Page numbers followed by an "n" indicate a footnote.

About the Author

Rob Neyer worked for fifteen years as a columnist and blogger for ESPN, from 1996 to 2011, and later worked as a national writer and editor for SB Nation and Fox Sports. A Kansas City native, Rob has lived in the Pacific Northwest for more than twenty years, and in 2018 served as commissioner of the West Coast League, the premier collegiate summer baseball league west of the Mississippi. This is his seventh book.